We can dream our dream and we can dream our world if we remember, like Harriet Tubman, that we can fly.

—FROM *Dreaming True*

"I am profoundly convinced, after many years of working in these areas, that the futures we see in dreams or intuitive states, for ourselves or others, are possible futures. The actions we take (including action to unfold the full meaning of the dream) can change the probability that any particular scenario will be enacted. Once we wake up to the fact that we dream the future—maybe all the time—we can play the powerful improvisational game of changing the future for the better."

—Robert Moss

Praise for *Conscious Dreaming* by Robert Moss

"A triumphant contribution. . . . Contains revelations for the advanced dreamer as well as the neophyte."

—PATRICIA GARFIELD, AUTHOR OF *Creative Dreaming* AND *The Healing Power of Dreams*

"Highly recommended for anyone wishing to explore dreams and how they can be used constructively in the craft of life."

—LARRY DOSSEY, AUTHOR OF *Healing Words* AND *Recovering the Soul*

Also by Robert Moss

Conscious Dreaming
Dreamgates

For orders other than by individual consumers, Pocket Books grants a discount on the purchase of **10 or more** copies of single titles for special markets or premium use. For further details, please write to the Vice President of Special Markets, Pocket Books, 1230 Avenue of the Americas, 9th Floor, New York, NY 10020-1586.

For information on how individual consumers can place orders, please write to Mail Order Department, Simon & Schuster, Inc., 100 Front Street, Riverside, NJ 08075.

DREAMING TRUE

How to Dream Your Future and Change Your Life for the Better

Robert Moss

POCKET BOOKS
New York London Toronto Sydney Singapore

An *Original* Publication of POCKET BOOKS

POCKET BOOKS, a division of Simon & Schuster, Inc.
1230 Avenue of the Americas, New York, NY 10020

ISBN: 0-671-78530-3

First Pocket Books trade paperback printing September 2000

10 9 8 7 6 5 4 3 2 1

Cover design by Anna Dorfman
Front cover illustration by Brian Bailey
Designed by Lindgren/Fuller Design

Printed in the U.S.A.

for Sophie

There are only two ways to live your life: one is as though nothing is a miracle, the other is as if everything is. I believe in the latter.

—ALBERT EINSTEIN

contents

preface

DREAMING TRUE

I have a dream today.
— Martin Luther King Jr., August 28, 1963

The common wisdom of most human societies, as far back as we can trace, is that dreaming is central to the human condition. Dreaming gives us direct access to the spiritual realms, and allows our spiritual teachers to speak to us clearly. Dreaming also helps us to keep body and soul together, by showing us dangers and opportunities that may escape our ordinary awareness. "Strong" dreamers, those who have the ability to provide accurate and helpful information—on the location of food in the hungry times, for example, or the movements of a hostile war party—are greatly revered and rewarded. The first business of the day, for many people in a traditional dreaming culture, is to come together and share dreams. In dreaming cultures, it is observed that in "big" dreams, we journey beyond the body and beyond the laws of spacetime, or receive visitations from beings who are not confined to physical reality. The dreamworld is a real world, more "real" than much of everyday life. Someone who is not in touch with his dreams is soul-gone, less than fully human.

This ancient wisdom was shared at some point in time by all our ancestors. It is still honored by traditional dreaming peoples such as Australian Aborigines, the hill tribes of Southeast Asia, and many Native Americans. It is a better guide to the possibilities of dreaming than scientific findings based on monitoring brainwaves.

We need to know about these things for ourselves. Dreaming is not a spectator sport (although in dreams we can certainly look in on many interesting situations). Theories about dreams are worse than useless if they come between the dreamer and the *practice* of dreaming. True dream scientists are active dreamers who work carefully with their journals, share their dreams with others, and research the frontiers of dreaming inside the dreamstate itself. As we explore the meaning of our dreams, and what we should do with them, we can always benefit from another person's insights and suggestions. But the final authority on any dream is the dreamer herself. The only "expert" on *your* dreams is you.

This book focuses on a vitally important aspect of dreaming that is familiar, on some level, to almost everyone—and yet has been almost completely ignored in the modern literature. This is our ability to dream events and situations before they take place in physical reality.

Knowledge of the future may come to us in various ways, waking or sleeping. It may be an extrapolation or projection from information already available to us. In dreams, we sometimes access larger or deeper data banks than are available to our everyday awareness and make brilliant connections that escape our surface mind. The dreams that come from these processes may not always be "psychic"—because they do not introduce information that goes beyond what may already have come to us (perhaps subliminally) in waking life. But they sometimes offer marvelously clear and instructive scenarios about the possible future that should certainly be considered as examples of dreaming true. Since dreams of this kind often help us to prepare for future situations, or weigh the consequences of alternative courses of action, I call them *rehearsal* dreams.

Then there are those dreams in which the body shows us what may be going on inside it. I call these *bodytalk* dreams. Sleep researchers call them "somatic" dreams or—when they show us developing symptoms—"prodromic" dreams. Bodytalk dreams give us impeccable X-rays of our present condition and show us where it could lead. Best of all, they offer us fresh and powerful imagery that we can use in healing and recovery.

In dreams we also have access to information about the future that goes far beyond what is stored in the body and the personal unconscious. Four psychic functions—dormant in most of us in waking life, apart from occasional intuitive flashes—come richly alive in dreams. These are *telepathy,* the ability to pick up another person's thoughts or feelings at a distance; *clairvoyance* or "distant seeing" (which Pentagon types like to call "remote viewing"—and is just that); *psychokinesis,* the power of the mind to influence physical events or objects; and *precognition,* which could be defined as knowledge of future events that does not come from any source available in ordinary reality. In practice, lines between these four psychic functions are often blurred. If you dream about an incident in another town that you read about in tomorrow's paper, did you (a) have telepathy with someone you know in that town; (b) have a clairvoyant sighting of the incident at the time it took place; (c) help to bring it about through your own (possibly unsuspected) mental powers or (d) experience precognition of tomorrow's newspaper headlines?

The boundaries are porous, but it is useful to draw them on the ground, if only so we can enjoy playing hopscotch over them. The key point is that all four of these psychic functions—which are often regarded in waking life as extraordinary gifts or otherwise attainable only through prolonged and dedicated training—come spontaneously alive in dreams. This is the most natural thing in the world, according to ancient dreaming traditions and 21st century science. The ancient wisdom is that in dreams, we travel beyond the body and beyond time and space, and receive visitations from other travelers, who may include ancestors or angelic beings. The new science suggests that time travel is a physical, as well as a metaphysical possibility,[1] that the mind is never confined to the body and the brain, and that consciousness—once released from self-limiting beliefs—can take us to the ends and the inner workings of the universe.

Once we wake up to the fact that we dream of the future (maybe all the time) we are ready to play a more exciting game. This is the game of using dream information to change the future for the better. The futures we see in dreams are *possible* futures. If we catch our dream messages, and act on them, we can improve our chances of bringing about a happy event—or avoiding an unpleasant one.

As we become more active dreamers, we'll make a bigger discovery: that nothing in our physical reality is necessarily as fixed as we may have told ourselves, or been told by others. Dreams are our bridge to a deeper reality, in which the events and patterns of our waking lives are forged. We return from our dream travels with images and energy that can carry us beyond our personal histories, our self-limiting beliefs and our stuck places. Dream images give us power to heal our bodies, our relationships and our environment and return to our soul's purpose in this lifetime. They put us in touch with what one of the most gifted dreamers I know, a Catholic sister, calls our "Moreness." When we connect with that Moreness, in ourselves and others, we are more generous and creative and brave.

I have a dream: that we will again become a dreaming culture, where dreams are shared and celebrated every day, in our families, our workplaces, our schools, our clinics and our religious communities. By creating a safe space for each other to share and work with our dreams, we will get over barriers of prejudice and misunderstanding. As we share our dreams, we'll move beyond taboos, tell our troubles, achieve healing and resolution—and have wonderful fun.

In our dreaming culture, we will check our dreams for guidance on the probable outcome of the choices we are making. As dream scouts, we will bring through dream guidance on the possible future for the benefit of others, and for the community as a whole. In the workplace, we'll ask for dream guidance to bring through creative innovation and resolve personality conflicts.

Dreamwork will be central to medicine and healing. We will avoid invasive medical procedures (and save on health costs) by heeding dream messages that preview what could go wrong in our bodies—often years before physical symptoms develop—unless we take appropriate action. When we do become ill, we and our physicians will use dreams as a source of fresh and powerful imagery for healing and recovery.

Instead of teaching our kids that dreams are "only" dreams, we will encourage them to tap into this wonderful source of insight and creativity. Starting in pre-K, schoolkids will be encouraged to build communication and storytelling skills by telling their dreams. They will gain credits for keeping dream journals. They will do projects on Einstein's dreams, dreams in art and literature, dreams in social evolution and world cultures.

The challenge before us is to marry the best of our science and scholarship to the ancient arts of dreaming that recognize dreams as both wishes and *experiences* of soul and offer a path for evolving consciousness that can help us build more compassionate and creative communities. When we remember what dreaming can be, we gain the power to remake our lives, and our world.

introduction

THE UNDERGROUND RAILROAD OF DREAMS

"A friend with friends."

—PASSWORD OF "CONDUCTORS" GUIDING ESCAPING SLAVES TO FREEDOM ON THE UNDERGROUND RAILROAD

HARRIET TUBMAN'S DREAMS

Harriet Tubman woke up with more than a jolt to the gift of dreaming true. She was a black girl, known as Minty at the time, on a slave plantation in Tidewater Maryland. She may have been eleven years old in 1831, when the gift hit her like a cannonball. She did not know her exact age. Where she lived, slaves were prohibited from learning to read and write, and they followed time through changes of seasons and crop cycles, through death in the family or the sale of loved ones to other masters.

The girl blocked a barn door to delay an angry overseer who was going after a black man who was running away. The overseer grabbed a two-pound metal weight and hurled it after the man. It struck Minty full in the forehead, opening a crater through which blood poured out. She was not expected to live, but somehow—treated only with the herbs and roots from the woods that her mother knew—she survived, with a huge dent in her forehead that marked this tiny but stocky and powerfully muscled woman more clearly than any slave brand.

Marked though she was, she succeeded not only in escaping her own slave master—despite the violent opposition and threatened betrayal of her husband—but in returning to Maryland from the North again and again, to help other slaves make their escape. Harriet started by bringing out family members in small, careful groups. As the situation in the South grew more desperate and the Civil War loomed, she became bolder, bringing out larger parties of complete strangers. She came and went safely through the gauntlet of bloodhounds and patrollers, bounty hunters and hired guns. Traveling without maps or compass, she found her way from the Maryland shore to Pennsylvania and New York and later—when the Fugitive Slave Law made it necessary to seek safety beyond U.S. territory—all the way to Canada. She conducted more than 300 slaves to freedom, never losing a single "package." On the Underground Railroad, they did not call her Harriet or Minty. They called her "Moses," the one who gets you to the promised land.

By her own account, Harriet Tubman's astonishing achievement was the gift of her dreams.

She had been a dreamer before, but that terrible bump on the head kicked her experience of dreaming to a new level of clarity and power. At first this seemed more like a curse than a blessing. She would experience an urgent need to go to sleep for an hour or two, like a violent narcolepsy. If she failed to obey this urge at once, she might fall where she stood. It could happen at any time—when she was tilling the field, holding the master's baby, or later when she was exposed and vulnerable, leading a group of frightened runaways along a back road. But she did not simply "black out." She dreamed, and the dreams gave her specific guidance and directions. The things she saw in her dreams seemed *more* real than ordinary scenes, the colors vivid, the senses richly alive.

While she was still in slavery, she dreamed that rough men on horseback came riding among the cabins, ripping mothers away from their children and husbands away from their wives to send them off to the Deep South in chain gangs. Waking, she could still hear the echo of the women's screams. She learned from a dream like this one—she had many—that her master was planning to sell her to slavers from the Deep South. She knew she had to get away, and dreamed of following the North Star to freedom north of the Mason-Dixon. She talked about these dreams with her husband John, but—though he was a freedman—he did not want to hear them. He ridiculed the idea that she could find her way through the woods. He even told her the fact she kept having the same dreams over and over meant she was simple in the head. Who but a fool would dream the same dream again and again?

It was one of these recurring dreams that convinced Harriet that she could do it, despite what her husband said. In this dream, she was flying. She flew over cottonfields and cornfields, and saw the corn tassels floating in the breeze. She flew over the Choptank River and saw the mirror-bright gleam of the water below her. She flew over hills and forests. She would come to a barrier—sometimes a fence, sometimes a river—that she couldn't fly over. "It appeared like I wouldn't have the strength, and just as I was sinking down, there would be ladies all dressed in white over there, and they would put out their arms and pull me across."

Harriet's dreams showed her the specific route she would take, and the houses and barns where she would be given shelter along the way. She had no conventional map, and would not have known how to read one, but her dreams gave her an aerial map, as well as close-up views of places along the trail. And the vision of the women in white gave her deep confidence that all the help she needed was available—not only from the network of Quakers and Abolitionists who actively supported the Underground Railroad, but from spiritual powers that supported her life.

Harriet's biographies[1] contain many detailed and convincing stories of how she used dreams to get slaves to freedom as a conductor. There is one episode, from November 1856, that is especially revealing. Harriet had returned to Maryland's Eastern Shore to bring out a group of four slaves that included Joe Bailey, a strong, handsome man who had been brutally flogged by his master with a rawhide whip the day before, and was still bleeding profusely from his wounds. Bailey's master was out to get him back, and the little group with the bleeding man and the tiny woman with a hole in her forehead, badly disguised by a mannish hat, was anything but inconspicuous. To top it all, as she marched her party down a country road, Harriet's head started to ache violently. She crumpled to her knees, and collapsed there, in plain view, into one of her involuntary "sleeps." Bailey had trouble convincing the other frightened slaves not to abandon her.

When Harriet came round, she ordered the group to follow her along a completely unexpected course that seemed to be taking them deeper into the slave dominions. They came to a river that looked far too deep to wade, and nobody could swim. Harriet insisted they must all go into the river; she was sure there was a place where the water was shallow enough to wade across. The other slaves were not convinced. Joe Bailey asked if she had crossed the river before. She told him she had crossed it in a dream, the dream she had just had when she fell asleep at the side of the road. Her dream had shown her that they *could* get across, and that crossing the river would mask their trail from the patrollers and bloodhounds who were homing in on them. She had seen a cabin on the other side where they would be given food and shelter. Only Bailey followed her when she stepped into the icy river. The water was up above Harriet's chin before the stream got shallower, but she found her ford. The others followed her, and they were greeted on the other side by a black family who sheltered them in their cabin. When Harriet led her group back the way they had come the next day, they found evidence that hunting parties had tracked them all the way down that country road; if they had followed their original route, they would have been taken.

Harriet dreamed that President Lincoln freed the slaves three years before he issued the Emancipation Proclamation. She was staying in the home of a New York minister at the time. She came down to breakfast in high excitement, singing "My people are free! My people are free!" Her host, the Reverend Henry Garnet, tried to calm her, cautioning her that emancipation would never come in their lifetimes. Harriet trusted her dream. "I tell you sir, you'll see it, and you'll see it soon."

When Lincoln issued the Emancipation Proclamation in 1863, Harriet declined an invitation from her abolitionist friends to join a grand celebration, telling them, "I had *my* jubilee three years ago. I can't rejoice no more."[2]

Harriet Tubman's story is a remarkable example of how we can dream our dream in the most literal sense. I don't remember learning anything about the Underground Railroad, let alone Harriet's dreams, when I was a schoolboy in Australia. The history we were taught in those days focused on the pink bits on the map, Britain's colonies and Commonwealth. When I literally followed my dreams to a new home in Troy, New York, in 1990, I was surprised when a sturdy little black woman bobbed up on my mental screen from time to time, usually as I lay in bed before falling asleep. She wore period clothes and often appeared in a mannish hat. When her forehead was bare, I noticed there was an odd shadow there, suggesting a hole or deep indentation. There was no communication between us. She seemed less like a visitor than like a hologram.

I did not identify her until I was working on this book. One night I asked for dream guidance on how to make my subject matter more accessible for people who might need help in getting back in touch with their dreams. I dreamed I was teaching the history of the Underground Railroad all over North America. I woke excited but puzzled. When I discussed my dream with my youngest daughter, Sophie (who was then aged nine), she told me she had learned in school that dreams had guided fugitive slaves. "But the teacher didn't want to talk about that part."

I got on the internet and sat stunned, in front of the first photograph of Harriet Tubman that came up on the screen. It showed a sturdy black woman with a determined face, seared by hardship—and a shadow suggesting a dent on her forehead. I had no doubt this was the person whose "hologram" had appeared to me in those twilight states.

I rushed out and got hold of all the books I could find on Harriet Tubman. I became more and more excited as I learned how dreams had guided her, step by step, through all her successful missions as a conductor on the Underground Railroad. I discovered she had come to Troy, my home town, and led the angry crowd that freed an escaped slave who was about to be shipped back to the South under the Fugitive Slave Act.

The story of prophetic dreams in world history is too often told—when told at all—as a chronicle of wild-eyed men on mountaintops, or of white men in helmets or stovepipe hats dreaming of death and slaughter. Harriet Tubman's dreams are a fine example of how the dreams of "ordinary people" have contributed to human survival and human liberation—of how we can literally dream our dream.

Whatever life throws at us, on our darkest nights, we can all draw courage and practical guidance for the journey from Harriet's story. We can learn to dream the way she did, and use our dreams to navigate through the trials and obstacles of everyday life, opening paths to a better life and creative fulfillment for ourselves and our communities. Harriet Tubman was an extraordinary woman, but her gift of dreaming true is a gift that is the natural birthright of all of us, if we are only willing to claim it.

WE ARE PSYCHICS IN OUR DREAMS

Harriet saw people and places in her dreams before she encountered them in waking life. So do we. As a matter of fact—a fact you can very easily check for yourself—we do this every night. We are gifted psychics in our dreams. We are not confined by conditions of space and time. We see round the corner. Sometimes we see people and events we won't encounter in waking life until years later. We foresee world events; we know what's in next Tuesday's paper. We see things that are happening at a distance. We know what other people are thinking and feeling.

In dreams, we talk to the departed in the most natural way. We travel beyond the body into other times and other dimensions. We have glimpses of other life experiences, from the past and the future.

Dreams not only take us beyond the body; they put us in closer contact with our bodies. We talk to our bodies in dreams, and our bodies show us what they require in order to stay well. We get previews of symptoms we may develop—but may be able to avoid if we act on dream diagnoses now.

Dreams prepare us to meet the challenges and passages of life in other equally natural ways. They hold up a mirror to our present lives and relationships, taking us beyond our blind spots. They show us aspects of ourselves we may have repressed or denied, at considerable cost to ourselves and others. They reveal the natural path of our energies. They rehearse us for challenges that lie ahead, exposing the probable consequences of our present actions and attitudes. Above all, dreams put us in touch with our heart's desire, the secret wishes of the soul.

All this dream information and guidance comes not only for our benefit, but for that of others. Quite literally, we dream for other people. In some of these dreams, we seem to step into their situation and glimpse the world through their eyes. Sometimes we seem to pick up someone else's mail, receiving a dream message addressed to them.

All of this goes on effortlessly and naturally, night after night.

If we are not in touch with our dreams, we are missing out on a lot. We are missing life-helping and sometimes life-preserving messages. We are missing the easiest way to develop our natural intuition and tap into personal sources of creativity and healing. We are turning our backs on a doorway into a deeper reality and a dialogue with our larger Self. Above all, we are missing the movies—the sheer fun and adventure of nightly experiences that can bring wonderful energy and creative play into everyday life.

It is sad that in modern Western societies, we have fallen into the habit of speaking of dreams as "only" dreams, as something less than *real.* The materialists of the Victorian era dismissed dreams as vain fancies or wild conceits, shadowy and insubstantial. The reductionist scientists of our era try to convince us that dreams are merely the product of random neuronal firing or the wash of chemicals in the brain, or part of a nightly flushing-out of waste products from the day's ingestion of information. When I read research reports along these lines, I wonder how much time the authors have spent with their own dream journals.

We not only see the future in dreams. We can use dream information about the possible future to create better futures. It is true we often dream of future events in dreams that we may seem powerless to influence. Common examples include natural disasters, major public events or the death—maybe sudden or violent, maybe the cumulative effect of a whole life history—of another person. But even when we cannot change an outcome we have foreseen, we can work with the information. If you dream a tornado flattens a specific neighborhood in Oklahoma, for example, you may find it possible to pass on a helpful advisory—or at any rate adjust your own travel plans. If all you remember from your dream is a tornado in Oklahoma, on the other hand, you had better not go running around yelling about it; nobody in tornado country is likely to be very impressed. And if your dream is a generic tornado dream, without clear indication of time or place, you'd probably do better to work your dream another way, by asking yourself where in your life something with the emotional force of a twister is likely to blow up.

As the last example makes clear, working with dreams to create better futures requires learning to get clear and specific information from them, and to recognize which elements in our dreams should be taken literally and which are symbolic. We often go astray when we try to interpret dreams on the basis of a blurred or fragmentary memory of a dream. The meaning of dreams is inside the full experience of the dream itself, as opposed to our tangled or broken memories. Learning to go back inside dreams to clarify their messages is one of the core techniques of dreaming true.

In our dream travels, we not only enter other times, but other dimensions where we may encounter spiritual sources of insight and healing. In big dreams, we may be open to a higher guidance we screen out in the midst of our hurried or ego-driven agendas. The guidance may come from a dream messenger—an angelic being, a departed loved one, an animal guardian—or direct from the Source. We might call this the Higher Self. I sometimes think of this spiritual source as the God we can talk to. Learning to work with the spiritual and transpersonal aspects of dreaming is central to the art of dreaming true.

I believe that many of us have the ability to become *practicing* psychic dreamers, bringing through life-helping information for ourselves and others, providing we are willing to set aside self-limiting beliefs and *practice.* Here are five reasons why:

1. *We are born dreamers.* We dream our way into this world. Rapid eye movement (REM) associated with vivid dreaming has been detected in unborn children, and recent research suggests that in the third trimester they may spend *all their time* in this state.[3] Physiologists believe that the REM sleep of the unborn contributes to the maturation of the nervous system. I think it may contribute far more. It is entirely possible that, in dreaming, we rehearse for the challenges of adapting to a physical environment while we are still in the womb.

   The process continues through infancy. Newborns spend 50–75 percent of their sleep time in the REM state—and they sleep a lot! Psychologists find it hard to assess the dreams of very small children because they lack verbal skills. But many parents notice young children's efforts to communicate dream activity, and as we grow older, some of us remember dream experiences from very early childhood. Two of my daughters reported vivid and exciting dreams quite frequently between the ages of two and four. When they started telling me about their dreams, they did not describe them as dreams. They talked as if they had gone somewhere and seen or done something. They talked about what had *happened* during the night. In general, by my observation, when children start talking about dreams they do not put a frame around their experience by saying, "I had a dream." Older people train them to do this—too often, alas—by telling them repeatedly, "It was *only* a dream." For small children, dreams are *real.* To learn more about this, talk to young children, ask them to share their dreams, and ask permission to write them down.

2. *We have the material (we all dream).* We all dream. By the most conservative estimates, we dream in four to seven cycles of dreams every night. And this only takes account of dreams associated with REM sleep. Laboratory research that began in 1953 suggests that we experience especially vivid dreams during REM sleep, when the brain is very active, the eyes move back and forth rapidly under the lids, and the large muscles of the body are relaxed. REM sleep occurs every 90 minutes or so, four or more times a night, and periods of REM sleep usually lengthen as the night goes on. The last phase of REM-state sleep may last 45 minutes.

   More recent research suggests that we may be dreaming *all the time* during sleep, and that some of the most powerful experiences are not confined to the REM state.[4]

   Anyone who says, "I don't dream" is only saying, "I don't remember" (or "I don't want to remember").

3. *Almost everyone has had the experience of déjà vu.* Even those of us who rarely remember dreams have had the experience of *déjà vu.* The sense of *déjà vu*—of having "already seen" something—is very frequently the surfacing of memories from a dream we may have forgotten until waking events catch up with it. *Déjà vu* ("already seen") is most commonly the experience of *déjà rêvé* ("already dreamed").

4. *Our ancestors were very good at this (it kept them alive).* For much of human evolution, we have relied on our intuitive

antennae to keep us alive. Before we became the dominant species on the planet, I suspect that it was our ability to dream-scout the movements of larger predators that saved many of us from becoming their lunch. In traditional indigenous cultures, up to the present day, strong dreamers are respected for their ability to scout the movement of enemy war parties and to locate food in the hungry times. Such abilities were shared by *all* our ancestors, and they are still alive in us, even if dormant.

5. *We learn this by doing it.* "Dreaming is a discipline," I was once told by a dream teacher who appeared to me—as such guides often do—in the twilight zone between sleep and waking. We become better at dreaming true through practice. In relation to spontaneous sleep dreams, the key elements in the practice are (a) keeping a dream journal and working with it intimately over time; (b) using simple techniques to clarify dream messages; (c) sharing dreams with one or more partners on a regular basis; and (d) taking action to honor and celebrate our dreams and bring their energy and insight to bear in waking life. If we follow this approach, we will soon find that we are evolving into more *conscious* dreamers. A conscious dreamer is not only keenly alert to the many levels of meaning and possibility in dreams, but is able to embark on conscious dream journeys and to read the symbols and synchronicities of waking life and use them as navigational beacons.

DREAMING A PATH FOR THE SOUL

Dreams show us a way through the thickets and hazards of life. They also open a path for the soul, a way of getting in touch with our heart's desires and manifesting them in physical reality. This is the ancient wisdom of dreaming, reflected in the practice, and even the language, of cultures in which dreams are shared and honored on a daily basis.

For the Temiar, an indigenous people of the rainforests of Malaysia, dreaming is central to healing and to living well. Like all ancient dreamers, the Temiar believe that dreaming is about much more than individual psychology. Dreaming is traveling. The dream soul leaves the body and makes a journey. It may go upriver and see what is going on in the next village. It may encounter a spirit guide, which may be the spiritual aspect of a tree or a mountain or a tiger (since everything is alive and has a soul). Fortunate dreamers bring back gifts that may help the whole community. One of the most important of these gifts is a dream song, or *norng*. These dream songs are central to healing and calling on spiritual help. Many people may come together to perform a dream song, providing a chorus for the dreamer's recitative, imitating birdcalls or the sigh of the wind in the leaves, or pounding out a beat with bamboo tappers and wooden drums. Marina Roseman, an anthropologist from the University of Pennsylvania, lived among the Temiar and recorded some of their dream songs.[5] They have extraordinary power; you can hear and almost *smell* the tiger rising from his afternoon nap to go hunting as the singer's gravelly voice invokes this powerful animal guardian.

The dream song is a song of power. It is also a pathway. This is what the word *norng* means: a path. It may be a path through the jungle, or a path for the soul. The Temiar say that one of the most common hazards of life is that we can lose our soul, a piece of our vital energy. This happens through shock and trauma and very often through unfulfilled *longing*. We yearn for love, for creative fulfillment, for a better life, for freedom from fear and pain. But we're not getting there. Maybe we have despaired of getting there. The heartache and disappointment are just too much. We've given up on our life dream, our heart's desire. We've numbed ourselves, blunting the pain—but also the joy—of life. So a part of our soul has gone away. It doesn't want to stay around with this numb, joyless bag of meat and bones. It would rather dance with the nature spirits, drift on a river of flowers, hang out in a faerie world where lovers are true and children are never abused. And while this part of our bright energy is out there, twinkling like a firefly, we become duller and less alive, prone to illness and misfortune, out of touch with our destiny and our deepest dreams.

A dream can bring us back to ourselves. Dreaming can open a path for soul to return to us, so we can be whole and fully know love and joy and hope, and live the life we dreamed before the part of us that is the beautiful dreamer took flight and didn't come back. Through dreaming, we learn to sing the soul back home.

Dreaming True is about finding our way—our way through the forest, and our way to fulfilling the secret wishes of the soul—with the help of dreams and the powers that speak through dreams.

Part I is about *how* to dream the way Harriet Tubman dreamed: how to dream the future, clarify the dream messages, use the information to make wiser choices and bring through life-helping guidance for others. Some of the most important chapters in Part I involve working with a dream journal. Now, Harriet Tubman did not keep a dream journal, since her slavemasters banned her from learning how to read and write. (What we know of her dreams is what she shared with other people.) But if Harriet were with us today, I think she would be a very active dream journalist, and I'll bet she would be urging children as well as adults to journal their dreams. A dream journal is an invaluable road map, showing us bends on the road of life that may lie many years in the future. It is a magic mirror that shows us who we are and how things *really* are. Keeping a dream journal is a way of effortlessly building writing and storytelling skills, hatching new ideas, and entering creative flow. Above all, it's a way of holding onto our deepest dreams and entering into a daily conversation with the God we can talk to.

As we look over our personal journals, we'll notice that we dream in many ways, even in a single night. We have big dreams and little dreams. There are dreams that really are brought on by a "bad bit of beef," as Scrooge tried to dismiss the visitation by Marley's ghost, and dreams that are actually visitations by the departed, or other spiritual entities. There are dreams in which we seem to be back in school, and dreams in which we seem to travel to other times or other dimensions. Yet *all* of our dreams—even the trivial "spicy pizza" dream—may be telling us something more than we already knew, or were willing to recognize or act upon, in our everyday minds (if only that we shouldn't gobble pizza so fast). In Part II, we'll study the variety of dreams: what we dream, how we dream, where we go in dreams, and what part of us is dreaming.

In Part III, we enter a deeper dreaming. We'll learn to become conscious dream travelers, time-jumpers and dream hunters.

We'll push deep into the borderlands of possibility. If we can see the future and change it, how about changing the past as well?

We will rediscover what ancient dreamers knew: that we not only dream the future, but that through dreaming we can become active co-creators of our future, bringing positive energy and insight from the dreamworld into physical reality. The great discoverers, inventors and artists have all created in this way. From the invention of the sewing machine needle to Einstein's theory of relativity, from Cornelius Vanderbilt's vision of skyscrapers in a then-undeveloped midtown Manhattan to Billy Joel's song "River of Dreams," creative breakthroughs are intimately linked to dreaming. Peak experiences of dream creativity (which often come in the twilight zone between sleep and waking) deliver both the *big* creative breakthroughs and the flow state in which we can follow through and bring them into full manifestation—a state in which time seems as elastic in waking reality as in dreaming.

By asking for dream guidance and working with it intelligently, we can create better futures for our communities. Part III contains simple, practical advice on how to create a safe space where dreams can be shared and used to heal conflict and bring through creative innovation in the workplace, at school or church, with family and friends, at the mall or in a hospital ward. We'll see that we can dream a path for others, help them to find their way and bring back missing soul. When we trust ourselves to do this, we become conductors on the Underground Railroad of Dreams. Wherever we go, we are friends with friends, and we remember we can fly.

part one

THE ART OF DREAMING TRUE

The only source of knowledge is experience.
—Albert Einstein

chapter one

JOURNALING FOR DREAMING TRUE

It is difficult to retain what you have learned unless you practice it.

—Pliny the Younger

Keeping a dream journal is central to the art of dreaming true. If you don't record your dreams, you are likely to lose them. At the very least, you will blur the vital details you need to work with. You will lose the chance to catch and use previews of events that come months or years before they manifest in everyday reality. You will most certainly lose the tremendous rewards of the most important book on dreams you are ever likely to read, which will become (if you let it) your private encyclopedia of symbols, an ever-available wise counselor, doctor and friend, a place where you can discover and study the larger story of your life—and a magic mirror that will never lie to you (although you may succeed in fogging or soiling the reflecting glass).

If you are not already keeping a dream journal, please start one! Goethe's advice is true for this, as for every major departure in life: "Whatever you think you can do or believe you can do, *begin it.* Action has magic, grace and power in it."

PLAY THE DATING GAME WITH YOUR DREAMS

If you rarely remember dreams, or have been going through a dry spell, don't worry about it. Catching dreams is fun; don't make it a chore. Think of it as going on a blind date with a friend you can trust with your soul. By the very fact that you are reading this book, you have said to the source of your dreams: *I'm ready to play!*

Here's how to play the dating game with your dreams:

Make a date with your dreams. Get yourself all the equipment you'll need: writing materials, or a tape recorder (preferably voice-activated) if you prefer, and one of those glow in the dark pens if you're worried about waking a sleeping partner. Put these within easy reach by your bed. Pick a time of the week or the day when you can wake naturally and allow yourself some extra quiet time. Try to avoid excessive alcohol or anti-depressants.

Tell your dreams you are ready to play. Before going to sleep, write down your intention, and give it some juice. "I want to have fun in my dreams" or "I want to go on a dream vacation" are good intentions. But go where the energy is. If there is a big challenge looming in your life, ask for guidance. If there is something you need to face that you have been avoiding, you may have been blocking the dreams that can bring you healing and resolution. So ask for help with that. It is *always* okay to ask for help. It's best to do it in a generous spirit. If you are in need of healing, don't moan about your symptoms. The powers that guide us through dreams are less interested when we bleat about our kidneys or our need for cash than when we say something like this:

> *Grant me the measure of health my body requires to serve the purposes of the soul.*

I have borrowed that one from Aelius Aristides, a famous Greek orator who found healing, inspiration and foreknowledge of future events in his dreams and walked very close to Asklepios, the god of medicine and dream healing. This invocation is quite adaptable. You might use something along these lines to ask for help with finding your dream job, your dream house, or the resources you need to keep body and soul together.

Whether your intention is a fling with a dream lover or help for a dying friend, go with the energy and remember to play. Write it down, put it under your pillow and sleep on it. You may be amazed how many things you can solve in your sleep.

You may need to use your imagination to relate whatever comes to you in the night to your initial question or intention. Say you ask for guidance on your relationship—as a woman in one of my workshops recently did—and you dream you have to escape from a resort hotel because a bomb is about to go off in the middle of your suite. There probably *is* a connection, even if you can't see it (or just don't want to see it) at first glance.

Write something down when you wake up (even if it's not a dream). Whenever you wake up—even if it's at a cruel and unsocial hour—write something down. Do this in the bathroom if that's why you awoke. Dream memories are fleeting. If you wake without dream memories, don't worry. If you just lie around in bed for a while, you may find a forgotten dream floating back, and then the dream before it, and the one before that. While working on this section of this book, I woke without dream memories. I spent a few moments in bed, gently rolling from side to side, as I tend to do during the night. Suddenly a dream scene reopened:

Drawing Dreamlines on the Roadmap

> I have a very large map, a photograph or holographic view of a landscape and a road winding through it. I draw lines at various angles from my position as observer to points on the road. These define the time-gap between dreams and episodes in waking life. They may also describe angles of perception and/or interaction with future events. The map, which is now a whole living landscape, can be "crumpled" so that points that are separate in space and time meet up. There is a scientist figure with tousled white hair who is eagerly monitoring my experiments. He looks like Einstein.

I was delighted to have recovered this dream vignette; it gave me confidence I might be able to thread my way through some of the knottier questions about dreaming, relativity and the holographic universe that we will explore in Part III. Later I was able to go back inside this dream and have a most provocative discussion with an Einstein figure. Had I simply jumped out of bed after telling myself I did not remember my dreams, I would have missed the fun.

If you still find you do not remember your dreams, don't worry about it. Write *something* down. Write down how you feel in your body, your heart and your head. Free associate. If you are up to it, fill those three "morning pages" Julia Cameron recommends in *The Artist's Way.* The gifts of your dreams may come spilling out. We all wake up with a dream hangover, even if we don't remember the dreams that caused it. As the song says, it can be the "sweetest" hangover, full of creative zest.

Make a date with a journal. The most important book on dreams you will ever read is your own dream journal. Make a date with your journal to write up your dream notes and review them. Always date your dreams and give them titles. Going back and rereading your journal regularly is critical to developing self-awareness and dreaming true. You'll discover what symbols mean for you. You'll learn to monitor match-ups between your dreams and subsequent waking events. You'll notice that some of your dreams overlap—or may be fully interactive with—the dreams of other people.

While you are on the way to becoming a full-fledged dream journalist, treat your journal like a sensitive lover who needs flowers or billets-doux at least once a week. Write something in your journal, even if it's not a dream. When you simply journal your observations of other people and the incidents of everyday life, you'll soon become alive to the play of synchronicity and symbolism in the world around you. The world is our mirror, as dreams are. When we wake up to the dream-like qualities of waking life, our dreams come back (and vice versa).

Make a date to share dreams with a friend. Many writers know that one of the best ways to get cracking with a project is to make a date with a friend to share work in progress. Most of us perform better when we are on a deadline—as long as we don't freeze up with performance anxiety! So give yourself a benign deadline. You'll share a dream with a special friend at least once a week. You might agree to get together to do this, or you might do it by phone or e-mail. This is something that needs to be done in *live* time. Your friend's role is not to interpret your dream, but to hold that special space for you in which dreams may be safely shared—and encourage you to bring dreams into that space. Leading dream circles, I am filled with delight by the way dreams simply come through for newcomers who may have had a hard time recalling dreams before. Now they are coming into a space where dreams are cherished. As you get deeper into this, you may want to join a dream group or form one of your own. But first and last, you need to select that one person who will be your dream witness.

GETTING OVER NIGHTMARE BLOCKS

Maybe you have come this far, but find your nightmares are blocking you. Have you come up against things in dreams you are unable to face? In my personal lexicon, a nightmare is an *unfinished* dream. We encounter something so fearful or disturbing that we jolt ourselves out of the dream. We lie in bed in a clammy sweat, hearts thumping against our ribs, and give thanks it was "only" a dream.

There is a sizable industry devoted to helping people suppress nightmares, by giving them drugs to stop them from remembering their dreams or by suppressing the dream function, or by offering soapbubble solutions (like rescripting dreams in a cute or inauthentic way, without going back to confront the terror on its own ground).

We should give thanks for our nightmares.

Perhaps that seems shocking. But I think it's like this: Dreams come in gentle and timely ways to show us challenges that lie ahead. If we ignore our dream messages, the dream messenger becomes louder and more strident, like a friend who will phone or come round in the middle of the night because she has vital information for us. That information may involve something very challenging or unpleasant. Maybe the message is that we could lose our job, our relationship or our health. And maybe we don't want to face such possibilities. So we slam the door on our dreams even as they grow more vocal and dramatic. Now the dream messenger pursues us in terrifying guises, and we flee from the nightmare—the aborted dream—back into the dream of waking life, mumbling "It was only a dream." What happens in the end is that the issue presented in the dreams will bite us in the throat in waking life.

If we have missed the gentler, timelier dream advisories, let us at least give thanks for the nightmares that can rouse us, like a firehouse bell in the night, to take action before what we most fear and hide from takes form in physical reality.

How do we get beyond nightmare fears?

First, we need to stop running, turn around, and brave up to what is pursuing or threatening us. Start by getting yourself calm and strong enough to ask whatever you fear in the dream, "Who are you? Why are you pursuing me? What do you have to tell me?"

Try to go back inside the dream and dream it onward to resolution and closure.

Ask help from your dream allies and spiritual protectors. Yes, you have some even if you haven't thought about it since you were a kid, and they will take the forms you believe in. I learned something important about this from a child; when it comes to dreaming, kids are great teachers, if we will only listen. I once gave a scared little girl—a friend's daughter—a plastic soldier to protect her against the scary things she was meeting in her dreams. The toy soldier looked like a Roman centurion. A couple of years later, when I had forgotten about the incident, she told me she had faced creepy things in the night but that "Lex" had defended her. When I asked who "Lex" was, she said indignantly, "Don't you remember him? You gave him to me. Now he's *seven feet tall.*"

Tell yourself you will stay with your dreams from now on and try to resolve their issues inside the dreamstate. If you are scared or startled out of a dream, try to stay with it, slip back inside it, and dream it onward to resolution and clarity.

Remember that, once confronted, nightmare adversaries often turn out to be helpers or messengers in disguise. However, some dreams we flee from relate to events developing in waking life that require action in physical reality. Your work with these dreams will not be confined to the approach outlined above. It will require you to clarify the dream message by the techniques explained in the next chapter, and decide carefully what you need to *do* about it in your waking environment.

chapter two

KEYS TO DREAMING TRUE

Dreams are the facts from which we must proceed.
—C. G. Jung

Now that you are catching your dreams and recording them, how can you tell whether they involve future events, and whether you should look at them literally or symbolically?

Here are some keys that will help you unlock your dream messages. They'll work at any time, but they'll probably work best at four distinct stages of your waking life: when you first awaken; when you start your day in the outside world; when you have time for quiet analysis and reflection; and whenever you're ready to decide what action you should take to honor the dream and apply its insights.

EXPLORATIONS ON WAKING

It's best to try out the first set of keys as soon as possible after you awaken, perhaps while you are still lying in bed. If you can't do that, because you have to rush off to work or get the kids ready for school, then try them at the first quiet moment you have, or inside your head on the morning commute (you'll find the ride will go faster).

1. Trust Your Feelings

Before you do anything else with your dream, listen to what your body and your feelings are telling you. They will give you an instant and usually entirely reliable sense of what is going on here. Trust your heart and your gut to tell you whether the dream message is basically positive or negative, whether it relates to a situation developing in physical reality, whether this is your "stuff" or someone else's, and whether you need to do something about this *now.*

2. Reality Check

Ask yourself whether it is remotely possible that you will encounter the scenes and events in your dream in waking life. Do not skip over this question because the dream content seems "weird" or "bizarre." You may have previewed a sci fi movie you will see next month, or a bizarre scene that will confront you at the next street corner. Or you may have seen something from an odd angle.

Do not shy away from running this reality check on dreams that involve frightening or unpleasant scenarios.

Don't overlook the trivial or humdrum dreams. Much of our everyday lives can be pretty mundane, and "humdrum" dreams may contain quite exact previews of situations that will confront us as we go about our daily rounds.

3. Write a Personal One-liner

Don't struggle over this; simply sum up the content of the dream as briefly as possible. It is extraordinary how both the meaning and the gravitas of the dream—how it leans toward action—jumps out when we do this.

A woman dreamed she had sex with a guy at work she wasn't attracted to in waking life and then hung out with more of the guys from the office, smoking cigars (something she also does not do in ordinary reality). Her dream was fun; she came out of it happy and energized. She decided her one-line dream motto was, *I can have more fun at work!* This would include getting closer to colleagues she hadn't gotten to know very well—though not necessarily having sex with them! (Getting into bed with someone in a dream is often a metaphor for intimacy or friendship, and "blowing smoke" doesn't necessarily involve inhaling.)

Another dreamer went to a series of gatherings stark naked. Initially she was embarrassed but nobody else seemed to mind, and no one harassed or came on to her. She decided her dream motto was, *It's okay to show myself to others. I don't have to hide who I am.*

4. Ask the Two Vital Questions

The two vital questions we should ask of any dream (our own or a dream that is shared with us) are:

What do I need to know? and *What do I need to do?*

I am constantly delighted by how clearly these questions bring the issues reflected in the dreams into focus, and orient us toward doing something to manifest the energy and insight of the dream in waking life. When you have the answer to the first question—*What do I need to know?*—you might ask who or what in the dream is best able to respond. You are now prepared to go back inside the dream to take a closer look at this element. Maybe you will able to conduct a dialogue with a dream character and get a direct response to your question.

A man dreamed a woman who had lived in his home many years before turned up in his backyard with a group in an immense silver tour bus. He felt deeply moved as he watched her drop a seed on the ground. Then the tour bus took off.

He decided he needed to know more about the seed and the tour bus. Thinking about the seed brought up images of death and rebirth; something is buried in the ground in order to rise above it. The big silver tour bus brought associations from a very funny Albert Brooks movie, *Defending Your Life,* in which buses like this take people from a processing center to different locales in the afterlife.

It occurred to him now that his dream might be preparing him for the death of someone strongly connected to the place where he lived. He decided what he needed to do was get in touch with her. Having answered the first question, his answer to the second was "Make a phone call."

5. Go Back Inside the Dream

The meaning of a dream lies inside the dream itself: that is to say, inside the full dream *experience,* as opposed to the memory of the dream, which is often fragmentary or garbled. The best way to get at the meaning of a dream and determine (for example) if the message should be taken literally or symbolically is to reenter the dream. The best time to go back inside the dream is fairly soon after waking, when you are still connected with its rhythms and scenes. But if you miss that moment, don't despair. By my observation, dream reentry is possible at any time, even years or decades after the dream. In my workshops, people sometimes travel back inside dreams from early childhood with magical results. To go back inside your dream, all you need is:

A quiet, protected environment where you will not be disturbed. Ideally, you are still snug in bed, with images and sensory impressions from the dream still dancing in your head and your energy field. If you are reentering the dream at a later time, you may want to light a candle or perform a simple personal ritual to reinforce the fact that you are moving into a different and sacred space, the dreamspace.

The ability to relax. If you can't laze in bed after waking but want to go back inside a dream later on, you may find that soft meditation music or simply following the flow of your breathing until you are quite relaxed will help get you ready. Personally, I prefer the primal heartbeat of shamanic drumming, which works to eliminate mental clutter fast and fuels vivid experiences of conscious dreaming.

Clear intention. Focus on your answers to those two key questions: *What do I need to know?* and *What do I need to do?* Part of your purpose may be to dream the dream onward, past the point where you left it, to seek resolution or healing or simply enjoy the adventure.

A vivid picture. Your memory of a scene or image from your dream is your doorway into another landscape. Bring up the image on your mental screen and let it grow strong. As you relax your body, breathe gently and evenly, tensing and releasing muscle groups to free any tension or blockage you are holding, and let your awareness begin to slide or flow into the image, into the dream.

If your purpose is to clarify whether a dream relates to a future event, once inside the dream you will want to pay close attention to the location. *Location, location, location!* The real estate agents' motto is an excellent mantra for dream explorers. Look for that character or element inside your dream that may hold the answer to your question. As a test of whether this dream demands action in waking life to alter the outcome, see if you can change the script in a way that seems authentic. If you see the same events played out as before in a realistic setting, this may be a clue that the dream will either be played out in physical reality or that action in physical reality is required to change the outcome.

There are many, many reasons for seeking to master the technique of dream reentry. You may find that a "dream character" is a spiritual guide, and your renewed encounter may be the prelude to closer communication with a personal guardian or mentor. You'll quickly find yourself practicing the ancient and liberating art of dream travel, which will not only help you to scout out the future in this reality but to enter many other dimensions of reality at will. And you will have placed yourself on a path of boundless adventure.

TAKING YOUR DREAM INTO THE WORLD

The next steps make a wonderful start to the day as you go out into the world.

6. Share the Dream With a Friend

We are often too close to our own issues to see things that a complete outsider may notice at a glance. We gain precious insights by sharing our dreams with other people, provided the sharing follows a simple but indispensable protocol.

We start by holding the space for each other. Listening to a dream is as much of an art as telling a dream. It requires paying attention. To attend is literally to "stretch" ourselves, to stretch our understanding and our inner senses so we can begin to find ourselves inside the other person's dream. We shouldn't let others tell us their dreams unless we are willing to hold the space for them and give them this kind of focused attention. Similarly, telling a dream is an art. We should relate the dream simply and clearly, starting with the title, and avoid losing our audience by dragging in extraneous information. When we learn to tell dreams this way, we quickly develop powerful communications skills that can help us in many areas of life. We become storytellers and storymakers, capable of holding an audience and helping others to find their own power of story.

When we comment on each other's dreams, we must agree never to play expert. We can offer our insights in a much more helpful and human way, by saying, "If this were my dream, I would think about . . ." If we develop the ability to look deep inside the other's dream, we might vary this and say, "In my dream of your dream . . ." But we must never lean on the other person and try to tell her how it is.

We should try to start the day by sharing dreams with someone close to us. We can do this at the breakfast table or during a coffee break at the office. Most offices would actually run much better, and produce more productive and creative work, if employers *encouraged* their staff to start the workday by sharing dreams in pairs, or in groups. This does not have to be a lengthy process. When you share dreams on a regular basis, you'll find your ability to tell a story and hold the attention of your audience grows rapidly and dramatically. (If it doesn't, you'll lose your audience.) You'll learn to tell your dream clearly and simply, without flopping about and hauling in unnecessary details. At the same time, you'll find yourself recalling *relevant* and helpful details you may have forgotten as you revisit the scene and respond to questions. The process does not have to take a lot of time. With practice and a regular dream partner or group, you can coach each other to tell a dream, take a few questions, and receive helpful feedback in about ten minutes.

If you don't have a partner you can meet with frequently, maybe you can find a phone or e-mail partner. E-mail works surprisingly well for dream sharing, though you'll miss the body language and some of the raw energy that comes with face-to-face encounters.

7. Ask the Consequence Tree

Among indigenous dreaming peoples, some form of divination is frequently used to get a second opinion on the dream message. You might look for guidance from the flight of birds, the patterns of tea leaves, the fall of cards or yarrow sticks, the images that rise from the heart of a crystal or the surface of a looking pool. My daily practice is simply to pay attention to the play of synchronicity in the world about me. If I have a question about a dream message—or of any other kind—I play the game of telling myself that the first unusual or striking thing that enters my field of perception as I go about the world that day will be guidance from nature. This is a good game to play on the morning commute. Sometimes I get my answer immediately. Sometimes it emerges from a series of small incidents that reveal a pattern. Oh yes: if the issue is big enough, and the answer remains unclear, I may turn to the I Ching, or the Tarot, or scoop up a rock and look for images on each of its sides.

In my family, we sometimes refer to the game of looking for a sign in nature as "Asking the Consequence Tree." I borrowed this phrase from my daughter Sophie. We were driving in early fall, and noticed a maple that was half green and half fiery red. It reminded me of the "fiery and ever-living tree" in Celtic mythology, and I started talking about this. After hearing me out politely for a bit, Sophie said thoughtfully, "Dad, I think that's a Consequence Tree. It shows people the consequences of what they're doing and thinking, if they'll only stop to look at it."

Look around you any day. See how the world mirrors and comments on your dreams and concerns. A man wrote to me that he had been puzzling over the next step he needed to take in his personal growth, and woke from a dream that intrigued him but did not offer clear answers. Still thinking about this, he entered a bookstore in Colorado. "A book flew off the shelf and hit me in the forehead, right in the third eye position." The book was *Conscious Dreaming.* Sometimes the message hits us slap in the face!

ANALYSIS AND REFLECTION

8. Look for Clues to Precognitive Elements

As you journal dreams, you will come to notice personal markers that will help you identify the dreams that contain information about future events. The signatures of dream precognition include the following:

> *The literal, realistic quality of the dream.* The action conforms to the general rules of ordinary reality. People do not fly around the sky and dragons do not burst out of underground chambers. Indeed, the action may be so routine—a meeting at the office, fighting the rush-hour traffic—that you may be inclined to dismiss the dream as humdrum or trivial.
>
> *A realistic but unfamiliar locale.* This may be a place you will visit in the future, even if you have never considered going there. A woman had repeated dreams of traveling in Italy. The next summer, her fiance surprised her with a pair of plane tickets to Italy.

Weird or unlikely content, but you remain an observer. Alternatively, the dream content may appear bizarre, or you may witness extreme or unlikely situations but remain an observer. In the dream, you may be witnessing something at a distance from you (perhaps in both time and space) in which you will not be personally involved. You may also be watching a movie or a TV program you have not yet seen in waking life.

The appearance of old acquaintances with whom you have lost contact. You wake up wondering why you dreamed of someone you have not seen in ten years. The dream may indicate that this person will unexpectedly reappear in your life. More frequently, when we dream of an old acquaintance we are dreaming of someone *new* who will turn up in our lives. When we dream of people we have not yet met, we often misidentify them upon waking, as people we already know. This may be one of the ways our dream editor helps us to hold onto slippery material. If you dream of a former lover, ask yourself (along with all the other questions you might have!) whether your dream is introducing a *new* lover. If you dream of a former boss, check whether the dream may contain a preview of a future boss and/or a future job. If you dream of an old friend with red hair, be ready to meet someone new who has red hair.

An encounter with the departed. The departed appear to us in our dreams for many reasons, and to my mind this is the most natural thing in the world. When a departed person appears in our dreams, it is appropriate to ask whether he or she is actually (a) the individual we remember, speaking to us from the other side, or meeting us *on* the other side; (b) an aspect of ourselves that is like that person; or (c) a dream guide that has assumed a familiar face, the way gods and goddesses disguise themselves as human friends in the dreams of the *Odyssey.* Whatever the answer, the appearance of the departed in dreams is often a sign of a message coming through, and that message frequently contains information about the future. Since the departed are no longer confined to physical bodies or physical laws, they may find it easier to see things that lie beyond the range of the senses than we generally do, though their information is not always reliable. The appearance of the departed in dreams is often believed to herald death, and it is true that departed loved ones often appear to guide the dying through their crossing to the next life. But the departed, like other visitors, turn up for all sorts of reasons, not only in connection with death.

Communications themes are also markers of a message coming through that may be telepathic, precognitive, or both. Victorian dreamers would dream of a letter or a courier. Now we get a dream phone call or (with increasing frequency) a dream e-mail. One woman dreamed of a man who suggested that they swap URLs. Since (in waking life) her homepage was highly personal, something she shared only with a few friends, she wondered if her dream cyberphile might play a significant role in her future personal life.

Watching or reading the news. We read newspapers and magazines and watch TV news in our dreams, just as we do in waking life. Sometimes we dream about future news events as if we were there at the scene. If our dream is presenting a dramatic version of something we will later witness only through the filter of a journalist's perspective or a cameraman's focus, our dream report may suffer from their possible distortions. An overt news motif—seeing a newspaper or watching a TV report in the dream—carries the clear signal, "There is *news* in this dream." If we remember a specific news event, this might give the clue to when other elements in the dream could be played out in waking life. You can take a proactive approach to this. Some dreamers, like some remote viewers, try to train themselves to sneak a look at the news headlines (or the stock market listings) from a specific date in the future.

You see something in the dream that indicates a future date. Perhaps you do succeed in catching that newspaper date. Or perhaps the passage of time is suggested in subtler ways. Maybe the season in your dream is different from the season in physical reality, or someone you know looks older. Maybe your dream features a new model Corvette or a Microsoft program that is not yet on the market. A world event—in the background or foreground of the dream—may be the clue to the passage of time.

You get a direct message. Someone may simply appear in your dreams and tell you something about the future, or where to find the information. The dream messenger may be a departed loved one, a spirit guide, or your guardian angel, but can also appear in a very homely guise.

Some psychic dreamers comment on the "insert" quality of messages coming through in their dreams. They may be in the midst of one dream experience when something else—a sudden image, a phone call—interrupts, just as a flash of intuition or a literal phone call might shift our attention in waking life. This insert effect is a good marker of "mental radio" or telepathy. For some dreamers, there is the sense of a "subtitle" running through a dream episode. Asked how she knows that a dream relates to future events, one active dreamer explained, "I seem to sense the difference, as if a subtitle is running through the scene, saying: *This is for real, pay attention.*"

Finally, there is the phenomenon of *direct knowing.* Sometimes we wake to find we have no recollection of our dreams at all, and yet have this sense of direct knowing about something at a distance from us in time or place. Like *déjà vu,* this is often the gift of a dream we have forgotten. Better than *déjà vu,* this kind of sixth sense allows us to prepare for something before we run into it.

9. Study the Code of Your Personal Dream Symbols

Some dreamers notice personal symbols in dreams that serve as markers of a certain kind of event that may be developing in external reality. For example, at least a dozen women dreamers have told me over the years that they dream of fish—often shoals of tiny fish—when someone they know becomes pregnant. Before tests confirmed that my wife Marcia was pregnant, I had a similar dream in which both of us were wading in a deep river where tiny silver fish were swimming rapidly upstream. It does not require any great imaginative stretch to notice the similarity between little fish and sperm swimming towards the egg.

From such correspondences, books of the drugstore dream dictionary or "gypsy dreambook" genre are born. If I were in favor of book-burning (which I am not) I would make a bonfire out of all the published dream dictionaries because they encourage us to trust in outside authorities and generic interpretations instead of the fresh, custom-made and highly specific insights of our own dreams. Nonetheless, it's fun and can be most revealing to compile a personal dictionary of symbols, one that is just for you and perhaps the people with whom you share your own dreams. Your personal glossary will emerge quite effortlessly after you have been journaling dreams for a while, even for as short a period as a few months. As you study recurring symbols, you will begin to notice that some of them may be signatures of certain kinds of coming events. For instance, you may notice that in some of your dreams, a wedding scene may be a *literal* preview of a coming event. In other dreams, a wedding may be a *symbolic* warning of a different kind of potential event, such as death. Or your dream wedding may be an episode in a separate reality, perhaps a glimpse of another time or a walk along a path not taken in this life, in which you married (or failed to marry) your high school sweetheart. The wedding in your dreams is not the same as the wedding in my dreams—unless we are having a mutual, or interactive, dream.

DREAMS INTO ACTION

The last key involves moving into active mode, bringing the energy and insight of dreams into waking life, and honoring the powers that speak through dreams.

10. Determine What Action Is Required—and Do It!

Under dream reports in my journals, I frequently make a note that begins "Dream-directed action" or simply "indicated action." Dreaming is about living in this world as well as in other worlds. Dreams give us specific clues to things we can do to improve our own lives and those of people around us. Dreams call for action. Keeping a journal, writing your personal one-liners, sharing dreams with a friend are already action, but there is a great deal more.

The action indicated may involve a specific strategy to avoid unpleasant events foreseen in the dream. A dream may ask us to change our diet, our habits, our work or relationships. I have abandoned book projects, withdrawn from partnerships, cancelled plane trips and even tried eating kale because of specific dream advisories. Alternatively, if the dream promises wonderful things, we need to devise ways to harness the dream energy and steer towards its fulfillment.

Above all, we need to improvise personal rituals and creative play to honor and celebrate our dreams and the powers that speak through dreams. We can do this by turning our dreams into stories and songs, pictures and theatre, and by sharing their gifts with those around us.

chapter three

WAKING UP TO DREAMING TRUE

Many things unknown, and unwished for, nor ever attempted by our minds, are manifested to us in dreams . . . which we knew not by any report; and these dreams need not any act of interpretation, which belong to divination.

—Cornelius Agrippa of Nesseheim, 1531

Quick: Have you ever dreamed something before it happened? If so, what was the *first time* you remember having had this experience?

I have put this question to many dreamers, and if you have not (yet) woken up to the fact that you are dreaming the future, you may be inspired by some of their replies.

* "I dreamed Grandpa visited me on the night he died. He told me he loved me and was going to a better place. Nobody in the family wanted to believe me, even though

we got a phone call in the middle of the night, telling us he had died."

* "I dreamed the space shuttle *Challenger* disaster before it happened. I saw the problem was with some kind of seal on the left side, though I didn't know it was called an O-ring until they told us that on the TV news."
* "I dreamed my husband returned a shirt I had never seen to a department store and they would only give him $32.99 for it. The next afternoon my husband called me to tell me his mother had sent him a shirt he didn't like for a birthday present. He took it back to the store, but they would only give him $32.99—the sale price, not the regular price—because he didn't have a receipt."
* "I dreamed of marrying a dark-skinned girl with beautiful long black hair in a little white church by the ocean in California. Six years later, I met that girl and married her in the little white church in Novato, California."
* "I dreamed someone had painted a happy face on a rock on the side of the road I take to work. A week later, I saw the happy face on that rock. I'm certain it wasn't there before."
* "I dreamed I was floating over the position of my Marine company on a battlefield in Korea, watching the enemy movements. I had this dream while sailing to Korea. When it came to the battle, my dream helped me to make the right tactical decisions, based on the prior intelligence that came, not from G2, but from my dream."
* "I dreamed that Fergie was cavorting topless by a swimming pool. Then the tabloid papers in England published pictures of her, topless with her boyfriend."

This is a random selection of anecdotes and—before the hardheads get out their heavy artillery—I will concede that, reported in this form, they are just that: anecdotes. As we go along, we will see that there are ways of recording dreams that give them more standing as *evidence* of precognition. More interesting, for those of us who want to use dreams to enrich and empower our lives, is the possibility that we can use some of these glimpses of the future to make wiser choices and shape our future for the better.

The first dream I recall that showed me the future terrified me, because I thought it meant we were going to war. I was six at the time, living in Brisbane with my mother and father, who was a major in the Australian army. In my dream, I saw my dad strapping on his service revolver and leaving the house in the middle of the night, in full battle kit, to join a convoy of soldiers. I tried to talk to my parents about the dream, but did not get much of a hearing, because they did not believe in dreams, at least not at that time. A week or so later, the scene was played out in waking life. There was a strike of railroad workers that threatened the banana and pineapple crops, and the army was sent out in the role of strikebreakers. Crying and uncomprehending, I watched in my pajamas as my father strapped on his service revolver and went out into the night, to join the military driver who was waiting for him.

In itself, this is merely another anecdote. It proves nothing to anyone but me, and even I might wonder if my memory is exact. At six, I was not keeping a dream journal, and have long since lost track of dates and details. But that incident—and many similar ones that followed—sowed a lifelong curiosity in me. Much of this book is a response to the questions that rose in me then. If we can see the future, does that mean that the future already exists? What does that say about our common-sense notions of time, and of reality itself? If the future we see in dreams is one that can be changed, what is this future that can both exist and not exist? And if we can see events, large and small, that will happen or that might happen, why don't we make more use of this ability?

I used to be a journalist, and when I was a correspondent in the wretched war in Cambodia, I believe it was a dream that kept me alive. A daring photojournalist had talked me into going out in a jeep on the main road from Phnom Penh that soon became notorious as a death trap for reporters and cameramen. I wasn't very happy about this plan. In my dream the night before we were supposed to leave on our expedition, I woke in a cold sweat from a dream in which I seemed to have been blown out of my skin. I did not take that ride. My friend did, and he did not return. You could argue—and you might be right—that my terrifying dream simply dramatized my fears.

But now I have been a dream journalist (rather than the other kind) for many years, I have collected many examples of dreaming the future in a more organized way, with the dates and details that were lacking when I was a shy, sickly kid or a young man pretending to be a hardboiled reporter. Throughout this book I have included excerpts from my personal logs that illustrate what, for me, has become a routine fact of life: if we pay attention, we will notice that we are dreaming the future all the time. My favorite examples are the trivial or silly ones, because they demonstrate just how routine this precognitive faculty may be:

* I dream that 68 people are enrolled for one of my dream workshops. Thirteen months later, when I arrive at a retreat center for a workshop that was not even thought of at the time of my dream, I find that 68 people are enrolled. The rest of my dream report—a quite complex narrative—proved invaluable in dealing with situations that came up during the weekend retreat.
* I dream that I go to a hotel where I am told that my credit card will also function as my room key. Three months later, unexpectedly obliged to check into a midtown Manhattan

hotel that I had never visited before, I am surprised (and yet not surprised) when the woman at reception tells me they have a new system: my credit card will be my room key.

* I have a movie-like dream in which a silly dog is decked out in fake antlers for a Christmas pageant. The dog runs out on the road but is magically revived by a bizarre character. The next day, I miss an airline connection. On the "wrong" plane, I watch in in-flight movie ("Michael") in which a silly dog is decked out in fake antlers for a Christmas photo shoot. The dog is killed on the road, but is magically revived by a bizarre character, a low-flying angel played by John Travolta.

It is fascinating to look at how we wake up to the fact that we have a natural ability to dream things before they happen—and then awaken (if we are lucky, or thoughtful, or simply ready to push the envelope) to the deeper realization that if we can see the future, we might be able to use the information to do some good.

Fire Above Fire

Sometimes it takes a jolt to wake us up to what dreaming can be.

Rita Dwyer was a rocket scientist when she got as fierce a jolt as most of us can imagine. Back in 1959, she was working as a research chemist for a pioneer aerospace company in New Jersey when an experimental rocket fuel exploded in her laboratory. She was instantly engulfed in flames, literally burning to death. Dense clouds of chemical fumes completely hid her from the view of her colleagues. As they scrambled to evacuate, it is doubtful that any of them would have been able to help Rita—except that Rita's friend and coworker Ed Butler had dreamed the event.

In his dream, Ed was working at his desk in the office in his shirtsleeves, without protective gear, when he heard the explosion. He ran to the door of Rita's lab, heard her scream, but could see nothing but smoke and fumes. He called her name and went in, finally seeing her and pulling her out by her foot, the only part of her that was not in flames. He put Rita under a deluge shower (a safety feature between the laboratories) which quelled the flames, then ran for the red phone used for emergency calls. At this point, Ed woke up.

When the rocket fuel exploded in Rita's laboratory in waking life, Ed was working in the office in his shirtsleeves. Step by step, he now reenacted his dream. He ran with unselfconscious heroism into the blazing laboratory, grabbed Rita's foot, and dragged her to safety. She was burned over much of her body, and for many months her life was a physical torment. She is alive today only because her friend remembered his dream—and acted on it when waking events caught up to the dream.

I first heard Rita's story when I listened to her speech as outgoing president of the Association for the Study of Dreams at its conference in Santa Fe in 1993. She is a petite, vibrant woman, quite beautiful—although she must avoid direct sunlight because her face and much of her body is sheathed in skin grafts—with a great and giving heart. As I watched her and enjoyed her passion for the limitless adventure of dreaming, I realized I was in the presence of one of those moving spirits who can help to make our society what is desperately needs to become: a society in which dreams are cherished and honored. A friend's dream gave Rita back her life, and in turn she devoted a vital part of her life to exploring and celebrating dreams.

By her own account, she was a "hard scientist" at the time of the accident in the lab, with no training in psychology nor any particular interest in dreams before the event. She now embarked on a search to see if dreams really could predict the future and if so, how the knowledge might be used. Her friend Ed—who had never mentioned dreams before the fire—now told her that he had had several dreams about the explosion. He called them "rehearsals." Modestly refusing to accept any praise for his bravery, he said that his dream rehearsals had enabled him to perform his heroic act without thought or fear; he simply reenacted his dream. For Rita, still very much the scientist, the question became: Were the dreams Ed experienced "anomalies," or could anyone—including Rita herself—dream of future events and make use of the information?

This question spurred her to decades of research, listening and learning from others but also focusing where the most important dream research will always be centered: on her own dream journals. She recorded her dreams and examined them for evidence of precognition. She was a tough examiner. Over the years, whenever she found occasional "hits" that seemed to be giving her dream snapshots of the future, she queried whether these were true cases of precognition, rather than processing of information she might have picked up from subliminal hints or things she had read or seen in the media. Her inner skeptic was only finally satisfied when she had a dream preview of the 1980 eruption of Mount St. Helens, fire echoing fire. A month before the volcano erupted, Rita woke from a terrifying dream: the setting was her childhood home, which she now observes often is the site of her precognitive dreams.

> As I look up at the distant mountains, I see lightning flash at the top of one, the sky is dark, and then mud/lava begins to flow from the top, moving fairly rapidly to the lower areas and threatening to overtake me and my older brother. He runs faster than I and leaves me behind. I fear the lava will catch up with me and wonder if I should climb a tree to escape it.

She told her husband her dream immediately upon waking. When she saw a report in the morning paper about activity observed at Mount St. Helens she wondered if she had tuned into the news—which would be an example of dream clairvoyance, (or telepathy) rather than precognition. Yet she had a deep certainty within herself that what she had seen was going to happen. Weeks passed, and there were no further reports from Mount St Helen's.

Then about a month after the dream, Rita's husband came to her and said, "Your volcano has erupted!" What made the event proof of precognition came in the newspapers the next day. One of the accounts related the sighting of lightning at the top of the volcano before its eruption, and Rita would never have expected that to happen from her waking knowledge of volcanoes. The scientist in her was finally satisfied she had dreamed a specific event before it took place.

As she went on monitoring her dreams for glimpses of the future, she noticed many more that anticipated situations at a distance in which there seemed to be nothing she could do to affect the outcome. Some involved tragedies like plane crashes; some anticipated trivial or silly incidents like the report of an elephant escaping from the London zoo.

But she never forgot her friend's dream "rehearsal" that had saved her life. She scanned her dreams for the early warnings we can use to change the future, to help ourselves, our loved ones, and others as we develop our ability to tune into this early warning system that never shuts down.

"If we change the future by acting on our dream information," Rita observes, "the outcome is not always as we had dreamed. We don't get run over by that red truck, or we don't get an illness, or have our purse stolen. Scoffers will say there is no proof that these dreams were precognitive. And dreams of this kind are unlikely to be reproduced in the laboratory, because each dream is specific to the individual and not programmable. The only way to convince non-believers is through careful journaling and noting 'hits' as they occur. And through our daily 'walking our talk,' showing by example just how valuable dreams can be."

Rita has lived by her dreams for decades and she has made a tremendous contribution—nationally and internationally—to raising consciousness about the importance of dreams and the need to heed their wisdom.

In her personal life, she is poised and alert to the possibility of using early warning dreams to help family and friends. By paying attention to her dreams, she believes she has been able to avert accidents, and to anticipate and respond early to medical emergencies in life-helping ways. Now an adept dreamworker who guides others to explore dreams on many levels, she never discounts the possibility that dreams may forecast situations developing in waking life.

Rita shared some recent episodes in which she dreamed medical advisories for people connected with her.

In one dream, a friend showed Rita a sore on her thigh. Rita told her she should see a doctor because it looked "angry" and in need of attention.

The next day, Rita saw her friend and told her she had dreamed that her friend had a sore on her leg. The other woman blanched and asked, "Where on my leg?" When Rita pointed to an area that was hidden by her skirt, her friend confided that she had a mole there which had become irritated. Up to this point, she had done nothing about it except to cover it with a bandage. Rita's friend decided to take her dream advice. She saw her doctor immediately, and found that the mole was precancerous and had to be removed.

In another health dream, which did not turn out quite so happily, Rita became aware of her father's previously undiagnosed terminal illness. When this very hale and hearty man caught a case of the flu one winter, he was left with a bad cough. Rita had a dream which was short and clear; it told her that her father was much more seriously ill than anyone in the family had realized. Because of her dream, Rita urged her father to go to the doctor. X-rays of his lungs revealed secondary cancer sites which had metastasized from Hodgkins' disease, the primary site being a lymph node in his arm. He died six months later.

While the dream did not save his life, it did prepare the family for his passing, and gave him time to get his affairs in order and share quality time with his loved ones.

LEARNING THROUGH BABY STEPS

Rita went through the fire, in the most literal sense, and emerged with the gift of dreaming true.

Even when it does not involve personal trauma, for many of us the first recollection of dreaming true may involve death or disaster. Unfortunately, some of us are frightened away from the very thought of dreaming about the future when our dreams involve unpleasant events. We may feel stricken or powerless after dreaming of some terrible calamity. Worse, if our dream is fulfilled in waking life, we may feel guilty, as if we are in some way responsible for a tragedy because we dreamed it before it happened.

It is the small, mundane or merely curious dreams about future events that are often most helpful in training us to recognize and work with precognitive dream messages. There is nothing of earth-shattering consequence going on here. We're not likely to be scared off by doubting our ability to get the message straight or figure out what to do with it (though we may fail to record and subsequently remember the dream simply because it does seem so insignificant). Let's find out more about the dream of returning the $32.99 shirt, and what flowed from it.

Returning the Shirt for $32.99

The experiences of the Idaho woman who shared this dream are an excellent example of how we can learn the art of dreaming true through baby steps, gaining confidence by catching "little" dreams and matching them up with subsequent events. Siskanna's story also reveals how as we start drawing on our intuition through dreams, we quicken our natural intuitive abilities in waking life.

Siskanna dreamed that her husband was in a store returning a shirt. The saleslady told him that she could only give him $32.99 for it and he said fine. When Siskanna woke up, she thought, "What a stupid dream!" thinking it was absolutely without significance. She wondered why she had even remembered such a mundane, meaningless dream. The next day, her husband called her at work. She casually asked him what he had been doing during the day. He told her that his mother had sent him a birthday package, including a shirt that he wasn't crazy about. He reported that when he returned it to the store, the saleslady could "only" give him $32.99 for it. This was the sale price of the shirt, not the regular price, but without a receipt it was the best she could do.

The dreamer was struck by how specific her dream information had been, about such a seemingly trivial episode. This experience encouraged her to watch her dreams much more closely. She soon found she was noticing more and more precognitive dreams. Like the dream of her husband's shirt, many of them seemed quite mundane. It gradually occurred to her that her dream consciousness might be teaching her through "baby steps" to receive and work with information about the future. She comments, "If my first precognitive dream had been about a murder or some other serious and potentially disturbing matter, my own fears would have probably shut down the process completely." The mundane dreams reassured her that dream precognition is real, and that it is safe to explore. She began to develop an intuitive feel for when a particular dream might contain information about the future.

She dreamed one night that her husband was driving her car, while she rode in the passenger seat. The car seemed to be moving through a dark, empty space. A male figure loomed up out of the dark and pointed insistently at the rear wheel of the car. In the dream, Siskanna told her husband to pull over. "That man was pointing at the wheel and I think something might be wrong."

When Siskanna woke up, she felt certain her car had a flat tire. She threw on her robe and rushed to a front window to check. When she pulled back the curtain, she saw she was right; a back tire was flat. Her husband was working in the yard but had not noticed the flat. She asked him to change the tire for her before she left for work, which he did. This "little" dream accomplished something. At the very least, it saved her from discovering the flat at an inopportune time, and arriving late for work.

In this second example of learning through babysteps, the dreamer was helped to recognize that if she could see future problems in dreams, she may be able to avoid them.

Siskanna continued to pay close attention to her dreams. She now noticed she was dreaming about strangers and possible future events relating to them.

She noticed something else. As she paid more attention to her precognitive dreams, she found her waking intuition coming more strongly alive. She found that when she was in the car, she had developed "an uncanny way of knowing" when a cop was in the vicinity. Driving in a remote area in the Idaho desert, she got "that feeling" and told her husband to slow down—just before a patrol car came into view over the top of a low hill. Waking intuition has alerted her to more serious situations. Walking in town, on her way to the bank, she picked up a disturbing mental image of her husband rolling over an embankment in his truck. Deeply concerned about the safety of her husband and their young son—who had left with his father that morning—she tried to "check" on them psychically. What she picked up was that her son was completely out of harm's way, and her husband would be fine. To her great relief, she later learned that, though her husband's truck had rolled over four times on the road she had glimpsed, he had escaped with minor cuts and bruises, and he had dropped off their son to play with friends before the accident.

She thanks the power of intuition awakened by her work with her dreams for her own escape from a much worse incident. She was taking evening classes at the university, and began to get a distinctly "creepy" feeling as she walked back to her car along a dark path near the river. She angrily rejected her fear, dismissing it as the "ingrained cultural fear of being a woman alone in the dark." She continued to walk that dark path, feeling afraid and angry. Her feelings became so strong she resolved to try to write her way through them. She produced a story for her fiction writing class in which a young woman was attacked by a knife-wielding man on the path. She turned in her story on a Friday, but its completion brought no sense of resolution, so she decided to stop walking the path. The following day, a young woman was raped and stabbed to death on the path near the river. Siskanna speculates that the murderer may have been imagining his crime for many weeks. "His thought projections were strong enough, and relevant enough to me, that I picked up on them. The intuition helped me to change my own behavior, perhaps just in the nick of time, to avoid imminent danger to myself. I agonized over whether or not I could have done something to save that woman for many months. I must rest with the knowledge that I was able to save myself—and I am much more quick to listen to my intuition after that experience."

Avoiding the Head-on Collision

My friend Wanda Burch is one of the most gifted psychic dreamers I know. Since her early childhood in the Deep South, she has had "clear" dreams about events taking place at a distance from her in space or time. She often passes on important dream messages to others. She was compelled to take her own dreaming abilities with utmost seriousness when her dreams started warning her, in her early twenties, that she was likely to die at 43. As she approached that age, her dreams warned her, quite specifically, that she had developed breast cancer before physical symptoms had manifested. I told part of the inspiring story of how she was then able to work with her dream images to guide herself through healing and recovery, altering the "destiny" announced in her early dreams, in my book *Conscious Dreaming.*

Wanda's story is an object lesson in how to work with future dreams. If we do not like the future that seems to be announced in our dreams, we should not jump to the conclusion that the future is fixed. We should maneuver and experiment and test the boundaries.

Here is a more recent example of how Wanda works with warning dreams to change the future for the better. I can vouch for this story, because she shared the dream with me before the event took place that *almost* played it out.

Wanda dreamed she was driving to work. She was following her usual route, and the scene was almost tediously realistic and routine. She had no idea she was dreaming. There was snow on the ground, and the road was icy in places. She came to a bridge. As she drove across, she noticed a small red car—a Honda—coming the other way. As both cars neared the midpoint of the bridge, the woman driver of the other car lost control on the ice and skidded across the road. Wanda woke up with a start and sat up in bed, her heart thumping. She felt sure she had just been involved in a head-on collision with the red Honda. She had to check to make sure she was safe in bed, her husband peacefully asleep beside her, under the covers.

What would you do, if this were your dream?

You might decide simply to give thanks that it was "only" a dream, and dive back under the covers for some possibly much-needed sleep.

You might go looking for an instant interpretation of a "car crash" dream in one of those dictionaries of dream symbols.

You might ask yourself where in your life—maybe at work or in your relationships—you could be moving toward a "head-on collision." That would be a good question to ask, but it does not address the literal, realistic quality of this dream, and the weight of dread that came with it.

You might start to become excessively fearful about icy roads, or driving in general—and end up bringing about an accident in waking life.

Wanda did none of these things. She lay down again in bed and pictured the scene she had dreamed, confirming details: the two lane bridge, the ice on the road, the red Honda, the woman driver. Then she wrote down her dream and resolved to keep it in mind as a travel advisory. Notice that her memory of her dream contained specific details, including the precise location, an approximate time—morning commute—ice on the road and the specific circumstances of the possible accident. If all she had retained was a sense of fear and the memory of a car crash at an unknown time and location, her story might have a different ending.

Two weeks after the dream, there was snow on the ground and the road was icy as Wanda drove towards work on her morning commute. As she stopped for the light before the two-lane bridge, she saw a red Honda on the far side and remembered her dream. Because of the dream, she decided not to drive onto the bridge until the red Honda had crossed. When the light turned green, she sat with her foot on her brake pedal, despite the angry horns of drivers waiting behind her. When the Honda reached the midpoint of the bridge, the woman driver lost control, skidded across the median, and plowed into the railing. Wanda and I are both convinced that the red Honda hit the railing of the bridge, instead of Wanda's car, because she remembered and worked with her dream.

We can't describe Wanda's dream as fully precognitive, because it was not enacted exactly as she dreamed it. Her dream was more valuable than that. The way she worked with it—avoiding panic or denial or the temptation to psychologize its message away—is a splendid model of how we can use dream information to change the future for the better.

chapter four

WHEN DREAMS SEEM FALSE

It was Smerdis the Magus, not my brother, of whose rebellion God warned me in my dream.

—King Cambyses of Persia in Herodotus, *Histories*

The five most common reasons why we misinterpret dream messages about the future are:

1. We mistake a literal event for a symbolic one, or vice versa;
2. We misidentify people and places;
3. We fail to figure out how far in the future the dreamed event might be;
4. We see future events from a certain angle, that may not reveal the whole picture;
5. We confuse realities, confounding a dream that relates to external reality with dreams that are real experiences in other orders of reality.

Let's explore each of these problem areas.

LITERAL OR SYMBOLIC?

In general, we need to take dreams more literally and the events of waking life more symbolically. But of course dreams have many levels of meaning, and they often speak to us in symbolic language because symbols help us to move from what we know in the surface mind to what we do not (yet) know. Even when dreams relate very closely to situations in external reality, they give us symbols to explore—sometimes by pointing us to the symbols of everyday life.

A woman dreamed her car had a flat tire. In the morning, she went out early to check and found that, indeed, a rear tire of her car was flat. She was grateful that her dream had prodded her to check before her husband left for work, so she could ask him to change the tire for her. This is a very small, quite typical example of how our dream radar helps us pick up and deal with practical problems. Yet the incident also offers an opportunity to explore symbolic meanings. If my car has a flat, I might ask myself where—in the rest of my life—things might have gone "flat." I might think about whether the vehicle with the flat might symbolize my job, my relationship, or my ability to choose my own course and go my own way.

Similarly, if my dream features a messy kitchen, and I find in the morning that my pets have knocked over the garbage and a late-night snacker has left dirty dishes in the sink and a trail of gloppy peanut butter over the cutting board, I might notice that while my dream gave me a fairly literal scan of the situation downstairs, it may also be pointing me to a deeper symbolism, involving all that the state of my kitchen represents. In my life, the kitchen is the place where I am nourished and fed. It is a place where the family comes together in easy, relaxed ways. In many of my dreams, my kitchen also symbolizes my creative center, the place where I cook things up, sort out the ingredients for my books, and decide how to present my dishes. If my kitchen is in a mess, is there a mess I need to deal with in any of these larger senses?

We need always to examine the possibility that dreams mean just what they say, and could be played out in external reality. But this is a preface, not an alternative, to playing the great game of symbol exploration. Dreams contain signs of specific events developing in physical reality, and we should watch for these signals and use them. But symbols are more than signs, and *everything* is a symbol.

Let's look at a few kinds of dreams that are often misunderstood because we err on the side of being either over-literal or over-symbolic.

Dreams of Natural Disasters

A dream of a natural disaster—earthquake, hurricane, volcanic eruption—may symbolize a coming crisis in your life. In this context, it is very interesting to examine the damage. For example, which buildings, if any, were collapsed or flattened? If a bank was destroyed, maybe there is a message about your finances. If a church or a college building was blown apart, perhaps you need to look at the possible overthrow of your entire belief system or mind-set. If your home was damaged, maybe a big change is coming in your personal life and relationships. If the whole landscape seemed to be swallowed by a force of nature, the change may extend to your entire way of being in the world: the transvaluation of all values.

Don't rush to interpret a dream of being swept away by a power of nature as wholly negative—unless your *feelings* are telling you that. A tornado may flatten your house; a dream twister may also whirl you away into a sparkling, magical reality, as Dorothy was carried off to Oz. But *nota bene:* if you dream of a twister and you live in tornado country, before you start thinking about symbolic levels of meaning you had better ask yourself whether you have received an advisory about an entirely literal event that could take place in the future. The first questions you will need to ask are quite specific ones about place and time. When is this happening? Perhaps the season in the dream, or the age of a familiar person, might give you a key to that. Where is it happening? Try to identify the location. If the neighborhood is unfamiliar, consider the possibility that you are previewing an event at a location you will visit in the future, or picking up information that could be relevant to someone you know in another state or another country.

Prior to the hurricane that leveled many of the buildings on Kauai in the early 1990s, a friend who was living in the islands dreamed that his office was destroyed. He took this as a warning about his professional career. He flew to the mainland to explore job opportunities. When he returned to Kauai, he found that his office—and most of the village around it—was no longer there. Fortunately, he now had a new office and a new job waiting for him on the West Coast. He concluded that his dream had given him a double message, both literal and symbolic.

The strongest symbolism in many precognitive dreams is actually the symbolism of the events and situations in waking life to which they orient us. Having your office flattened by a hurricane is a very powerful symbol—so powerful that it mobilized the Kauai dreamer to take care of his job security before he realized that his dream scene was also a preview of a physical event.

Celebrity Dreams

Suppose President Clinton, Whoopi Goldberg or Princess Diana appears in your dreams. The celebrity figure could be:

a. An aspect of yourself (the part of you that is like Bill Clinton or Princess Di);

b. An analog for someone you know—the person who behaves like Clinton, or has Whoopi's sense of humor;
c. Precognition: you glimpsed a future news report, or a movie, or a physical encounter;
d. Tapping into a collective thought-form. These are generated when many minds and many people's emotions are focused on a particular image or individual. They take on their own life; this is how saints appear to the faithful in dreams and visions after their deaths;
e. Distant seeing: you saw into some aspect of the literal life of a famous person.

In working with celebrity dreams, it clearly makes a difference whether you know the famous person. If not, ask yourself whether it is remotely possible that you will one day have contact with this person. Be open to the unexpected; you may never get into the Oval Office, but you just *might* be in the crowd when the President makes a stop in your home town. Maybe one of your friends has access to the famous person. Since friendships create psychic bridges, it might then be possible for you to pick up accurate information about the famous person via your friend without either of you even being aware of the mechanism at work.

STRANGERS WITH FAMILIAR FACES

That celebrity in your dream could be someone you have not yet met who will remind you in some way of the famous person, because they have the same twinkle, the same laugh—or maybe the same cocaine habit. Maybe you wonder why you are dreaming of someone you knew in school whom you haven't seen in twenty years. Then someone who is a dead ringer for your old friend (minus the braces) walks into your life. You dream of a former lover or a bank manager who was once mean to you. Then you discover the dream was actually about a new lover who wasn't in your life at that time, or the difficult fellow at the new bank you have to deal with over a loan you hadn't even considered taking out at the time of the dream.

When we dream about people we have not yet met, we tend to tag them with the identities of people we do know. While this often leads to puzzlement and confusion, I think it is an example of the helpful role of the dream editor who gets to work as we surface from sleep. Some dreamers, like gifted intuitives, are able to bring through the names and specific descriptions of the new people they encounter in dreams; some even bring back phone numbers and street addresses. But many of us, on surfacing from sleep, might have little more than the memory of some kind of interaction with "people I don't know" without the editor's tags.

So let's hover for a moment and determine if that really was Bill or Janet in the dream, rather than someone we don't know yet—or don't know well—who may remind us of them in some way. You might notice a discrepancy in the way the dream character looks. The Bill you know doesn't wear a moustache, but his doppleganger does in the dream. Janet doesn't smoke—or does she?—but the character in the dream was outside the hair salon puffing away.

When I dream of a former editor or a former partner but am not 100 percent certain that my dream character really is that person, I sometimes put the name inside quotation marks in my dream report ("Michael," "Trina"). Or I might add a notation like "someone who reminds me of ____."

Sometimes we dream the correct name of a person we have not yet met, but the name also belongs to someone we know, so we misidentify the dream character with his namesake. I think of this as the Cambyses problem, because of the wretched fate of an ancient King of Persia described by

Herodotus. While Cambyses was campaigning in Egypt, he dreamed that a usurper called Smerdis seized his throne. The only person he knew (or at any rate thought about) who was called Smerdis was his own brother. Cambyses concluded that his brother was guilty of treason. No slouch at acting on his dreams, the King despatched assassins to bump off Smerdis. Later he was appalled to learn that there was a second Smerdis, one of a powerful caste of magician-priests, who had taken advantage of the confusion at home to steal the throne. The episode drove poor Cambyses mad. Herodotus quotes him as wishing he had never dreamed. While I can understand that sentiment, under the circumstances, it is worth noting that it was not the dream that doomed the King; it was his misinterpretation. The dream contained quite accurate intelligence—more accurate, it seems, than all the King's spies could bring him. It was his assessment of this intelligence that was faulty.[1]

I run into the Cambyses problem quite frequently—though never (I am glad to report) with such darkly disturbing consequences—because I have learned to bring back a great amount of specific information, including names and addresses otherwise unknown to me, from my dreams. A recent example springs to mind. I had several dreams of friendly encounters with a man who spoke with a crisp Anglo-Australian accent. His name was Malcolm Fraser. When I woke, I wrote in my journal that I had met the former Australian prime minister. I had met *that* Malcolm Fraser many years before, and it was not beyond the bounds of possibility that our paths would cross again. But this did not happen when I visited my native country a few months later, and I forgot my "Malcolm Fraser" dreams until I was setting up for a workshop in Chicago a year after that.

A fit, friendly-looking man with white hair strolled into the space.

I knew him at once.

"Have we met before?" I asked.

"I don't think so," he replied in a crisp Anglo-Australian accent.

He stuck out his hand and introduced himself. "Malcolm Fraser." He told me he had been born in England but lived for many years in Australia.

Then I remembered the dreams, and the dreams made sense. It had seemed odd to me at the time—though certainly encouraging—that a prominent Australian politician would be so deeply interested in dreamwork. *This* Malcolm Fraser proved to be deeply engaged in exploring consciousness, and brought wonderful energy and insight into our Chicago dream group.

How do we recognize the strangers who wear familiar faces in our dreams? Often we *won't* recognize them until they show up in waking life. But if we want to take advantage of our dream previews of new people who may be coming over the horizon—and where our engagement with them could lead—we should take a second look at the names we give to our dream characters. This can be as simple as asking ourselves, *Suppose it isn't X, but someone who will remind me of him/her?*

THE TIME-LAPSE PROBLEM

One of the greatest challenges in reading dream messages is to recognize material that relates to possible events that may lie far ahead on the road of ordinary life. If an event follows a dream within a day or two, we may notice the match-up—if we remember and record our dreams!—and may be able to benefit from the dream information. But many precognitive and early warning dreams precede the events they foreshadow by much longer periods. By my observation, we start dreaming of encounters and events that pack a strong emotional charge months, years or even decades before they manifest. Active dreamers have told me they have clusters of dreams relating to future romantic partners *three to nine months* before the first encounter, and sometimes much longer in advance.

In the two case studies that follow, I received an important dream message about a challenging situation at a workshop 13 months before it took place, and a woman dreamer received dream warnings about a traumatic relationship some 20 years before she met the man involved. In each case, the time lapse between dream and waking event made it hard to recognize the connection and work with the material. I would probably have missed my dream connection had I not been helped by synchronicity. The woman dreamer missed hers, and with it the chance to avoid or mitigate a great deal of emotional distress.

Dreaming a Workshop 13 Months Before It Takes Place

I had an hour of free time before I needed to leave home to conduct a weekend workshop, and I devoted it to leafing through some old dream journals. As I was closing the books and binders, getting ready to take my stuff out to the car, a couple of typed sheets fell out of one of the volumes. They contained a lengthy dream report from 13 months before. I glanced at the first line: "68 people are enrolled for one of my workshops." What followed was a complex narrative, involving several challenging situations. Most of the characters in the dream were unknown to me. Yet the dream report gave me interesting profiles of several of them—a woman who appeared to have suffered soul loss as a result of childhood abuse, same-sex partners who were approaching a breakup, a man who was burdened by the legacy (both genetic and spiritual) of family members who had died but remained attached to him. On a whim, I folded the dream report and put it in my pocket.

When I reached the rural retreat center where my workshop was being held, I was told that 68 people had enrolled. This came as a surprise, since when I had last checked, we had less than half that number. The registration numbers were not only gratifying to my ego; they confirmed that my dream from 13 months before was about *this* workshop. When the circle formed, I studied faces, keenly interested to see whether I could identify any of my dream characters. By the end of the weekend, I had matched most of them with workshop participants. My dream report gave me specific information on several tricky situations that developed, so that I was prepared for them and was able to manage them better than might otherwise have been the case. Yet that information might not have been available to me but for the gift of synchronicity that wafted those particular pages out of a journal from the previous year.

The Noseless Woman

Starting at the age of six, Dawn had a recurring nightmare that continued into her teens.

> I am sitting on a park bench in a foreign country. I watch people going by. Everything is innocent and uneventful until I notice a particular woman among the strangers. She frightens me more than any other person I have ever seen, more than any demon I could conjure. She has no nose. She doesn't look scary or deformed. But the knowledge that she has no nose terrifies me. I feel she is evil. After watching her in horror for several moments, I wake myself up, trying to escape from her.

In adult life, Dawn puzzled over what the dream may have been telling her. She played punning games with the main motif, asking herself if the woman who scared her represented someone who commits "no-nos" or is ignorant ("no-knows").

Then, twenty years after she first dreamed of the noseless woman, the dream began to be played out in physical reality.

Dawn became engaged to a man whose parents had emigrated to the United States. Though American born, he spoke with a foreign accent and was often mistaken for a foreigner. Though Dawn was initially warmly received by her fiancé's family, she soon began clashing with the young man's mother, a very controlling woman. A full-blown feud erupted in which the mother used all her influence to get Dawn's fiancé to call off the wedding shortly before it was due to take place. The emotional effect on Dawn was devastating. She left her home and her job, moved to another part of the country, and battled for years to regain her confidence.

In the course of these dramas, Dawn finally grasped the significance of her childhood nightmares. "The no-nose people had entered my waking life." Her fiancé's mother had had expensive rhinoplasty, not in itself an uncommon procedure. What was extraordinary was the fact that, ten years before she had met him, Dawn's fiancé had lost his nose during radiosurgery for a brain tumor. He had not been forewarned that he might lose his nose, and although his nose had been reconstructed by gifted plastic surgeons, the procedure had been traumatic and shocking for him.

The story has a surreal quality, like one of Gogol's tales.[2] Yet it is a vivid and arresting example of how we may receive early warning long in advance of possible events in our lives that carry a strong emotional charge. Dawn is convinced that her dreams were warning her, twenty years before the event, of the bitter confrontation that wrecked her marriage plans. "As early as age six, I sensed the terror of the woman from the foreign land who had no nose. What I failed to realize is that she had a son."

Dating Dreamed Events

How can we avoid missing or misreading those dream messages that may relate to the distant future and to people and places we have not yet encountered in physical reality? One of the key steps is to look at the dream closely to see if there is anything that could help to date the dreamed event. Maybe the season has changed. Maybe someone in the dream looks older.

Here are a number of clues to look for:

1. *The season.*
   What season is it, in the dream? If you are dreaming in summer, and a familiar landscape in your dream is covered with snow, this may suggest that the situation reflected in the dream will be played out in the winter. Remember the change of season may also be symbolic or somatic; ancient dream interpreters noted that it may indicate that something in the dreamer's body is out of tune with nature. Notice, too, that it is possible to mistake the season in a dream when the dream reflects changeable weather. In the spring of 1999, I had a series of dreams that appeared to anticipate events in the fall, since I noted that leaves from the maple trees around my house were thick on the ground. Because of drought conditions over the summer, the leaves started falling in August that year, and I saw other elements in my dreams played out two months earlier than I had expected.
2. *The age of people you know.*
   How old are the people you recognize in your dream? Look at the children (if there are children in the dream) especially closely. Many of us are poor guessers of the age of adults, but are bound to notice if a toddler has turned into a fourth-grader, let alone a teenager. If someone you know appears to be two years—or ten years—older in the dream, this may indicate the time lapse before waking events will start catching up with the dream. The longer the time lapse, then the more room for maneuver you may have to influence the possible course of events.

3. *Events and anniversaries.*
Is there a special event—a wedding, a concert, a football game—going on in the dream that you might be able to date in ordinary reality? I once dreamed that Rod Stewart was giving a concert in my backyard. When Rod Stewart came to Albany, New York three years later to perform at the Pepsi Arena in my "backyard" (ten miles from my home) I noticed that waking reality was also catching up to other elements in my dream.

For Wanda, a church auction provided the clue to when her dream might be enacted. In the fall of 1997, she dreamed her mother had died. In the dream, she was going through boxes of things that had been shipped to her from her mother's house, which had been sold. She sorted out things she did not want and took them over to donate to the local church auction.

When she woke from this very realistic dream, Wanda considered what it might be telling her. Though elderly, her mother was not seriously ill at that time. Wanda wondered whether the church auction might be a clue to when the most important dreamed event—her mother's death—might occur in waking life. Her local church held its auction every other year. One had been held just before the dream. The next auction was scheduled for September 1999.

Over the intervening period, Wanda's mother sold her house and moved to a nursing home. Boxes of her things started arriving at Wanda's house. The old lady died in August 1999. Wanda donated several boxes of her effects to the church auction that was held on September 25, 1999, exactly as she had done in the dream.

4. *What's going on in the world?*
Maybe there is an element in the dream scene—even the far background—that can help to tell you when the main

action could be played out in waking life. Maybe you just "know," in the dream, that President Clinton is no longer in office. Maybe Larry King Live is running seven mornings a week as well as seven evenings. Maybe there's a new Corvette on the road, or your neighbor has installed solar heating, or Ben and Jerry have a new flavor of ice cream. If you're getting really good at this, you might be able to catch a date on a newspaper; some active dreamers make this one of their targets, in both sleep dreams and conscious dreams.

ANGLE OF SIGHT

When I was a kid, I used to enjoy a popular guessing game that consisted of trying to identify a familiar object seen from an unusual angle. Our dreams show us events from unusual and often highly personal angles, with the result that we may have a quite accurate preview of something but do not comprehend exactly what is going on because we do not see the whole picture.

There are countless variations on this theme. Here are a few:

* *Seeing just a piece of the puzzle.* John dreamed he ran into a close friend, driving an old blue Ford pickup. Waking, he was surprised because his friend did not own such a vehicle and he found it hard to imagine the friend would want to drive one. Later that day, he ran into his friend's estranged wife. She was riding around in an old blue Ford pickup, identical to the one John had dreamed. The truck belonged to her new boyfriend. John's dream had given him just a piece of the puzzle, but a very interesting one. It showed him two things he had not known before: the boyfriend's blue pickup and the actual state of his friend's old "vehicle," his marriage.

* *Seeing through someone else's eyes.* Our perspective is different from normal. We are not our usual selves in the dream, but we are not disembodied spectators either. It's as if we have stepped inside someone else's head and are looking out through their eyes. Many psychic dreamers frequently experience this phenomenon. It is very common among close siblings, and very frequent with twins, who often seem to dream each other's dreams. For example: One teenage twin dreamed he was out biking and was offered a ride from family friends he didn't know well. They drove him out past an enormous scrapyard to look at a show of veteran cars. The next day, his twin *brother* was out biking when family friends offered him a ride. They took him past a huge junkyard to a show of veteran cars.

  One of the challenges of working with dream material that is seen through someone else's eye is to determine what is our stuff and what belongs to someone else. This troubled a woman dreamer who had recurring dreams about violent alcohol abuse and infidelity involving her "husband." When she agreed to go back inside the dreams and look around more carefully, she realized she was actually inside her sister's house. Her dreams proved to be an accurate scan of problems developing in her sister's marriage.
* *Distinguishing the news from the event.* Often, in dreaming the future, we pick up the news of the event rather than the event itself. J.W. Dunne often dreamed what was going to be in the newspaper—for example, the devastating explosion a volcano in Martinique. Today, we may be even more likely to dream about what will be breaking news on CNN, or online. We also pick up gossip and rumor about coming events, and other people's interpretations of them. Though dreams themselves are "the facts from which we must proceed" (Jung) the facts available *inside* dreams about news events must be looked at as warily as (say) you would watch

the TV news or listen to a mayor reporting on the state of the city, to separate the spin and the distortions from the hard kernel of truth.

CONFUSION OF REALITIES

There were press reports in 1999 about a woman in England who dreamed she encountered a radiantly beautiful lady. She woke convinced that the beautiful lady was her true self, and decided this meant she should make every possible effort to *look* like the radiant woman in her vision. She spent every penny she had, and went deep into debt, hiring plastic surgeons to try to reproduce the face from her dream. Somewhere along the way, she saw a picture of the famous museum bust of Nefertiti, and recognized the face from the dream. Apparently this did not give her pause. She went on, trying to resculpt her face into the likeness of the face in the dream mirror, until she had endured several dozen operations and spent nearly $500,000.

This sad story illuminates the problems that stem from confusing different orders of reality. In the dreamstate you have had a vividly *real* experience, but the only reality you have been taught to comprehend is the physical plane. You have seen the face of the radiant Other—perhaps your soul-friend, your deeper and truer Self—and you confuse this with skin-identity, something to be brought about by the plastic surgeon's knife. There is the same sadness, to my mind, in some of the stories of alien abductions. There is no doubt that many, if not all, of the people who report such experiences have lived through something quite *real* and sometimes terrifying. But when they leap to the conclusion that in order to be "real" an experience must be *physical,* they may fall into the trap of confusing different orders of reality, and end up telling fairytales. (Fairytales may be real, but usually not in the reality that includes sliced bread and college credits.)

The counterpart to this story of misplaced literalism is the sometimes even more tragic confusion that results when we dismiss the possibility that dreams may be closely connected to physical reality. One young woman went to a series of analysts, troubled by a recurring dream in which a knife-wielding rapist broke into her apartment. She had been offered a good deal of advice on the possible symbolic meanings of her dream. Speculation ranged from surfacing memories of childhood abuse to her fear of her own shadow. None of her analysts had explored the possibility that her dream might preview a situation that could be played out, quite literally and horribly, in waking life. I was brisk, though I hope gentle, with her. "Location?" I asked, first off the bat. "Where is this taking place?" She told me she wasn't sure. I led her back inside the dream with my voice. She was astonished to find the dream apartment was her present apartment in the Bay Area; she hadn't recognized the locale in early dreams because she had only moved in within the previous month. She noticed that renovations and redecorating had been done, projects she had not started on yet. If the dream menace reflected a possible future, this meant we had time to work with—time to reshape things. She eagerly agreed to look very hard at the physical security of her space.

When we don't dream true

All the problem areas described so far can be found in a single dream, or a series of dreams.

A tall, attractive young woman approached me during the break at one of my workshops on dreaming true. "I need to talk about dreaming *un*true," she said.

Sandra explained that for several months she had been caught up in a tremendous emotional roller-coaster. It involved a love triangle between herself, her long-term boyfriend, and another woman. The boyfriend had recently moved out to live with the other woman. Sandra had heard they were officially engaged. Still very much in love with her former partner, she found hope in her dreams that there might be a chance of resuming their relationship.

In six or more dreams, she had enjoyed the experience of being intimately involved with her former lover. Although the gulf she found between her continuing dream romance and waking separation was depressing, she worked with the idea that her dreams might be telling her that she and her boyfriend would get back together in the end. She now asked for specific dream guidance on whether her ex-lover would actually marry the other woman. As an observer inside her dream, Sandra watched the other woman as she signed her name on a series of business documents. When she woke up and thought about what she had dreamed, Sandra seized on this detail. She told herself that the marriage would not take place, because the other woman was using her own name.

A couple of days later, Sandra learned that a date for the wedding had been set. "My heart just fell through the floor," she told me. "How could my dreams lead me so far astray?"

I gently suggested that her *dreams* were not "untrue," but her *take* on them might be. We discussed three problem areas. The first involved the *time lapse.* It is often hard to tell exactly when a future situation we foresee in a dream will manifest in waking life. Professional psychics have the same trouble figuring out when future events will come about, even (or perhaps especially) when their information comes from spirit guides or "control personalities," who are not focussed on calendars and linear sequence in the way that we are. If there were any chance at all that Sandra's dream reunion with her lover might come about, it might lie in the distant future. The second problem area was the *angle of perception.* In her last dream, Sandra watches the other woman signing her own name and draws the conclusion that she won't get married. But many women today continue to use their maiden names after marriage. So this element in the dream did not answer the question about the marriage. (The answer might have been found in the papers the other woman was signing, but Sandra did not recall what they were.) The third troublespot is *confusion of realities.* While some of us might be inclined to dismiss the romantic reunion dreams as wishful thinking or fantasy, I am prepared to believe—as the dreamer most certainly did—that these were entirely real experiences. The question that arises is which order (or orders) of reality they belong to. If we break up an intimate relationship, a part of ourselves may stay in that relationship, on the psychic level, for a long time after the rupture. Or a part of ourselves may gravitate to that person in dreams. It was indeed possible, in my opinion, that Sandra was involved with her former lover on the psychic plane, and might *remain* involved unless one or both of them took effective action to cut the psychic link between them. But this situation did not, in itself, provide any clue as to whether there was any chance of the two of them coming together in waking life.

We briefly explored the possibility that Sandra's dreams of her former lover were actually a rehearsal for a new partner who might be about to step into her life, maybe someone she had not even met yet. She didn't think so, but she brightened as she mulled it over. "Oh, those would be the Pierce Brosnan dreams!" she exclaimed. She proceeded to tell me that she'd had some juicy encounters with the actor in other recent dreams—and was *very* open to the prospect of someone who would remind her of him walking into her life.

I believe our dreams, in themselves, are always true. It is we who create "false" dreams, by garbling and distorting our messages.

chapter five

LISTENING TO NIGHTMARES

Choosing one holographic future over another is essentially the same as creating the future.
—MICHAEL TALBOT, *The Holographic Universe*

There are plenty of dreams we *don't* want to come true.

Stephanie dreamed she woke up in bed with a stranger, in a room she did not recognize. She had a crashing headache and a filthy taste in her mouth. As she stared at the mess of underwear, cosmetics and pills strewn all over the bedcovers and the room, she had a gathering sense of dread. The man beside her smelled bad. She asked him, "Did we have safe sex?" He smirked and said, "Nah. There's no fun in that." Stephanie woke up sick to her stomach, with the bad taste in her mouth and a deepening sense of dread.

She did not know who to ask for help. Most of the people she knew tended to shrug off dreams as "only" dreams or just looked up dream symbols in books. Her dream felt *real.* Every time she thought about it, the sense of nausea and borderline panic returned. She sent me an e-mail. I asked her to start with that indispensable reality check. Did she know anyone who resembled the man in the bed? Where was his room? Could she have been fed one of those date rape drugs? Was there any possibility of the dream being played out in waking life?

Stephanie's response was one of recognition and deep relief. When she thought about the man in the dream, she realized he strongly resembled one of the owners of the bar where she was about to start part-time work. Some features of his anatomy she could not confirm and had no wish to find out about. The owners of the bar, the help and their friends partied after hours on Saturday nights, and Stephanie had been invited to join them after her first shift. She decided not to go that night, and that if she joined the gang on other occasions, she would be very careful about whom she allowed to pour her drinks.

This was not a precognitive dream because (so far as I know) Stephanie has not blacked out and had unsafe sex with a stranger. It was a warning and a rehearsal. It showed her, in an utterly convincing way, the consequences of not taking very good care of herself in a particular situations. The depth of her emotional response, and the physical hangover from the dream, made sure she paid attention.

When we wake up to the fact that we dream the possible future, we can start doing the interesting thing, which is changing the future for the better. Sometimes, when we see painful or tragic things before they happen—things we seem powerless to influence—we can be tempted to become overly pessimistic or fatalistic about such things. What's the good of seeing the victims of a plane crash before the aircraft goes down, if we can't influence the outcome? What's the use of foreseeing death or disaster if we can't do anything about it? If I dream the assassination of JFK, or the death of JFK Junior, or the space shuttle *Challenger* tragedy before they happen—as many people claim they have done—doesn't that merely suggest that the future is set? Why should I want to know about terrible things I can't change?

We have already seen that dreaming the future is not just—or even essentially—about dreaming the "terrible" things, although these dreams may be more likely to stick in the memories of people with spotty dream recall who do not keep journals. Our ability to change the future is clearly conditional on our access to appropriate means and levers of influence. At one extreme, unless you have godlike powers, you may find it hard to stop the hurricane or the volcanic eruption you foresaw in your dream. But you may be able to make good use of that information if it includes a specific scenario. In a conscious dream journey, I saw a new eruption of Vesuvius in 2023. If I'm still around at that time, I'll leave the Bay of Naples out of my travel plans. If I'm not around, I hope the people who inherit my journals can make use of that information, if only to test the dream prediction.

The "observer" dreams in which we preview world-historical events or natural disasters show us developing situations involving the nation, the human collective, or the fate of the ecosphere that we may not be able to influence in any direct way—although such dreams may drive us to join the Sierra Club, deed land to a conservation league, and vote for or against a certain political candidate.

At the other end of the spectrum are the dreams—a majority of dreams, for most of us—where we are at the center of the story, and where its denouement or rescripting depends essentially on us. A Yoruba divination priest, a *babalawo,* once told me he thinks that we are profoundly mistaken when we tell ourselves that we cannot change our lives. He maintains that there are only two things in life that are extremely difficult to change. The first is our basic character, the constellation of personality traits and karmic traces (if you like) that we are born with. The second is our maximum allotment of time and energy in this world. Our lifeline can be cut short by violence, by suicide or by self-destructive habits, but it is awfully difficult to stretch it out longer than the contract allows for (though I have seen even this done). Beyond this, says my friend the *babalawo,* almost anything can be changed. And this comes from a priest of a tradition that maintains that we agree to a specific life contract before we come here! It's a further incentive to push the boundaries, test the limits, and see how—with dream help—we can go about re-creating our lives and our world.

WHEN WE DON'T TRY TO CHANGE THE FUTURE WE DREAMED

If we do not take appropriate action to change the events we foresee in our dreams, we may be obliged to live those dreams. Hollywood has given us an instructive fable in the 1998 movie *In Dreams* in that. I would not recommend this movie in other respects; it is dark and violent and may leave some viewers with the impression that dreaming true is a curse. Yet if we follow the story closely, it is an excellent object lesson in what can happen when people fail to recognize that they are naturally psychic in dreams and should use the information they get to change the future for the better.

A woman played by Annette Bening has a recurring dream of a young girl's murder by a deranged man. She associates her dream with a past event: the well-publicized disappearance of a young girl from the neighborhood. Only when she is caught up in the horror of her own daughter's abduction and murder does she grasp that her dream was about the future. Nobody in her environment, including the dreamer herself, believes in dream precognition. When she first encounters a psychiatrist, she asks him to give her something to stop her dreaming, as if the dreams are the problem. She has lost her daughter and is about to lose her husband by the time she realizes her dreams are showing her the future—and the killer's mind—and that they require action to avoid the enactment of the events foreseen. By this time, she has been institutionalized and sedated with megadoses of drugs. Nobody thinks her horrific dream of her husband's corpse being chewed by the starving family dog in room 401 of an abandoned hotel is anything more than a hallucination—until they go there and discover the scene exactly as she described it.

I wish Hollywood could make the point that "dreams come true" in a happier way. By the end of this movie, everyone we might care about is dead. Yet, trying to surface from the horror and carnage of this film is a vitally important message: that the ability to dream the future is a gift, not a curse, if only we can learn to recognize such dreams for what they are and to take appropriate action to avert unwanted events (and help manifest happy ones).

There is another cautionary tale in the story of the French actress Irene Muza, who saw the future not in a sleep dream, but under hypnosis. She was hypnotized and asked if she could see her future. She replied, "My future will be short. I dare not say what my end will be: it will be terrible." When they roused her the experimenters decided not to tell her what she had said. She had no memory of it. A few months later her hairdresser accidentally spilled mineral spirits on a lighted stove. Muza's hair caught fire—she was engulfed in flames and died in hospital a few hours later. The question arises: Could she have been saved if her own vision had been reported to her? Or if the experimenters had pressed her for more information under hypnosis? I believe she might have had a chance had she been encouraged to retain the detailed memory of what she saw under hypnosis, and to work with it, the way we can work with dreams, since reports of the tragedy suggest she saw far more than she told the nervous experimenters.[1]

SAVING THE BABY: THE RESEARCH OF LOUISA RHINE

Dr. Louisa Rhine had more than a researcher's interest in the possibility of intervening to change events foreseen in dreams.

As a young mother, she dreamed she took her children camping with friends. They found a lovely wooded spot on the shores of the sound between two hills and pitched their tents under the trees. She realized she needed to do some washing for the baby, so she walked down to the creek where it broadened out a little. She put the baby and the clothes down on clean gravel near the bank. Noticing she had forgotten the soap, she started back to the tent. Her toddler threw a handful of pebbles into the water. When she came back with the soap, she was horrified to see her baby lying face down in the water. She pulled him out but he was dead. She woke sobbing, and was tremendously relieved to find her baby safe with her in bed.

Dr. Rhine worried about her dream for several days but (as she noted in the *Journal of Parapsychology*) "nothing happened and I forgot about it."

That summer friends invited Dr. Rhine and her children to go camping. They cruised along the sound until they found a lovely wooded spot on the shore between two hills and pitched their tents under the trees. Dr. Rhine realized she needed to do some washing for the baby. When she set the baby and the clothes down on a patch of clean gravel by the creek, she noticed she had forgotten the soap. As she started back to the tent, the baby picked up a handful of pebbles and threw them into the water.

At this moment—but only at this point—Dr. Rhine remembered her dream. "Instantly my dream flashed into my mind. It was like a moving picture." The baby looked just as she remembered from the dream, his yellow curls bright in the sun. She caught him up and carried him away from the creek.[2]

It is not at all unusual for parents to dream that their children are at risk. If Dr. Rhine had remembered nothing more from her dream than the scene of her baby floating face down in the water—dead, perhaps she (and certainly many of those around her) would have dismissed it as a typical "maternal anxiety" dream. But here the dream scenario is quite specific.

The greater part of Dr. Rhine's dream was played out, exactly as she had dreamed it several months earlier, before she had received the invitation to go camping. If we trust her account (and we must remember that she was a scrupulous scientific reporter) she accurately previewed a scene she had never seen in waking life. The episode with the laundry is played out down to the last detail *until she remembers her dream.*

Did she *change* the future—a future in which her baby drowned? Dr. Rhine thought so, and so do I. In this case, as in many others, the difference between the future that can be changed and the future that appears to be set is *awareness.*

Louisa Rhine's experience as a dreaming mother drove her subsequent research as a scientific investigator. She studied more than 450 cases of apparent precognitive experiences in which (1) the experiencers recognized *at the time* that they were seeing future events and (2) the events foreseen were unpleasant, of a kind that anyone would want to change if they could. In two-thirds of these cases, no effort was made to change the future event, usually because people either forgot their warning messages, or feared ridicule if they discussed them with people around them.

Rhine focused on 191 cases in which people tried to prevent a foreseen event from taking place. In 31 percent of these cases, the attempted intervention failed—usually because the dream or intuition had failed to provide enough specific information to provide effective guidance. Either the details were foggy and fragmentary, or the warning came in symbolic images that were not clearly understood.

More encouraging is Rhine's finding that in 69 percent of the cases, people were able to take effective action to avoid unwanted events that they had foreseen. One of the most striking cases involved the dream of a streetcar operator in Los Angeles. His dream was strikingly realistic. He was operating a one-man car on the old "W" line going south on Figueroa Street. He pulled up at the intersection with Avenue 26, waiting for the signal to change. When the light changed, he crossed the intersection and waved to the motorman of a northbound car. Without warning a big red truck cut in front of him, making an illegal turn from a street exit. There was a terrible accident. The truck overturned, leaving its two male occupants sprawled dead in the street, and a woman passenger screaming in pain. The woman shouted at the dreamer, "You could have avoided this!"

The streetcar driver woke up terrified and sweating. The dream stayed with him the following day, when he was operating a car on the "W" line. On his second run, he felt queasy as he sat at the Avenue 26 intersection, waiting for the light to change. As he crossed the intersection, he saw a number 5 car approach and the motorman waved at him, as in the dream. The full force of the dream now came back to him. He acted on it by shutting off the power and slamming on his brakes, bringing his car to a stop—just in time to avoid a collision with a truck that shot directly across his path, making an illegal turn. It wasn't a big red truck; it was a panel van with a red banner on the side. But there were three people riding in it, as in the dream. The woman made an "okay" sign with thumb and forefinger as they passed.[3]

THE *TITANIC* DISASTER AND THE BLIND SPOT OF A PSYCHIC RESEARCHER

On her maiden voyage in the north Atlantic on April 14, 1912, the great ocean liner *Titanic* struck an iceberg and sank in less than three hours. More than 1,500 of the 2,207 passengers and crew were drowned. The event made a deep impact on the collective psyche. The boat's builders had boasted that the *Titanic*—which seemed to symbolize luxury and technological mastery—was "unsinkable." The wreck of the *Titanic* two years before the outbreak of World War I sent a message that things were sliding out of control in the Old World's arrogant establishment.

In conventional terms, few people had conceived of such a disaster. Yet the wreck of the *Titanic* was anticipated in other ways: in premonitions, in precognitive dreams, and in prophetic fiction. Fourteen years before the disaster, Morgan Robertson published a novel called *The Wreck of the Titan* in which an 800-foot ocean liner struck an iceberg while sailing at 25 knots; many people drowned because the huge liner had only 24 lifeboats. In addition to the remarkable resemblance between the names of the fictional liner and the real one, the *Titanic* was 882 feet long, was traveling at 20 knots when it it the iceberg, and was carrying only 20 lifeboats.

One of the more famous passengers who went down with the *Titanic* published his own accounts of the sinking of a big ocean liner, both as fiction and nonfiction. British editor and psychic researcher W.T. Stead wrote a story in 1892, *twenty years* earlier, in which he pictured a liner sinking after hitting an iceberg. In the story, the captain of another boat, the *Majestic,* received a telepathic cry for help from the sole survivor of the wreck. The most interesting detail is that in his story, Stead used the actual name of the skipper of the *Majestic,* Captain Smith, who later became the captain of the *Titanic* and went down with his ship in 1912.[4]

Dr. Ian Stevenson made a detailed study of nineteen recorded cases of possible ESP relating to the sinking of the *Titanic.* He identified ten clear cases of precognition, six of which were experienced several months or longer before the event, four within ten days of the sinking. Some passengers who had dreams or premonitions of the disaster acted on them. Some shrugged them off, or perhaps forgot about them.

One of the most interesting cases is that of an English businessman, J. Connon Middleton, who had booked passage on the *Titanic* the month before it sailed. Ten days before the voyage, Middleton dreamed he saw the ship floating keel upwards, with her passengers and crew bobbing around her in the water. He had the same dream the following night. The dreams disturbed and depressed him. His sense of dread was deepened by what may have been a glimpse of his possible postmortem situation, "floating in the air just above the deck." Four days after the first dream, Middleton canceled his trip.

Ian Stevenson's research led him to raise the excellent question of why some people act on perceptions of the possible future, and others do not. He noted that "a cultural climate hostile to psychical experiences may influence percipients not to act on perceptions when a more favorable climate might encourage them to do so."[5]

Ironically, W.T. Stead was very far from being "hostile to psychical experiences." This crusading journalist and social reformer was dedicated to the scientific investigation of the paranormal. He founded a magazine, *Borderland,* devoted to these areas, experimented with mediums and automatic writing, and created a psychic bureau dedicated to demonstrating the soul's survival of physical death. Stead was surrounded by "sensitives," two of whom warned him several months before the tragedy that he faced the risk of death by water. Yet he blithely sailed on the *Titanic* and went down with it. Perhaps we all have a blind spot in relation to some things in our own future. Or perhaps Stead's early warning of the circumstances of his own death had come to him so many years ahead of the event—through whatever intuition led him to write his shipwreck story two decades before—that he failed to use the information when waking events caught up with his premonition. Making the link between an early premonition and a much later event, and *acting upon it,* is a challenge for all of us.

The saved family vacation

The possible future we can change for the better very often involves much smaller things. My dreams frequently show me possible problems with the spaces I use for my lectures and dream workshops, enabling me to take timely action to set things up better. While traveling in Europe, I dreamed that an incredibly noisy fan made it impossible for people to hear my lecture. On my return to New York, I drove out to a college where I was scheduled to speak during the summer and had them turn on the air-conditioning. The fan was so loud I would have been stuck with a choice between roasting or remaining inaudible—had I not respected my dream advisory and thereby been able to arrange the transfer of my lecture to a different auditorium. On another occasion, I dreamed I was trying to conduct a shamanic dream circle in a lecture theatre with sharply sloping rows of seats that were bolted to the floor, making it quite impossible for people to sit comfortably in a circle and stretch out on the floor, as this kind of workshop requires. This dream prompted me to make another check of a planned venue; when I found it closely resembled the scene from the dream, I was able to prevail on the workshop hosts to give me a more comfortable space. I could multiply these examples very many times.

You might say: Wouldn't it be prudent to check something as fundamental as the space where you are going to teach without needing a dream to prod you? And you would have a good point—if there were time to attend to every detail. An Irishwoman with the magical name of Maedb concedes she should probably have checked her plane tickets before she had the dream that saved the family vacation.

Maedb dreamed she had set off by plane from her home in Canada to her native Ireland, expecting to enjoy a wonderful family holiday. But things rapidly went wrong. She found herself separated from her family. At the end of the dream, she was "up in the air," in a kind of limbo. As she surfaced from the dream, she heard my voice saying, firmly and crisply, "reality check."

She and her family were scheduled to fly together to Ireland a couple of weeks later. Because of her dream, she rushed to check that their travel documents were in order. She was alarmed when she found that her own airline ticket was missing. She called the discount agency she had used, and they told her that someone had called to cancel her ticket. She protested that this was impossible: they were a large family party, including two young grandchildren, traveling together. The travel agent told her there was nothing they could do because the flight was oversold. After prolonged pleading and negotiating, Maedb finally got a seat on the plane.

Except for the dream, she observed, she would probably not have checked the tickets until the morning of the departure—at which point it might well have been impossible to get a seat on the flight, and she would have been left "up in the air."

Don't trust the rearview mirror

Patrick dreamed he was driving his cherished '78 Sport Impala before dawn on a stretch of Highway 12 in north central California known locally as Death Alley. The dream was highly realistic. He was edgy and alert, looking frequently in his rearview mirror. The car behind him kept riding close, though Patrick slowed a few times to give the driver the chance to pass. When the car behind failed to pass, Patrick hit the gas pedal, putting a comfortable distance between the two cars.

At this point, an anomaly in the dream alerted Patrick to the fact that he was dreaming. As he moved to put a new cassette in the stereo, he realized the stereo was not in its usual place. His surprise nearly jolted him out of the dream, but he decided to stay with the dream and see what developed. At his mental command, a number from a recent Guns and Roses album came on his mental soundtrack. He remained aware he was dreaming, but as his awareness rocked along with the music, the dream seemed to exert its own momentum. Unsure why, he found he needed to turn left onto a little used road he had never noticed before. Still uneasy about the car that was following him, he flashed his left blinker three times as he approached the turn. The driver behind seemed to get the message because he dropped back, widening the gap between the cars.

As Patrick slowed for the turn, he saw several big trucks coming over a rise a quarter mile ahead. As they crested the hill, they accelerated to high speed. Patrick needed to make a decision. Should he come to a full stop on this dangerous road to allow the trucks to pass, and risk being rear-ended? Or should he chance a hard, fast turn in front of the speeding trucks?

Checking the rearview mirror, he saw the driver behind was swinging out onto the shoulder, leaving plenty of room to pass safely. So he came to a complete stop, waiting for the trucks to pass. He made sure his wheels were pointing straight ahead, so he would not get shoved into oncoming traffic if he were rear-ended. Even though everything seemed to be fine—and even though he was fully aware that he was dreaming the action—he remained nervous about being hit from behind. As the car from behind shot off in front of him, he began to relax, listening to the *whoosh* of the big trucks as he waited to make his turn.

He bent down to turn up the volume of his stereo.

As he straightened up, there was a bone-splintering crash. "My world went topsy-turvy and all I could think of was, *Why am I looking at the ceiling?* and *What are all those sparkling things flying around inside of my car?*"

Patrick came out of his dream, breathing hard. He was quite certain he had been rear-ended in the dream. He knew the stretch of road he was traveling in the dream, and he knew the time of the apparent accident: before sunup. Many details were clear since he had been conscious he was dreaming for all of the climactic sequence. Could the dream be a rehearsal for a future event? If so, Patrick had plenty of details to work with. And he recorded them right away.

Nonetheless, like so many of us, he forgot his dream until waking events caught up with it.

Two weeks later, Patrick, who is a photographer, got a job shooting pictures for a company brochure. The client requested that he should take some early morning pictures of the corporate building to take advantage of the golden light. The plant was located just off Highway 12. Even as Patrick wrote down the directions, he failed to make the connection with his dream. He did not think about the dream even after his alarm roused him at 4:00 A.M. the next day and he scrambled to get his camera gear together for the drive to the plant.

"So, there I was driving on Highway 12 in the pre-dawn, just me and this one vehicle behind me and I suddenly remembered the dream about five miles before the left hand turn I would need to make. Smiling yet a more than a little chagrined, I put on the Guns and Roses tape and turned the volume up loud, feeling rather smug that I was now prepared, if need be, to change reality due to my precognitive dream.

"And apart from the fact that my stereo was now in the right place, events proceeded just as they had in the dream. Double-checking my mirrors I saw the car that had bothered me in the dream. Nothing else on the road. This worried me a little because if events were to play out as foretold, there *must* be another vehicle behind him. But there wasn't . . . not that I could see as I tried to look past the glare of his headlights in the mirror. So I put on my blinker, turned it off, slowed, turned on my blinker again, checked the mirror—and saw the driver behind back off and swing over to the right, preparing to pass. The trucks crested the hill in front of me, six of them in tight convoy formation, moving fast. I came to a stop, looking a final time in my mirror as the guy came around the right side and I gave him a little wave. There were *no headlights* to be seen for a couple of miles behind me. I was sure of it.

"Then, feeling as if I'd avoided any problems and making sure my wheels were still straight ahead, I leaned over to turn up the music and—*WHAAAAMMM!*—I was seeing stars."

A drunk driver with his headlights off slammed into the back of Patrick's car at full speed, apparently oblivious to the fact that the Impala had stopped. The drunk driver never even tapped his brakes.

"This happened seconds before the first of the trucks passed me. If I had turned my wheels ready to go left, they would still be picking my teeth out of that truck's front grill! The seatback broke upon impact, throwing me into a reclining position, looking up at the ceiling. Those pretty little sparkly things I saw in my dream were bits of my shattered rear window flying around the interior of my car, lit by the lights of the passing trucks."

Patrick was extremely lucky to come out of this unhurt, though his car was wrecked. "Lessons to be learned?" he reflects. "I'm not sure. I recognized the premonition, and I could have acted on it to make different choices. I could have gone past my turn and found a safer spot to turn round and come back. That would have changed the parameters." He did not make that choice because, every time he looked in the rear mirrors, he could not see anything to worry about. "Who would ever think that a drunk driver would be way out there in the middle of nowhere driving with no lights on a moonless night?"

Ah, but Patrick *did* have a way of knowing. His dream showed him what never showed up in the rearview mirror.

There is a powerful metaphor here. Any one of us is liable to get into trouble if our vision of the future is controlled by what we can see in the rearview mirror.

WHEN WE FAIL TO CHANGE THE FUTURE FOR THE BETTER

The most common reason we fail to take advantage of life-supporting dream information about the future is quite simply that we forget, even when (as in Patrick's case) we believe in dreams and have worked on a dream on many levels. Another reason we miss the messages is that we allow our waking editor to reshape them in a way that fits in with our ordinary hopes and fears but distorts the facts perceived in the dream.

Then there's the problem of other people. Acting on the dream information may require us to engage the help or understanding of other people, as in Terry's story.

Terry dreamed she was forced to walk away from her car at twilight in a snowy and heavily forested area. There were several people standing around who were only mildly interested in the fact that she had to abandon her car. She woke with a deep sense of unease. She associated the people on the road who were disinterested in her plight with members of her family.

Three days later, Terry's family insisted on driving to a wooded area to cut a fresh Christmas tree. There was snow and ice on the roads, and Terry had a strong gut feeling—reinforced by her memory of the dream—that they should not go out that day. Family members laughed off her objections and dismissed her dream as "only a dream." Later that day, in the "twilight" of low cloud cover, Terry's car was totaled when she skidded on an icy patch of back road. She was "forced" to walk away from her car. Fortunately, she and her family escaped with only minor injuries.

"If I had been more firm with my family that day," Terry reflects, "I would still have my car in one piece. Of course they are not laughing any more."

Terry's experience is typical of that of many dreamers who have allowed others to talk them out of following dream guidance. We need to trust our dream intuition despite what other people say. Terry told me there was a special "tone" about her dream that made her quite sure she should take it seriously—and quite literally. Yet she let family plans, and the ignorance or reflex skepticism of others, get between her and her dream. Our dreams are wiser than the people who are constantly trying to tell us how things are and put our world inside a little box. We must trust our dreams and act on them.

When we fail to take action to prevent an unpleasant event foreseen in a dream, we must avoid going on a guilt trip. However painful, these episodes can be powerful learning experiences. I once dreamed I had to fight off a street mugger. Later, in my dream, I looked through mugshots to identify my assailant. I was surprised when I learned that the photo I identified belonged to a woman, not a man, and that the suspect's surname was the maiden name of a woman with whom I had embarked on a business venture. Waking, I was shocked by the implication that my female associate might try to rob me. Though I noted this down as a possible "dream motto," I edited it out of my waking mind. My refusal to heed the clear warning in my dream resulted in a situation, six months later, involving that very person, in which I lost several thousand dollars.

As an adult, I had the ability to act on that dream. As a child, I was often unable to take appropriate action based on my dreams, because the action depended on the consent or help of adults, and the adults in my boyhood environment did not want to hear about dreams. Many of us, as children, have gone through the frustrating experience of having our dreams—and their life-helping insights—brutally rejected by the adults around us.

I felt immense sympathy for the radio talk show host who once confided to me, on the air, a terrifying dream he had had as a boy. In the dream, he saw his mother on her back in what looked like a coffin. The rocky landscape around the coffin was covered with snow. He woke up desperately afraid his mother had been killed. He did not tell his family the dream; dream-sharing was not part of their life.

A week later, the family was out tobogganing on the snow-covered slopes of the Rockies. The dreamer's mother was unable to stop her sled as it hurtled towards a cliff. Moments later, the dreamer looked down, horrified, at the fulfillment of his dream: his mother lay inside the coffin-shaped toboggan with a broken back that left her paralyzed.

The man who shared this childhood dream with me, still anguished decades after the event, asked me if he could somehow have prevented the tragic accident had he known more about dreams and how to work with them. There is no way of answering such a question about the past. Certainly none of us should hold ourselves liable for failing to act on information we did not understand at the time. The challenge is to use what we know *now* to deal better with situations that may be developing *now.*

I put the radio host's question to the woman who had nightmares about "noseless" people many years before she met the "noseless" man and his mother. Since those early dreams, and the traumatic breakup of her relationship for reasons apparently anticipated by her dreams, Dawn had become an active dreamer, skilled in the arts of dream reentry and dream travel. If she had understood *then* what she now knew about dreams, might she have been able to spare herself some of the pain and grief?

"Yes," Dawn responded, "I could have used the 'noseless' dreams to avoid some of the pain. But only some of it. Had I understood how waking and dreaming experiences inform each other, had I known how to honor and act upon dreams, surely some major alarms would have gone off when I met my 'noseless' man and his family. Perhaps I wouldn't have been so trusting of them, leaving myself open to their power plays. At the very least, it would have been more difficult to deny the conflicts that did exist with them. The dreams would have confirmed all the danger that I sensed in my gut but didn't want to see with my waking eyes.

"If it were to happen today, I would certainly reenter the dream and ask the noseless woman in my nightmare more about herself, what she was trying to tell me, and how to proceed with the noseless folks I'd met. I would ask for protection and guidance."

Dawn added, with searching honesty and self-awareness, "On the other hand, I can't say definitively that I would have had the courage back then to make the necessary choices, even if I had been more knowledgeable about dreaming, and even if I had made the noseless connection and understood it as a warning. I was deeply attached to my fiance very early on. It's tough to admit, but I'm not sure there is any warning I would have listened to if it meant ending the relationship.

"That said, I feel that my whole approach to life is stronger since I have come to understand how to make use of dreams. Had I been personally empowered in this way at the time I met my fiance, the entire dynamic would have been different. Who knows how things might have worked out?"

I asked Dawn what tips she would offer for others, based on her own experience. She volunteered profoundly helpful advice: "Keep a dream journal, explore the meanings of your dreams, share them with others for insights. But the heart of dreaming involves courage and faith. Have the courage to face your worst nightmares, even if it means plunging headfirst into your fears, coping with discomfort, or changing plans. Have the faith to know that dreams can and will illuminate even your darkest paths; trust them. Know that if a dream returns again and again, or if it leaves you in a sweat, it's simply begging for acknowledgment and change in your life. Stick with it until you know what it's trying to tell you. For dreams may come bearing multiple gifts, long into the future. If the dream remains with you, let its applications evolve as you do. Never ignore the dream's literal meanings. Share it with a friend, reenter the dream, ask it questions, discern what it's trying to teach you, and then honor its lessons when wide awake."

HOW CAN THE FUTURE BOTH EXIST AND NOT EXIST?

What is this future we can see but also change? Sometimes our dreams of coming events are so vivid and sensory they feel less like dreams than memories of the future—a future that must in some sense already exist.

Maybe, in dreams, we dip into a kind of holographic soup of possibilities, selecting events that may later be manifested. What seems clear to me is that the futures we perceive in dreams are *possible* futures. We can alter the probability that any specific scenario will be played out in waking life by the action we take or fail to take. Even if a future course of events is in some sense predetermined, maybe (as some scientists speculate) we can accomplish a "holo-leap" into a parallel reality where the story has a different outcome. Sometimes we can effect these changes inside the dream, especially if we have learned the arts of dream reentry and conscious dream travel. Sometimes the change requires communicating information effectively to others, or recruiting their help. Now *there's* a challenge.

chapter six

DREAMING FOR OTHERS

Range him among your saints, who, with all-acknowledged powers, and his own steadfast scale for every thing, can . . . transpose himself into another's situation, and adopt his point of sight.

LAVATER, *Aphorisms on Man* #580

Dreaming, we see into the future of other people—from intimate family to complete strangers—as well as our own. Sometimes these dream messages come from that wide and noisy band of "human static" between individual channels. Receptive people may pick up a great deal of information that is not directly connected with them simply because it is "out there." I remember vividly a cry for help from Robin Givens that I picked up shortly after I moved to upstate New York. It came in the twilight zone between sleep and waking, as a lot of useful psychic information tends to do. With the cry—a literal scream—came the picture of a desperate woman, and then a series of rapid images—rushing past like the images in a movie trailer—of Mike Tyson. I saw him speeding madly in a car, at risk of wrapping himself around a tree. I saw him beating several people, male and female. I saw him caged behind bars, like a feral animal.

Many of us remember dreams involving the possible death or misfortune of friends or family members. When such dreams come close to the *natural* end of another person's life, they can help us to prepare ourselves and others for the separation and the onward transition of the dying person's spirit. Sometimes they reflect dangers we can help the person about whom we dreamed to avoid, if only we can get the message clear and figure out how to get it to the person who most needs it.

A psychologist in one of my workshops reported a series of dreams on successive nights that featured her cousin's husband. She understood that *recurring dreams* come to us again and again because (a) we need to get the message and/or (b) we need to do something about it. In these dreams, her in-law had a damaged arm. In the last and most troubling of the series, his arm seemed to have been cut off at the shoulder. All that was left was a pathetic bony stub, "no more than a chicken bone." The dreamer decided she needed to share these dreams with her cousin (the wife of the man who seemed to be losing his arm). She felt constricted and embarrassed when she started talking about the dreams. Her cousin, who respected dreams, told her curtly, "Just give me the facts," meaning the facts of the dreams. When the dreamer proceeded to relate, blow by blow, what she had dreamed, her cousin told her, "You are right on the money. I'm going to make my husband go in for cancer tests. His *uncle* has a cancer in his arm. The doctors want to amputate it at the elbow."

Did the dreamer misidentify a relatively unfamiliar dream character (her in-law's uncle) as a more familiar one? Or did her dreams alert her, and her family, to the possibility that her cousin's husband had inherited his uncle's specific problem—a possibility the family was encouraged to explore because of the dreams? Whether her information came by telepathy or precognition, the dreamer seems to have produced a helpful advisory.

Dead on the living room floor

Jasmine dreamed of finding her husband dead on the living room floor.

> I walk from the kitchen into the living room at night. My husband is laid out on the floor, naked. I'm shocked to see him there. I kneel down to see if there's life. My nose touches his cheek; he feels cold and dead. I need to get help. I'm not sure if I use the phone or send out a mental cry. I see the headlights of a police car coming down the drive. I go outside and see my husband's car. It's in terrible shape, horribly rusted, standing in tall brown grass that rises above the wheels.

When she shared this dream in one of my workshops, we immediately ran a reality check. Was it remotely possible this scene could be played out? She had the strong sense that the dream was showing her something that could conceivably happen. She described her husband as "stuck" with quite unhealthy habits.

We looked for a way to date the possible event foreseen in the dream. The clue was the state of the husband's car. Jasmine felt her husband's car would be in the condition she had seen if it were left unattended for a couple of years. If the car was also a metaphor for her husband's physical body, that could mean she was dreaming an event that could manifest within two years or so. The conversation now became deadly serious. How could she get the warning through to her husband, who refused to listen to dreams? We agreed she would try to speak to him in perfectly rational, commonsensical ways, about changes he might need to make in his lifestyle. Jasmine also decided—having learned some conscious dreaming techniques—that she would try to get through to her husband on a higher level. Even if he was not open to talking about dreams, maybe he could receive a message in his own dreams that would jolt him into paying attention.

JUST GIVE THE FACTS

So what is the best way to share dream messages that seem to be addressed to other people?

The absolute best way is the one recommended by the psychologist's cousin: *Just give the facts*—by which I mean, of course, the facts of the dream.

But I recommend this subject to two vital conditions:

1. *We need to have all the facts of the dream.*
   It would be worse than useless to call up a friend and say, "I dreamed you were in a car crash" or "I dreamed you had a heart attack." For starters, we are all suggestible and you could actually help scare your friend into driving off the road or having that heart attack. It is altogether different if you can say something like: "I dreamed you had a collision with a blue Dodge at the intersection of Lark and Hudson. It was in the fall, because the leaves were red, and there was a white delivery truck in front of the bookstore." One of my most clairvoyant friends once gave me a very specific warning about a health problem that might result if I refused to take a medication. Her description of the scene in which I experienced the crisis (and was told severely by a physician that it could have been avoided if I had only agreed to take

"that one pill a day") was very specific. It took me years to act on the dream advisory she passed on to me, but I never forgot it. And when circumstances in my waking life caught up with other elements in the dream scene, I finally went to the doctor and started taking that one pill a day.

So if we are going to share dream messages with the people for whom they seem to be intended, let's first make the effort to get the story clear and specific, especially if it involves major life challenges. All the techniques I have offered for clarifying our own dream messages are relevant here, especially dream reentry and the search for ways to date the dreamed event.

2. *We must establish a safe space in which to share the dream.* We should not go around dropping bombshells, and we may be wasting our time—and more important, the opportunity to share life-helping information—if we go blurting our story out to someone who flatly refuses to listen to dreams or believe in them. If we cannot establish a proper basis for dialogue, it may be better to go a roundabout route, by sharing the dream information with someone in the other person's life who is more receptive.

Remember it is not always necessary or appropriate to begin by saying, "I had a dream." In a traditional dreaming culture—like that of Australian Aborigines or some Native American peoples—that opening may win you a depth of attention and respect you would never achieve in any other way. Sadly, in many parts of Western society it will only win you a shrug or a snort of disbelief. So, if your information is sufficiently specific, you may be able to think up a clever way to pass it along without mentioning its source. I have done this on quite a number of occasions.

For example, in a conscious dream I once saw a potential danger for a toddler in a house I had never visited in physical reality because a window that ran all the way down to the floor on a high landing had been left open. I called a mutual friend and asked her to go round to that house and check the situation with the windows, explaining that this kind of risk had been on my mind because of the tragic death of Eric Clapton's child, who had fallen through an open window. I suggested to my friend that if the situation was what I feared, she should try to prevail on the owners of the house to nail the window shut. She reported back that when she visited the house, a window that went all the way down to the ground was open on an upper floor, and the toddler was playing on the stairs above. Thanks to her intervention, that window was nailed shut. My dream was never discussed, and the family involved was never informed of the role I played. It's said that you can accomplish anything if you don't mind who gets the credit, and I believe this is a useful maxim to remember when we are working with dream messages for others.

Here's another example of how to get a dream message through, from a woman I'll call Rose. This story involves both (1) checking the dream facts and (2) establishing a safe space in which the information can be shared.

Rose dreamed her son-in-law (we'll call him Ed) died of cancer. She woke deeply troubled, with a black sense of oppression. When she went back inside the dream, she noticed that her daughter's two children, infants at that time, looked about seven and eight. So she guessed that she was dreaming about something that *might* develop in six or seven years' time.

Seven years is a good big chunk of time, as any physician will tell you, when it comes to detecting and preventing a life-threatening disease.

But Rose was hesitant about passing on the message. She felt she could talk to her daughter, but she feared upsetting her. The situation was complicated by the fact that Ed had a violent temper and had ridiculed his wife for "listening to your mother's bullshit about dreams."

Rose finally discharged her responsibilities in the following way: She decided to have a quiet talk with her daughter and persuade her to get Ed to go to the doctor for a routine check-up. (Ed had not been to a doctor in quite a few years.) She would instruct her daughter *not* to recount the dream to her husband. At the best, Ed would be given a clear bill of health—and maybe some good advice on how to stay that way. At worst, he and his doctors might gain seven years in their effort to heal his cancer.

"Clear Air"

The question of whether and how to pass on a dream message to others may not arise when we are in a position to act on the dream information ourselves for their benefit. Repella (a cyber-name) woke from a dream remembering only a voice expressing amazement that someone had died as a result of "such a simple procedure." This sounded like something you would hear in a hospital. That thought set Repella's antenna quivering when she learned that her husband was going into a hospital three weeks later for a hernia operation, a "simple procedure" that turned out to be not so simple.

There were a number of complications, and three days after surgery Repella's husband was still in the hospital. She was with him in the ward when his IV monitor started beeping. She examined the machine. The computer was flashing the words, "Clear Air."

A young nurse entered the room, glanced at the signal "Clear Air" and did something to make the beeping stop. Then she left the room.

Alone with her husband, Repella remembered her dream fragment about someone dying as a result of a "simple procedure." The dream memory made her deeply uneasy and afraid. It also made her vigilant. She checked the IV tube and found that a large section was filled with air bubbles that weren't supposed to be there. She rushed out and got an experienced nurse, who suctioned the air bubbles out, avoiding a crisis.

One lesson here is that even a dream fragment can help us to help others, when we can link it to a developing situation and find the appropriate way to act on it.

DREAMING CREATIVE SOLUTIONS FOR OTHERS

Our dreams bring us many gifts, as well as warnings, for others. While I was in the midst of writing my historical novel *The Firekeeper,* my wife Marcia told me at breakfast time that she dreamed she was back in college. Her teacher had an unusual name. In her dream, Marcia had skipped some classes and was worried she would be presented with a test for which she was unprepared. Instead, her teacher wanted to talk about life, rambling on in a jovial, philosophical fashion that Marcia found very enjoyable. Waking, she realized that her teacher's name was Rahilly. He had been her French teacher in college and she had loved his name, which was pronounced "Riley."

She wondered why she had dreamed of him. I remarked that if it were my dream, I would think it was connected with the novel I was writing. I had just come to the Irish chapter, introducing my hero, Sir William Johnson, as a boy. I realized, when I thought about the dream, that I had "skipped classes" in a most specific way. I had given no thought to describing Johnson's early education, on which there was precious little in the historical records. As the son of a prosperous squire, he might well have had a private tutor. Rahilly would be a plausible and interesting name. It was also (I recalled) the name of a famous bardic singer of that period.

Marcia remarked, "Maybe I dreamed this dream for you."

After she left for work, I wrote the first pages of my new character introducing a completely fresh character, named

Denis Rahilly, as Johnson's teacher. A jovial, philosophical whisky-mystic who can talk the stars out of the skies, Rahilly helped bring the whole chapter alive. For me, this was a very creative example of how we can dream for others.

DREAMING OTHER PEOPLE'S DREAMS

We not only pick up messages for other people in our dreams. Sometimes, we seem to dream *their* dreams. A woman dreamer once called me and began the conversation by saying, "I think I had one of your dreams last night."

She proceeded to describe a specific place where I had lived in London as a postgraduate student—a walk-up bedsit (studio apartment) in a big row house in Kensington. When I quizzed her on the layout, her descriptions were precise and detailed. Indeed, she was able to tell me about things in the room I had completely forgotten. Yet I had never told her I had lived in this place, and had never thought about it in many years. She proceeded to describe characters and scenes that were meaningless to her but were deeply interesting and relevant for me. Throughout her dream, she remained a detached observer.

When there is a strong personal connection between two people—as there was between me and that woman friend, whom I often described as one of my "sisters"—entering another person's dreamspace in this way is by no means unusual. Even when the connection is not so close, from time to time we seem to pick up other people's dreams just as we might pick up their mail. This is less like a case of misdirected mail than like the mailman dropping off a special delivery at the neighbor's house because the addressee isn't home.

While the bedsit dream involved personal issues related to the past—and might be viewed as witnessing a holographic movie derived from my personal past—we also dream other people's dreams involving the future.

If we are seeing from someone else's perspective, it is often difficult to sort out what we are perceiving, even when we wake up the fact that we are seeing into another person's situation. An episode of the popular television series *JAG* ("Judge Advocate General") gave a good example of how we sometimes edit these dream perceptions in ways that blur the content. In the TV show, the hero is in search of his father, who is believed to be dead, but was reportedly sighted many years before in Siberia. A gypsy family harbors him, and the gypsy woman has a vision in which she is threatened with rape by Russian soldiers at a riverbank. Her husband, who would have defended her vigorously in waking reality, stands back, while the hero of the series charges forward, killing all but one of the soldiers, who then kills him. The gypsy describes the dream locale in great detail. Later the hero finds a woman in Siberia who had lived with his father and she tells him how his father died saving her from soldiers who had tried to rape her by a riverbank. The hero recognizes the locale from the gypsy's dream. She had dreamed of his father's death, not his own. She had entered the scene completely, in her dreaming, experiencing the fear and grief of the Siberian woman. But she identified the father she did not know with the son who was sleeping under her roof.

If we are dreaming from someone else's perspective, it is often difficult to sort out what belongs to whom. Louise's story is a tragic example:

"How could I have known it was my friend in the car?"

At the start of the holiday season, Louise had a very vivid dream of an auto accident. She was driving at night along a dark country road. Rounding a corner, she saw an old pickup truck with a man at the wheel and a woman passenger, rushing toward her in the wrong lane. They had a head-on collision. Louise woke deeply troubled, with the clear sense that the accident had resulted in severe injury and possible death.

She did not reenter her dream, but over the next weeks she had flashes of the collision during the day. She might be going about the business of the day, eyes wide open, when suddenly an image of the collision would flash into her mind. Her perspective changed. At times she looked down on the scene from above; at other times her view was confined to what she could see through the windshield from the driver's seat.

Needless to say, these continuing visions made her edgy. She tried to get a clearer sense of when and where the accident might take place. When she thought about this, she realized that she would be driving late at night on a country road—very similar to the one in her dream—to a party on New Year's Eve, quite a likely time to run into a drunk driver. In waking life, she would be traveling with a friend, while in the dream she was driving alone. Nonetheless, she decided to take exceptional precautions that night. She changed her route to avoid the stretch of road she now associated with the dream. She asked a friend for advice on defensive driving techniques. And she resolved to abstain from alcohol at the party.

On the night, Louise arrived at her friends' house without incident. Then came the shock. Her hosts broke the news that one of her closest friends had been killed the day before in a car accident. The description of this tragic event closely resembled Louise's dream. Louise's friend (who lived in another state) was driving home alone at night on a country road when a pickup truck crossed the center line and struck her head-on. She was killed instantly; the male driver and female passenger in the truck were severely injured. Louise had been very close to the woman who died since they had been classmates in college, but had moved away, and it had been more than a year since Louise had seen or communicated with her.

Louise's thoughts on this unhappy episode are very interesting. "I have racked my brains to see if there is any way I could have known that my dream might contain a warning for her. I can't recall anything in my dream or the subsequent waking visions that could have led me to believe that someone other than me was driving that car. But I wonder if in some sense there was a warning 'in the air.' My friend may have had a premonition, because shortly before the accident, and unknown to her husband, she took out a very large insurance policy that left her husband and daughter very well off. I have always wondered why I had no inkling that it was her and not me in the car."

WHOSE HEAD AM I IN?

When our emotions and perspectives are very closely enmeshed with another person's—as seems to have been the case with Louise and her friend—it may be very hard to disentangle what dream material belongs to whom.

We are all connected. Waking or sleeping, we move through overlapping energy fields and *mind* fields. Waking or sleeping, we need to hone the ability to recognize what belongs to us and what does not. This is critical to psychic well-being, as well as to dreaming true. If we don't practice this kind of mindfulness, we will be constantly blown this way and that by thoughts and feelings that are not our own.

It's not so hard to figure out that you are dreaming someone else's stuff when you become aware, inside the dream, that you are not in your regular body. Psychic dreamers often seem to have a natural ability to slip into someone else's head and see through their eyes without becoming utterly confused about what is happening.

I have learned a lot about this from a marvelously gifted psychic dreamer I'll call Perisia, an ancient name that was given to me in a dream I had for *her.* She was born in the Deep South, and says of herself, rather self-effacingly, that "Southerners have a particular ability for eavesdropping, for moving easily into the nuances of other people's lives." Her Irish grandmother was a folk healer and conjure-woman in the Alabama hills who encouraged her to tell her dreams. "I grew up listening to my grandmother's stories of dreaming dreams for and about other people, knowing life and death before they happened, foreseeing the grief or joy of others before they felt it." Dreams were interwoven with tales of fairies and elves, magicians and ghosts. The Otherworld was not remote; it was right *there,* accessible through dreaming. Perisia's time with her grandmother and, above all, the encouragement to trust her dream experiences, was the foundation of her gifts. She grew up knowing that it is entirely natural to see the future and meet the departed in dreams, because this is what she and her grandmother did.

The first dream Perisia remembered from childhood involved a neighbor who died on a hunting trip. He appeared to her and asked her to tell his family goodbye many hours before his wife received new of his death.

Perisia discovered early that in dreams, we are not confined to our ordinary identities. We can step inside someone else's situation (in our own time or another time) and see the world through their eyes. Though this can sometimes be confusing, once we recognize what is going on and work with the process, it can be the source of remarkable insights and information. Here are three examples of how Perisia has dreamed herself inside other people's situations and mind-sets:

Inside the stalker's head

In a series of dreams, Perisia found herself inside the head of a male stalker who was watching and following a well-known TV star. She could see through his eyes but could not see his face. She knew his name was John.

There were subsequent news reports that the police had arrested a man who was stalking the actress on the night of a screening.

Perisia had further interaction with the stalker after his arrest. This time, she found herself looking through a man's eyes into a confined space, a cramped room with a small table and a couple of chairs. She glanced down at his/her hands and forearms. She looked across the table at the female psychiatrist who was doing his evaluation. John was dealing stolidly, logically, with the shrink's questions.

Behind his personality was a second male personality—"smarter and more deceptive." He was saying, "This is a game. We know how to play it. We'll play it—and win."

From her unusual, multiple perspective, Perisia found that the psychiatrist's voice seemed hollow. Her words seemed to travel down a long tube, first to the prisoner, then to the second personality, whose name was Charles.

Her sense of the stalker's life deepened. He was a burly, cantankerous, friendless failure, who may have suffered childhood abuse. There was a flashback to an abused mother. His feelings were conflicted; there was a desire for sex and power, but also a desire to protect.

Perisia noticed a shift in her visual perception as she came in sync with each of the personalities. As John, she had something like normal vision. As Charles, she lost peripheral vision and developed something like tunnel vision.

In Richard Nixon's head

During Richard Nixon's final illness, Perisia dreamed she went to a hospital. Here is her account of what transpired:

> I am not myself. I am in someone else's "head," thinking in a different fashion, not like I usually think. I realize that I am in a hospital. I hear conversation and hear

enough dialogue to realize that I am Richard Nixon and that I am in a coma. I think of my own father for a moment and wonder what it must be like to be in a coma, hearing conversation and even understanding it but not being able to respond. Nixon is talking to someone but not someone in the room—he is negotiating the next state of his soul, denying nothing, arguing nothing, making no excuses for himself. He is methodical, intense, and aware of all his excesses, all of his problems, all of his mistakes, and all of his successes. He presents them all for review, barely waiting for the review to be presented to him; and he does not try to argue his way out of any of the ones that embarrass him, a position that seems to place him "ahead of the game." He is somewhat surprised by this process and understands more than he has ever understood about himself. He knows he needs to do something about the things he has done that do not place him in the best light, so he asks forgiveness for those things—the mistakes in his life that were made by him and the things that caused pain to others. He seeks forgiveness for actions now clear to him as mistakes. He seems surprised at how much influence he had, particularly good influence, good actions, that changed people's lives in a positive manner. He is forced to acknowledge many negatives and he is forced to look at all the sides of his life, which he does with a great deal of grace and sometimes with a great deal of regret. He is moving quickly to a point where he is ready to go. The thing he regrets most in his life is the lack of love in the later years of his life—love for other people whose gifts and talents he did not recognize, love that would have been given to him. He has a charge—he must learn love and teach love. He is ready to leave.

In My Mother's Place

In the last dream that will be shared here, Perisia was not aware she was in someone else's situation, no doubt because the "someone" was a close family member. Her dream might have been terrifying, except that she woke from it quite calm and detached.

In this dream, Perisia walked into a plush doctor's office to get the results of some tests. The doctor told her she had lung cancer and insisted on starting treatment. She was told to get into a large bathtub. She climbed in fully clothed, then noticed that excrement left by a previous patient was floating in the tub. She got out, demanding that the doctor must clean things up. In the next scene, she was standing with her father (who died many years before) at the end of the drive of her childhood home in her hometown. Coming down the street on a float was her mother as she may have looked in her early 30s. She was running for office and had lots of support—everyone was out on the sidewalks cheering for her. The dreamer's father was smiling and appeared to be waiting for his wife to join him.

Soon after this dream, Perisia received a call from the nursing home where her mother was living. Her mother's cancer had metastasized and spread to the lungs. Her doctor had increased her medication because she was in terrible pain. Her disease and the medications had thrown off all her body functions and she was losing control of her bowels. The first part of the dream, with its disgusting and disturbing details, apparently allowed Perisia to see into her mother's situation in the nursing home *from the inside.* The beautiful second scene, of the hometown parade, coached Perisia for her mother's eventual death and gave her assurance that there was plenty of support on the other side.

These three dream episodes are all quite instructive. We might wonder why a gentle, compassionate woman would dream herself inside the head of a stalker—or of Richard Nixon.

Perisia herself does not understand the apparent psychic link with the stalker, although this is one of many comparable experiences she (like many other natural clairvoyants) has had. Maybe she simply tuned in to a very active frequency in what Robert Monroe called the "Human Noise Band" while channel-surfing during the night. Maybe there is a past or future connection here with someone relevant to her that has not yet emerged. Maybe these dreams were a rehearsal for dealing with some comparable situation involving multiple personalities.

On the Nixon dream, Perisia commented, "It was helpful for me because it presented a side of a president who had not fared well in the public eye. Nixon used his skills to his advantage in the last negotiation of his life but the result was positive. He was willing to see himself and willing to move on." She felt there might be a lesson here for many others about making allowance for change. From this angle, her dream recalls one of the most rewarding aspects of dreaming: it allows us to see deeply into the situations of other people, to walk in their shoes and live in their skin. I think of my own cycle of dreams of being a black man and experiencing from the inside what it means to be a black man in a society where racism is still very much alive. To be able, truly, to enter another person's situation is to forego prejudice. *Tout comprendre est tout pardonner.* To understand everything is to forgive everything. There is an antidote here to intolerance.

Perisia's dream of sharing both her mother's physical humiliations—and her vision of a new life—took her deeply into the circumstances of her mother's deathwalk, and equipped her to offer clear counsel and direction on decisions that needed to be made—on her mother's behalf—in waking life. Once again, dreaming the dream of someone else's life helps us to understand, from the inside, who they are and what they need—at least when we wake up to the understanding of whose dream we are in.

Perisia comments, "I believe we can be *advocates* in these kinds of dreams. Dreams in which we walk into another's mind present us with rare opportunities to understand another human being—even the most heinous personality—from the inside, with all of our senses. What is the benefit of it? We can comprehend the most secret part of ourselves and of the selves of others and understand when and how healing begins, and how humans fit together."

chapter seven

BECOMING A BETTER DREAM JOURNALIST

> *The one who knows all secrets is here now, nearer than your jugular vein.*
>
> —Rumi, *Diwan of Shams,* 824

A dream journal is like a bank vault with a time-release lock, containing tremendous wealth you can only access fully after time—maybe years of it—has elapsed. Here are some of the things you will gain and learn by keeping a dream journal for *at least* a year:

* You'll find yourself constructing a personal dictionary of symbols vastly more interesting and rewarding *for you* than somebody else's version (because the snake in your dream is not the same as the snake in mine). You will also be able to monitor how your dream images evolve over time, revealing

new levels of meaning and perhaps your deepening relationship with your larger self.

* You'll be able to track recurring themes and serial dreams in which dramas seem to play out over many installments. You may notice you return again and again to locales and situations in dreams that appear to have no connection with your waking life. Sometimes these dreams foreshadow situations that may emerge in the future. Often they seem to be glimpse of parallel lives we lead in another reality. Sometimes we watch a shadow self walk a "ghost trail"—a path we abandoned in ordinary reality—on which we are still married to a former partner, living in a place where we lived long ago, working in a former job. These dreams may inspire us to reclaim energy we left stuck in those situations, or may simply suggest that the dreamworld (like contemporary scientific speculation) has room for infinite parallel universes.
* You'll become much more alert to precognitive messages like the ones I excerpted from my personal journals. You'll develop a knack for recognizing these messages in time to take appropriate action to avert a dreamed event you don't want or to help bring a happy dream into manifestation. As you log correspondences between dreams and subsequent waking events, you give yourself a spur to dream *truer.* Your dream source and your dream editor will both respond!
* A dream journal is a good place to monitor your physical, emotional and spiritual health. You'll discover in the process that your dreams are giving you a powerful stock of healing imagery you can use to help heal yourself and others.
* Your dream journal mirrors your evolving relationships with other people, including the departed people. I find it fascinating to study changes over time in how people connected with my life appear to me and interact with me in dreams.

* Your dream journal is also an excellent place to study the workings of synchronicity in everyday life. When we pay attention to dreams, our perception of meaningful coincidences and symbolic values in events around us seems to flourish, and vice versa. Going over a dream journal actually seems to *mobilize* synchronicity in magical and helpful ways.
* Dreaming is both personal and interactive, and your dream journal is an excellent place to study your interconnectedness with others. As you become more confident about sharing dreams with friends, you'll notice overlapping dreams in which you seem to share certain experiences or perceptions. Maybe you'll want to experiment with your ability to enter shared dreaming with one or more partners, or even embark on conscious dream travel. And of course you'll report your results in your journal.
* You'll also find it rewarding to record dreams that are shared with you, especially by young children, who are wonderful dream teachers because they emerged from the dreamworld very recently and haven't yet learned that dreams are anything but *real* (which is why small children often have a hard time using the word "dream" to describe experiences to adults who think dreams are "only" dreams).
* Every time you write or draw in your dream journal, you are releasing your creative juices, flexing your writing muscles, and giving yourself a chance to enter that blissful flow state in which you do something for its own sake, releasing the consequences—and come back to find you have something marvelous you can gift to others.

Dream journalism is a *discipline.* To become a dream journalist, you need to make a commitment not only to record your dreams on a regular basis, but to work with them and go back and review them.

When I record my own dreams, I add a good deal of comment, reflection and follow-up data, in addition to the dream report itself. If I am writing in a notebook, I leave facing pages blank so I can add thoughts and experiences related to the dream that may come later, perhaps when waking events catch up to the dream. The virtue of a loose-leaf binder is that it makes it easy to insert material of this kind, as well as drawings, doodles the results of dream-inspired research.

A two-page spread in your journal might be laid out as displayed on pages 104 and 105:

A FORM FOR YOUR DAILY DREAM JOURNAL

Date [include time of waking]
Intention [if you asked for dream guidance]
Dream Title

DREAM REPORT

Feelings on Waking:

First Associations:

Reality Check:

What Do I Need to Know?

What Do I Need to Do?

Personal One-Liner:

REENTRY AND FOLLOW-UP [fill in only applicable sections]

Back into the Dream [Dream reentry report]

Overlap (if any) with other people's dreams or experiences:

Results of symbol exploration and other dream research:

Action taken to honor the dream:

Follow-up: [Note correspondences with later events in waking life]

Time-lapse: [between dream and waking event]

INDEXING DREAMS

As your dream records grow, you'll want to index your dreams to avoid being swamped by all the information.

The simplest way to do this is to make a list of dream titles, with dates, at the back (or the front) of your journal. You may want to note strong—or confirmed—indications that a dream has precognitive information; I simply make the notation P/C. You may wish to flag dreams that come to you in the hypnagogic zone between waking and sleep (HG), or are fully conscious experiences (CD).

You'll find it fascinating to note recurring themes and locales.

THE SCHOOL OF DREAM JOURNALISM

Let's examine some journalistic techniques for improving your ability to get the scoop in your dreams, check and confirm your results, and get deep background information from reliable sources, especially very young ones.

Pretending We Dreamed Something After It Happened

One of the problems I notice, going through old journals, is that precognitive messages are often jumbled up with all sorts of other stuff in complex dream narratives woven together with threads from the past and the present as well as the future. Let's look at one technique that can help us to sift through the clutter and recognize the good stuff.

In his trailblazing book *An Experiment with Time,* first published in 1927, J.W.Dunne advises that at the end of the day, we should consider our dreams from previous couple of nights as if they came *after* that day's events. This approach takes advantage of the fact that we are generally more adept at making connections with what has already happened—and is therefore familiar—than with what lies in the future. Dunne's method also builds on our everyday notion of causality, which makes it easier for us to see waking events as the cause of dreams than the other way round. The trick is to pretend that dreams we have already recorded are the dreams we are going to have *tonight,* and to look at what we encountered or learned today for anything that might be regarded as the cause of the dreams.

Here is an example of how the game works:

Black and yellow dogs

> On a warm summer day, Wanda brought work down from her upstairs office to a room that opened onto the garden, so she could sit with the door open enjoying the glorious weather. Her assistant rushed in and said, "Wait until you hear this woman's story." She brought in a woman with unruly red hair, who sat down on a metal folding chair, facing Wanda, and proceeded to tell the story of a feud with a neighbor. The red-haired woman owned two dogs, yellow and black labs. She claimed her neighbor had fed them poisoned meat. The black lab would not accept food from strangers, but the yellow lab had eaten the meat and died the previous night. Now she was suing the neighbor.
>
> Wanda felt sure she knew the woman, even though they had never met. The story of the black and yellow dogs also seemed familiar.
>
> That evening, Wanda found she had recorded the following dream the night before the incident with the red-haired woman: "I am sitting in the garden room at work. A woman with wild, unkempt red hair sits down

opposite me on a metal chair. She is talking but I do not hear what she says. Instead I see two boxes in the air near her head, almost like dialogue boxes in a comic strip. In each box is the head of a smooth-haired dog, one yellow and one black. The box with the yellow dog's head gets smaller and smaller until it disappears. The black dog's head remains quite clear and prominent."

Waking, she thought this was a rather silly dream and almost failed to write it down.

This is a neat and clear example of dream precognition, because the woman Wanda encountered was entirely unknown to her in waking life and she had no ordinary way of knowing anything about the unpleasant episode with the two dogs—except through her dream. Her dream report was not cluttered with images and information extraneous to what was played out in the garden room on the warm summer day. Often, however, the precognitive elements in our dreams are jumbled up with all sorts of other material. Looking at dreams as if they are the result of the day's events trains us to recognize direct and indirect correspondences.

While Dunne recommended that we play this game with dreams and waking events that take place within a couple of days, it can be even more interesting to play it with dreams and incidents that are separated by much longer periods of time.

Indonesian Puppet Theatre

On September 16, 1999, disturbed by reports of the brutal murder of civilians by Indonesian-backed militias in East Timor, I paid close attention to news of the gathering of a multinational UN peacekeeping force, spearheaded by soldiers from my native Australia. When I checked the on-line version of *The Australian* newspaper, I read a report that as early as

February, senior Indonesian military intelligence officers had met with militia leaders and hatched detailed plans for the massacre of East Timorians, including priests and nuns, who favored independence.

The news story jogged my memory. I went through my journals and found a dream sequence that I had titled "The Kabuki Murders." The dream from which I woke I titled simply "Massacre":

> I grope my way through ground floor rooms in a house where a massacre has taken place. There are two bodies in the outer room and at least four in a bedroom. Several show the marks of torture. I step over and around the corpses carefully, not wanting to disturb evidence. I am a trained observer. In a little while, at the agreed time, I will make radio contact with the team that will bring me out.

In the previous dream from the same sequence, I had an encounter with my departed father-in-law, an Australian academic and writer who specialized in Asian studies.

Geoffrey and the Shadow Theatre

> Geoffrey shows me articles he has clipped from Australian newspapers. They include a long obituary, one of many on the table. He remarks on the huge quantity of news that remains to be read.
>
> He tells me stories from his "swashbuckling" youth, when he traveled widely in Southeast Asia.
>
> He shows me a souvenir from these times: an elegantly crafted teak cabinet. When I first glance at it, it seems to be a trunk. Then it's a tall, wide wardrobe. Then it seems like a mobile room. Inside is a vast collection of

theatrical pieces. There is an elaborate costume displayed in the first section, including a *kris* (a dagger typical of Indonesia and Malaysia) with a wide handle. In other compartments of the theatre box are hanging shadow puppets, the kind used in Indonesia. There are hundreds of these, together with backdrops and props.

Looking over these dreams as if they *followed* the September 1999 news reports of the murderous "puppet theatre" the Indonesian army conducted via the East Timor militias, they look like fairly straightforward dramatizations. In one scene, I am given a close-up look at a massacre. In the other, an Australian source shows me the puppet theatre that is behind it.

But I recorded those dreams on March 30, 1999, nearly six months *before* I read the Australian news story revealing the full extent of Indonesian puppeteering. When I originally wrote up the dreams, I did not link the "massacre" scene to possible events in Asia. There was no specific indication of the locale or the ethnicity of the murdered people, except that they were "foreign" and fairly dark-skinned. My first association was with the atrocities in Kosovo that had mobilized world outrage at that time. I felt that the massacre scene and my dream of Geoffrey and the Indonesian puppets were closely linked, but I could not explain this connection. I jotted down questions I could not answer at the time. "Whose obituaries?" "What performances should be staged with the theatre box?" Perhaps these questions were answered, tragically, in September.

The game of looking at an old dream as if it came after a new event is not intended to prove anything. And Dunne's trick is worse than futile if we use it to pretend to ourselves that we saw more of the future in our dreams than was actually the case. It is simply a way of noticing connections we might otherwise miss, and of schooling ourselves to recognize more of these connections before waking events catch up to the dream.

This exercise also helps us to notice those personal markers that can alert us to precognitive content in our dreams. There were at least three of these markers in the dreams I recorded on March 30. The first was the presence of a dead person, who appeared (as the departed so often do) quite alive and well in my dream. The second was the newspaper motif, underscored by Geoffrey telling me there was a *huge* quantity of news to be read. The third was the vivid, realistic and chilling quality of the dream in which I inspected the massacre scene. Nonetheless, despite these markers and some careful thinking and research at the time, I could not identify any clear correspondence between my dreams and external events—until waking events caught up with it.

Why would I dream about the East Timor crisis months before it happened? I don't find it difficult to answer that question. I am Australian, though I have spent most of my adult life outside my native country, and trouble in East Timor is trouble in my neighborhood. Political upheavals in Indonesia have threatened to embroil Australia in a regional war more than once. All of this would be of keen concern to Geoffrey, who was a leading expert on Asian affairs and international conflict—or to the part of me that is like Geoffrey, if you prefer a psychological explanation of his appearance in my dream. Of course, we also dream about world events that have no obvious connection to us. We discover in dreams that *Earth* is our neighborhood, and that all of humanity is our family.

Becoming a Dream Scientist: The Home Precognition Experiment

Harvard researcher and long-term dream journalist Dennis Schmidt told a conference of the Association for the Study of Dreams in 1996: "In the tradition of the naturalists whose patient observations prepared the ways to elegant understandings of physics, chemistry and biology, home journal keepers record and discover events and regularities that astonish and enlighten, and that elude experimental probing."

As we become dream journalists, we become able to make important contributions to an evolving science in which the study of consciousness will be central and the working definitions of reality will be very generous indeed.

While dreaming is a path of experience rather than of experiment in the laboratory sense, there are home experiments we can conduct that are wonderful fun, deepen our relationship with friends who are willing to share dreams, and can provide objective, scientific confirmation of our ability to dream true.

I would like to invite you to try out a simple home experiment for documenting and validating dream precognition. All it requires is your willingness to keep a dream journal and to share selected dreams with one other person, preferably in written form, as soon as possible after you have recorded them. There are four easy steps:

Guidelines for Home Precognition Experiment

1. Record and date your dream
2. Choose a friend to be your dream witness, or monitor. Share dreams you feel may include glimpses of the future with your dream monitor as soon as possible after you record them (*before* waking events catch up to the dream).
3. Record and date subsequent events in waking life that appear to correspond to your dream.
4. Share and discuss the match-up with your dream monitor.

This basic protocol may be old hat to those who have been working with their own precognitive and "early warning" dreams for many years. But it has hit me, in discussion with many everyday dreamers around the world, that this is a dazzlingly simple way for us to stage home experiments that can very rapidly (a) confirm that we have the natural ability to dream things before they happen and (b) enable us to present this phenomenon lucidly and coherently to others—who can now be encouraged to test their own abilities and stage their own experiments.

If we perform the whole experiment just *once,* we have powerful evidence of dream precognition of a kind I hold to be truly scientific—and a pathway for a dream science based on the raw data of experience. For anyone who succeeds in this, the implications go deeper than our world, since they imply that our consensual notions of time (and reality itself) are inadequate. The involvement of the dream monitor (who may be your regular dream-sharing pal) is crucial, because this supplies external validation that the dream came before the corresponding physical event, and that the dream report was not edited.

Synchronicity Games for Dream Journalists

If you are keeping a dream journal for the long haul, part of your basic discipline will be to go back to old journals and see what you make of those dream reports now. You may discover—as I frequently do—that something you dreamed five years ago appears to be manifesting now. If you spot this kind of match-up, forage around the old dream for other dreams that may reflect other things developing in your life now.

The journal review is easier if you index your dreams and flag them for different types of content. But if you have prolific dream recall and record much of what you remember, the sheer volume of material that piles up can still become daunting.

A fun way to do a journal review without making it a chore is simply to grab an old journal at random and open it up anywhere. It is often astonishing what will leap out at you. Perhaps when we do this we invite the presence of that benign energy that Arthur Koestler called the Library Angel (the one that brings about amazing finds when we just pick up or open a book at random).

Maybe synchronicity will guide you back to an old journal, as happens quite often to me. A recent example involved a silly incident at my local post office. As I stood in line one morning, I noticed they had put up a new digital display next to the old-fashioned clock on the wall. The message was about time, how the post office knows we value our time and tries to give timely service. Each time it was repeated, the date flashed on in red numbers: "06 AUG 94." I chuckled, because the date that morning, to the best of my knowledge, was September 8, 1999. I joked about it with the clerk when my turn came at the counter. A couple of other clerks came over to share the joke; it's a friendly post office. They asked me, "What's that date again?"

As I left the post office, it hit me that I had now said "Six August ninety-four" three times—in the place where I go to pick up and send messages. Was there a message here for me? When I got home, I plunged into the closet where I keep my dream journals. The journal I needed was on top of a pile of thick notebooks I used in that era. It fell open to a dream report titled "SS Exhibit in Holland." My sense of amusement left me. I was riveted, because a Jewish friend had contacted me that same morning, concerned about what she believed to be "neo-Nazi" elements in messages channeled by a Dutch New Age personality who claimed to be in contact with a "super-race." My dream pointed to documentary sources that might shed light on this whole murky area. I had recorded this dream report on August 4, not August 6, 1994. When I turned to the entry for August 6—the date on the crazy digital clock—I found a dream that seemed both to anticipate and explain a troubling personal conflict, involving the same friend, that had erupted five years later.

The interplay between synchronicity and dream journaling works the other way too. It's one of the things that makes a journal review fun. You look up an old dream, and something jumps out at you in waking life that seems to echo that dream. Sometimes this feels less like a waking event catching up with an old dream than as if the dream has somehow pulled something into play that wasn't there before. Another tiny example from my own journals. On the day I was writing this section, I opened an old journal at random and found a dream report from 1993 that mentioned a character called "Casca." My journal entry read like an outline for a thriller involving a brutal mercenary and a warrior chief. I was confused about the locale. The flavor was South American, but the action seemed to take place in the United States. Within a few hours of noticing this dream report—whose meaning was still unclear to me—I received an email from a friend who had just visited a site of the "moundbuilders" at Parkin, Arkansas. She described the savage encounter between conquistadors driven by greed for gold and a warrior chief called Casqui. She described the feel of the site as strongly South American.

Cynthia Pearson, a dedicated and adept dream journalist, has reported many experiences of this trigger-effect since she started entering hundreds of her dreams on a computer database. "A dream from the past," she reports, would often have "surprising pertinence to my waking experiences at the time I happened to enter it into the database, often years later." She has written a delightful essay on the interplay between opening up an old dream and the appearance of synchronicities in waking life; she calls these patterns "arabesques."[1]

Learning From Our Children's Dreams

Dream journalists, like other reporters, must learn sources. The best sources on dreams, of course, are dreamworld itself. The best sources on dreams in waking life are frequent fliers and dedicated dream journalists who can speak from personal experience. Some of these "reliable sources" may be white-haired; some are remarkably young.

For those of us who are privileged to spend time with children, one of our most rewarding assignments as dream journalists is to record and learn from children's dreams, especially when they are very small. We will learn more from this intimate observation than from all the theories of child psychologists, and it is something we can do every day, if we will only make a little time for it. When they tell us their dreams, especially when they are very young, children not only reveal their inner life and their take on situations going on around them; they remind us of the infinite possibilities of dreaming. They run with the animals, talk with the departed, travel to dreamworlds and dream things before they happen. All we have to do is listen and record. I will add the quick observation, as a parent as well as a dreamworker, that children are rarely looking for interpretation when they bring us a dream. They are seeking our attention and our respect for their experience. Our first requirement is to honor and cherish their telling. Sometimes our kids need help in dealing with nightmare terrors. The best thing we can do is to reassure them that they have powerful friends—including us—who will accompany them into the dreamspace and help them to deal with whatever is scaring them. Sometimes our kids bring us lessons in how to brave up to our nightmare fears. When she was four, my youngest daughter Sophie came into my room in the middle of the night and announced she had been chased in her dream by "scary monsters" of different colors. She seemed calm, so I asked what she had done to resolve this situation. "Easy," she told me. "I put on a dragon costume and I chased them back." When she did this, the monsters turned into a rainbow of many colors.

To encourage you to seize the opportunity—if you are lucky enough to have it—of recording and learning from the dreams of young children, I will share a few excerpts from my personal journals of dreams Sophie shared with me between the ages of four and five:

Astronaut Training
"Daddy, do you know what my dream was? Astronaut training. They showed me how to put on a helmet. I was bouncing."

"Who were your teachers?"

"The same like me."

"What do astronauts do?"

"They live in space. They bounce around with the stars." [January 17, 1994]

Meeting an Ostrich on the Beach
"I'm in a chair at the beach. I'm making sand castles. An ostrich comes by, making tracks across the sand. I'm cross because of the marks it's making." [February 6, 1994]

Flying Houses
"I dreamed of flying houses. I dreamed Daddy was dreaming and his dream made the lamps start rattling. When the lamps started rattling, the books came off the bookshelves and started walking and talking. Everything was shaking. The house started shaking and then it was flying through the sky." [June 19, 1994]

Daddy and Mommy Are Bulls Locking Horns
"Daddy and Mommy are both bulls, and they are fighting each other. I'm a small cow. I don't like Mommy changed this way." [August 15, 1994]

Punching a Hole in the World
(and Other Doors into Dreaming)

I drew a rainbow hoop for Sophie to color in. She turned it into a Rainbow Door. She told me, "If you go through it, you fall down a hole and come out in another world."

She asked if I would go on an adventure with her. "I want to hitch a ride on a shooting star," she told me.

We sat together on the sofa, eyes closed. She led me through the Sun Door. We visited the Tree Gate—she picked an apple tree. A horse statue came alive and guided us to the Wishing Tree, which will give you a wish when the time is right. Sophie wished for a rollercoaster ride, and got one.

We agreed it would be nice to have a special key so we could go through the doors of dreaming any time.

"Do you know any other doors?" I asked.

"You can go through a painting," Sophie said. "Or you can punch a hole in the world."

"Do you ever get scared on these journeys?"

"When I get into trouble, red, golden and blue birds come to help me. They live in my pillow."

She was making pretend beds for new "friends" when Marcia came home. When Marcia referred to "imaginary friends," Sophie's tone and expression became ominous. "*Invisible friends,*" Marcia hastily corrected herself. [January 23, 1995]

One dream in this series (the dream of fighting bulls) was a dramatic commentary on domestic tensions at that time, and instructed my wife and me to pay close attention to the impact our occasional disagreements could have on a small child. Another dream ("Flying Houses") may be, inter alia, an amusing commentary on my sometimes impressive "shamanic snoring." Other dreams are postcards from exciting adventures in a separate reality. In the last exchange, Sophie suggests doorways into conscious dreaming.

Our children remind us, if we let them, that there are not only many types of dreams but many levels of dreaming, that we do not have to go to sleep in order to dream and that when we imagine something vividly we are doing far more than "making things up": we may be punching a hole in the world, opening a path into a larger reality. In Part II, we'll explore the types of dreams and levels of dreaming more closely. We'll discover that as we learn to punch a hole in the world and become conscious dream journeyers, we can open paths for others, helping them to find and to manifest their deepest dreams.

part two

SEVEN LEVELS OF DREAMING

The dreamer is actually seven men and his earthly person becomes the seventh shaman.

—Robin Ridington, "Beaver Dreaming and Singing"

chapter eight

WAYS OF DREAMING

There were twenty-four interpreters of dreams in Jerusalem. Once I had a dream and went to every one of them and what any one interpreted, none of the others interpreted in the same way, and yet all of them were fulfilled.

—Rabbi Bana, in the Talmud

Suppose you dreamed you were flying high, having a wonderful time, but then had some trouble getting down because of the power lines (a fairly common twist on a universal theme). What could we say about this dream?

We could say it was the result of something you ate, like spicy pizza. Some physiologists would tell you that your dream images are byproducts of random neuronal processing in the brain. A Freudian might tell you that your dream is sexual: that flying is the sublimation of the sexual act. Other kinds of analysts might say your dream indicates a tendency towards escapism or excessive self-esteem.

All these explanations are *reductionist,* in one way or another. They tell us that dreams are "nothing but" something that is quickly explained, and not very interesting. They may each contain an element of truth, because dreams have many levels (and we *do* occasionally have "spicy pizza" dreams) but they will not take us where we need to go, because dreams take us beyond what we already know, in our surface minds. The most impoverished form of reductionism, to my mind, is the kind that tries to reduce the mind to a computer made of meat and describes dreams as the accidental results of physical processes in the brain. This is like pulling apart a TV monitor in the effort to understand where the pictures originate. The innards of the TV set can tell us something about how images appear on the screen, but they cannot tell us about the reality beyond the set in which those pictures were filmed, or the energy channels along which they come to us.

Let's go back to the flying dream. A more sensitive approach might suggest it is both a gift and a warning. In your dream, you enjoy that wonderful sense of liberation from everyday constraints—but then you have to come down to ground. If you were in a dream-sharing group like the ones I lead, you would probably be asked all of the following questions:

* Where in your waking life do you have trouble coming down to earth?
* What "power lines" do you have to contend with?
* Do you feel your flying dream was an out-of-body experience?
* Were you flying in something like your regular body, or in a different form?

If the dream carried a strong emotional charge, I would probably ask you to try to go back inside it, enjoy the sensations of flight again, take a closer look at the landscape—especially those troublesome power lines—and see whether you can take flight on further itineraries.

In dreams, flying is a natural human ability. It is wonderful fun, and gives us the ability to see things from a larger perspective. I don't want to *interpret* a dream of flying; I want to celebrate it. But in this particular dream, there is a caution about the need to watch those power lines.

Let's suppose that you get in your car, the morning after you had this dream, and on your way to work you see something suspended from a power line. When you get close enough, you are saddened to see it is a beautiful redtail hawk, hanging straight down. What would you make of your dream now?

You might conclude that it was either precognitive or telepathic: that you foresaw the death of the hawk, as if you were flying on its wings, or that you somehow tuned into its fatal flight. You might dismiss the follow-up as coincidence. If you happen to believe (as I do) that coincidence is never "only" coincidence, you might conclude that the message of the dream is greatly reinforced by the waking event, and that you will need to pay more attention to this problem of grounding, in your life and perhaps in those of others who are connected with you.

There are further possibilities. Maybe, in your dream, you flew on the wings of a redtail hawk. Maybe your consciousness fused, for a time, with that of a bird. Maybe you shared its flight, and its danger. Maybe you clashed with hawk, or embraced it, knocked it off its balance and contributed to its fall. In the view of the earliest dream specialists, the shamans, all of these things are possible. Dream shamans take flight, quite literally, in energy bodies that can interact with other beings, human, animal or otherworldly. They also shapeshift. If a Native American dreamer says, "I became a redtail hawk," he is not sharing a metaphor; he is telling you about a metamorphosis.

We won't get far with dreams until we come to recognize that they are not only products of the individual psyche but experiences of a multilayered universe, not only about what is in here but about what is out there. Dreams are transpersonal, as well as personal, experiences. Dreaming, we learn that the boundaries of our identities and possibilities are not nearly as fixed as we may have told ourselves, or been told by others. We fly like birds, and we know their language.

THE VARIETIES OF DREAM EXPERIENCE

As the example of the flying dream suggests, a single dream may contain multiple levels of meaning, both literal and symbolic, personal and transpersonal, somatic and sacred. A single dream sequence may reflect multiple levels of experience. This is especially true of dreams-within-dreams, in which we sometimes appear to move into deeper dimensions of being and understanding.

There are many ways of dreaming, and many ways of classifying dreams. The simplest typologies focus on content analysis. For example, a content analysis of the dream reports of 300 adults in the city of Cincinnati revealed differences between dream content associated with gender and age. Women reported more dreams than men, with more characters and emotions. Men's dreams contained more violence and aggression. People over 65 had more death anxiety than younger people, and so on.[1] Another way of classifying dreams is to look for common themes, either negative or positive. We dream of falling or flying; of being pursued or of being embraced; of being naked in public or of being well-dressed (or naked and sure of ourselves). Such typologies can be quite entertaining and help us to recognize how much we have in common with other dreamers, regardless of circumstances or cultures. But they are necessarily limited, because they draw on dreamers' reports of their dreams—which are often fragmentary or blurred—rather than the fuller dream experience and they focus on *what* seems to be going on in a dream, but not on *how* we dream, *where* we go, and *who* (i.e., what part of ourselves) is the dreamer.

A satisfactory description of the variety of dreams and dreaming must address all these areas—the what, the how, the where and the who.

WHAT WE DREAM

As you keep and review your dream journals, you will become more attuned to patterns and recurring themes in your own dreams. You will identify personal markers in dreams that flag not only possible precognitive content but possible messages about other specific areas of your life and relationships. If I dream of a gas station, for example, my first hunch is that my dream is telling me something about the business side of my life—especially my dealings with publishers, my principal source of income ("gas," or fuel for the road) for more than two decades. I will stop to ask if the gas station in my dream is a literal gas station, where a literal event in waking life could take place. But, having monitored the language of my dreams for many years, when my dream locale is a gas station I am braced for a message about publishers. If the dream focus is on my car rather than the gas station, on the other hand, I'll prepare myself for a different kind of message. I'll probably spend a little more time checking for a literal advisory, since dreams often tell me about literal car problems that may be developing. But on symbolic levels, the car in my dreams is very frequently an analog for my body. If my dream car is having problems, I may need to check my physical health. In your dreams, your vehicle—apart from being a literal car with possibly literal brake or transmission problems—might represent something that gets you around in life: your job, your relationship etc.

These are examples of how dreams mirror our situations back to us in creative ways that help us to see ourselves and our issues more clearly.

When we have *recurring dreams,* in which the same situation or issue is represented in similar form again and again, perhaps with deepening emotional emphasis, we are probably receiving a clear signal that we either need to get the message or *act* on it. A recurring dream should not be confused with a recurring theme or locale, which may simply be an agreed signal between the dreaming self and the waking editor on where to look for meaning, as my gas station locale tells me to think about publishing or a school dream might lead you to thing about tests or learning experiences that confront you now. A *serial* dream, though often confused with a recurring dream, is something different again. In a serial dream, the plot thickens over many installments, as in a long-running television series. Such dreams sometimes suggest a secret logic to our lives, our connection to a larger story—or to many stories, being played out in parallel life experiences.

What we dream about is related not only to present circumstances and the processing of past episodes and "day residue," but to the rehearsal and psychic functions of dreaming, that prepare us for situations that lie in the future, and to the social and transpersonal aspects of dreaming, which bring us in contact not only with other humans, but with the variegated realms of "gods, demons and others." We have already explored how we dream for others, pick up their stuff, see through their eyes. In *big* dreams, we also encounter messengers and spiritual teachers. Sometimes they call us and escort us into deeper orders of reality, into dreams beyond any ordinary conception of dreaming.

HOW WE DREAM

Dreams are not dependent on the REM state, and dreaming is not confined to sleep. We also dream in the hypnagogic zone, in waking reveries or daydreams, and in conscious dreams (waking or sleeping) in which we are aware we are dreaming. As Jung suggested, "It is on the whole probable that we continually dream, but that [ordinary] consciousness makes such a noise that we do not hear it."[2] Anthony Shafton offers the beautiful image of a dream aquifer: "One possibility is that we are always dreaming, that we live above an aquifer of dream activity of which we become conscious only when the ground conditions allow it to surface."[3]

In a study of shamanic healing, Holger Kalweit accurately observes that "we continually swing back and forth on a consciousness continuum between subwakeful and hyperconscious states. Indeed, we live in a mercurial universe of consciousness."[4] From this perspective, we are deluding ourselves if we suppose there is a "normal' state of awareness, or a solid line between dreaming and other modes of consciousness.

How do we dream? On our backs and our bellies and curled up in fetal position (and we may have different dream experiences depending on our body postures in bed). We dream without knowing we are dreaming, and we dream wide awake. Here are some of the ways we dream:

* *Spontaneous sleep dreams,* in which we are not aware we are dreaming;
* *Incubated dreams,* in which we have asked for dream guidance

and perhaps prepared ourselves through purification, meditation, invocation, personal ritual and/or lying in a certain position or at a special site;

* *Dream reentry,* in which we consciously go back inside a dream to dream it onward and explore the dreamscape;
* *Hypnagogic experiences* in the twilight zone between waking and sleep (and sleep and waking) in which spontaneous imagery arises;
* *Daydreams,* reveries and "mini-dreams" in which images appear spontaneously during waking or drowsy states, sometimes through a kind of "trapdoor" that opens up in our field of vision;
* *Creative visualization,* in which we bring a picture up on our mental screen and then step inside it and inhabit it with all of our inner senses;
* *Meditation,* when we do not dismiss the images that appear to us, but allow them to rise and fall or flow with them and allow a dreamlike sequence to unfold;
* *Conscious or lucid dreaming,* in which we are aware we are dreaming and are able to navigate the dreamspace and choose our actions and interactions;
* *Journeying or conscious dream travel,* in which we embark on conscious and intentional journeys across time and space and into other orders of reality;
* *Astral projection* or intentional out-of-body experiences, in which we deliberately shift awareness from the physical body to an energy body that travels independently;
* *Interactive dreaming,* in which we journey inside the dreamspace with one or more partners;
* *Dreams within dreams,* in which we have the experience of moving through different levels of dreaming and/or dimensions of reality;
* *Flow states* of waking creativity in which we have the dreamlike sensation of being "in the zone," able to bend the

normal laws of physics, fully attuned to the play of synchronicity and its guidance;

* *Continuity of awareness,* in which we are conscious of our moves—and the thoughts and emotions behind those moves—both waking and sleeping, are alert to the symbolic resonance of everything that enters our field of perception, and constantly test the limits of the possible.

The dream yoga of Naropa is founded on the core understanding that waking consciousness, dreaming and death are all illusory states that need to be transcended. This gives rise to three periods of practice: (1) during the day, remind yourself that you are dreaming; (2) at night, become conscious that you are dreaming and practice transforming and directing your dreams—for example, by traveling to one of the heavens and receiving instruction from a spiritual teacher, perhaps a Buddha; (3) control your reactions to what you see and experience in any of the bardo realms (or states of transition) so you can move beyond attachments and desires into the clear light of higher consciousness. The aim is continuous awareness.[5]

WHERE WE GO

Ancient dreamers understood that in big dreams, we go on a journey. In the languages of some indigenous peoples, heirs to ancient dream wisdom, the word for dream literally means "a journey of the soul." In the language of the Makiritare, a shamanic people of Venezuela, a dream is an *adekato,* or "flight of the soul."[6] In Tibetan dream yoga, it is taught that in dreams we travel through six distinct realms of awareness that are also dimensions of reality. When we travel in dreams through these domains, we interact with their inhabitants: with gods and demons, dakinis and hungry ghosts.[7] In most of the world's civilizations, the existence of parallel worlds, peopled by gods and spirits and accessible in altered states of consciousness—such as dreaming or death—has been accepted as common fact, and the ability to visit these territories intentionally has been highly prized. Frequent flyers have brought back vivid and detailed geographies of these dreamworlds, as described in my book *Dreamgates.* They contain heavens and hells, temples and bordellos, cities and gardens.[8]

If we are not very familiar with the dreamworld, we may think it is a realm of fleeting phantasms and mirages. But we learn through exploration that to many of its inhabitants, the dreamworld is quite solid. Annie, a New York artist, had a multi-layered dream that began when she took off her clothes, getting ready to take a bath. As she tested the water, a troop of "little people" came in. They did not seem to notice she was naked. When she became lucid and said, "Oh my God, I'm dreaming," the little people were dismissive. "I realized that for them, this wasn't a dream; it was their reality." They took her outside and she saw a shapeshifting neon sign. The word "ESSE" was flashing. As she focused on the sign, she realized the message was an old Latin tag, *esse est percipere.* Being is perceiving; what we perceive is our reality.

In Annie's case, she didn't travel through space, but into a different dimension, or frequency domain.

We don't have to stray far from home to unfold a basic proposition about dream travel. Frank Baum gave us the clue in *The Wizard of Oz.* It's in Dorothy's attempt to explain what had happened to her when she got back to Kansas from the wonderful world of Oz. "But it wasn't a dream," she insisted. "It was a place." I would amend Dorothy's statement just a little. If we have gone on a dream journey somewhere, we can say that it was both a dream *and* a place (or another dimension).

Since we travel, or seem to travel, so frequently in dreams, it might be more accurate to say we "go on" a dream rather than simply that we "have" a dream. So one of the ways of looking at dreams is to ask where did we go. Did we stay close to ordinary reality, checking up on the dog in the yard, or Aunt Rhoda in Chicago, or the scene at the office Christmas party? Did we go to something like a movie set, constructed by our personal dream producer to unfold a morality play or entertainment? Did we travel to an afterlife locale—which would explain why those dead people seemed so perfectly alive? Did we go astral slumming? Were we allowed to ascend beyond the astral for initiation, training or testing on a higher plane? Did we pass through a whole series of interdimensional boundaries, so that our memories of dreams-within-dreams reflect the experience of what leading-edge physics depicts as nested realities, the cosmic enchilada?

The ancient dreamers maintained—and may still maintain—stable locales in the dreamscape where students may travel for training and initiation. Homer wrote about one of these locales in the *Odyssey.* It is called the Phaeacian shore. It is on the borders between the dreamworlds and ordinary reality, a liminal zone. Odysseus washes up there, naked and vulnerable, after ten years of wandering the deep realms of the psyche and being initiated into the mysteries of the Goddess, which required him to die to his previous, brutishly macho self. The kingdom of Phaeacia is the realm of active dreamers. Sacred beings step into the dreams of humans and communicate with them as easily as the goddess Athena speaks to the princess Nausicaa. Humans speak to each other in dreams as fluently as Nausicaa speaks to her family and the shipwrecked Odysseus.

It is a meeting point and bridge between the worlds, and has been recognized and used as such for thousands of years (like other locales) in Western Mystery traditions. Since my boyhood, I have found myself traveling there, again and again, in dreams. Sometimes I am a pilot, sailing off high above the cloud canopy on dangerous missions in a seaplane or an old

Spitfire-type fighter plane. When my battles are done, I come down to the Phaeacian shore to relax and renew myself, to taste the unmixed wine and the wild figs, to meet old friends and companions—and find my way back to Ithaca.

Where we go in dreams (as in waking life, and most certainly after death) is very largely determined by which part of us is in charge.

WHO IS THE DREAMER?

Who are you, in your dreams? One of the gifts of dreaming is that we slip the bounds of the ego and the social persona. We get in touch with other aspects of ourselves, and (if we are lucky) with the *big* Self. The dreaming "I" is not the same as the waking "I." It can be more, and it can be less.

One of the great scientists of dream travel was Shahabuddin Suhrawardi (c.1153–1191), a medieval Persian philosopher and Sufi *experiencer* who was legally murdered by the defenders of Muslim orthodoxy for opening paths to direct experience of the sacred. He maintained that the degree of "truth" or "falsity" in dreams is closely related to which part of the dreamer's psyche is dominant in the dream experience. The dreams of people who practice meditation and self-awareness are likely to be "truer" than those of people who are caught up in ego agendas and unreasoning appetites. Dreams in which the lower self, or *nafs,* is dominant, are likely to be "mere fantasy" or experiences confined to the lower and most deceptive levels of the astral planes; the landscapes traversed in such dreams are "stages of lust" and worldly attachments. On the other hand, when the dreamer rises to the level of a higher aspect of soul consciousness (*ruh*) he is rewarded with clear dreams, or "free revelation" (*kashf*) which do not require interpretation. Such dreams are true visions of the soul.[9]

There is practical wisdom here. What we encounter in dreams, as in waking life, is greatly conditioned by the part of us that is dominant at the time. Our habits, appetites and desires steer us toward corresponding levels of experience.

SEVEN KINDS OF DREAMING

The Beaver Indians of the Peace River area in Northwest Canada say that the most powerful dreamer, the *nachi,* is not one person, but seven people in one. The *nachi,* or dream shaman, has traveled far into the hidden orders of reality. He has encountered six spiritual guides in other dimensions of reality, and each of them has conferred a blessing, a teaching, and the gift of a sacred song. To claim all of these gifts, he has been required to travel beyond the gates of death. When he has returned to himself and begins to function as a healer and teacher to his people, he carries the energy and the knowledge of six "grandfathers" with him. In himself, he is the seventh dreamer, but he is seven in one. He can do many things for the community. He brings healing energy from the dreamworld, mediated by the sacred songs that call it through; in the language of the Beaver Indians, *ma yine,* the word for medicine literally means "his (or her) song." He leads the hunt by going out, as a dream tracker, to find the game and negotiate for its life; what he chooses and arranges inside the dreamscape is believed to become manifest. Above all, he commands the songlines that lead to the higher world. He can teach others to scale them, like a climber's rope, for true initiation.[10]

There is magic in the number seven, as in all prime numbers. An energetic professor of English joined one of my week-long trainings at the Esalen Institute and told us, on the first day, that he had asked for dream guidance and received a *big* dream in which he was shown seven keys to seven locks. He understood that the seven locks—"though they were also something like canal locks"—secured the seven gates of dreaming. In his dream, he was able to turn a golden key in the first lock. Invited to go back inside his dream, with the help of shamanic drumming, Greg had a wonderful time opening further doors. He told us that the first key was intention: having the intention to dream and remember the dream. He is still exploring, working his way up to through levels of dream-within-dream and conscious dreaming.

As I look over the variety of dream experience, it seems to me that we can single out seven kinds of dreaming that are accessible, at least on some levels, to any of us who are willing to turn that golden key and make it our strong intention to remember and work with dreams. They are not levels of dreaming in the sense of a rigid hierarchy, but the sequence does take us from "little" dreams to "big" ones, from personal processing to transpersonal experiences and creative engagement with partners and communities, from blurry, fragmented dream memories to conscious exploration of the larger reality. When we are dreaming on the first three levels, we are usually unaware we are dreaming—though we can "wake up" to the fact that we are dreaming and continue the experience with lucidity, sometimes to much deeper levels. Dreaming with the body can also be developed as a conscious dream practice, and is central to the healing practice of both traditional shamans and medical intuitives.

These are the seven levels of dreaming:

Level 1: Dream Recycling. This produces dreams shaped by day residue, personal processing and external input.

Level 2: Dream Moviemaking. Our dream producers and scriptwriters creatively rework our personal material to show us how things are and where we are likely to end up if we go where we are headed.

Level 3: Dreaming with the Body. The body talks to us in dreams—and sometimes we travel inside it—producing self-diagnosis and images for healing and recovery.

Level 4: Psychic dreaming. Psychic dreams may or may not also be conscious dreams, out-of-body experiences, or visitations. They are possible because we live in a mind-field shared with other humans (and maybe all forms of conscious life) and because the mind itself is nonlocal.

Level 5: Transpersonal dreaming involves encounters with people and places that have their own objective reality. We go somewhere, we meet other beings, we receive visits. Basic types include social or interactive dreams and dreams of the departed. These may or may not be conscious dream experiences.

Level 6: Sacred dreaming involves contact with higher powers, spiritual guides and protectors. These may be experiences of calling, initiation, training or healing. A sacred dream may or may not be a conscious dream, but it usually involves either dream travel or visitation. To encounter higher beings, we must rise to their level, unless they descend to us. The confirmation of a sacred dream is its numinosity, the dreamer's experience of wonder and awe.

Level 7: Dreambringing. We are now *growing* dreams for ourselves and our communities. We have become dream creators, working on energy and imaginal levels to shape physical reality for the better. Though in some belief systems (as in some versions of Tibetan dream yoga) the highest level of dreaming involves moving beyond dreaming and the worlds of form, to my mind the consummation of the dreamer's journey is in what Joseph Campbell called the hero's return. We have soared to the heavens; we have braved the realm of death and its gatekeepers; we have conversed with angels. Now our task is to bring a dream—a healing image, a life vision, perhaps a path into the next world—to someone in need of a dream. When we do this, we become conductors on the Underground Railroad of dreams.

chapter nine

LEVEL ONE: DREAM RECYCLING

If you are in the body of a donkey, enjoy the grass.

—Tibetan saying

PROCESSING DREAMS

One of the most aggressively reductionist views of dreaming presents it as a kind of janitorial, or garbage collection process. For Crick and Mitchison, dreaming involves a random process of dumping information from memory. Dreams are not cognitive events; they are a "garbage out" function that reduces the risk of overload in the neural nets that support waking cognition.[1] This view is taken to its logical extreme by New York psychologist John Antrobus, who maintains that dreaming is one facet of a "cyclical sleep process" that may function "to give the non-central nervous system part of the organism a break for restorative purposes and to keep the cognitive engine warm so that it will run efficiently when the sun rises. However, I suspect we could do quite well without it."[2]

We do not need to devote any more space to this type of analysis, which can be blown apart by what you retrieve from your own dreams in a single night.

However, in the level of dreaming most closely associated with the preoccupations and activities of the previous day, we may find ourselves going over and around the stuff we took to bed with us, sifting and filing, clearing up and clearing out.

We work our way back through the "day residue," trying to sort out unfinished business and to integrate new data. In order to avoid spending too much time in this fairly unrewarding zone of consciousness, advanced dreamers and meditators recommend spending some time before going to sleep sorting through the day's business and trying to resolve it—or alternatively, to focusing on a good theme for dream incubation rather than undirected ramblings—before going to sleep.

However, the processing function can have positive results in accelerating learning and memorization. One study suggested that students in an intensive foreign language course who increased the time they spent in dream sleep performed better in their studies than those who did not.[3] I have caught myself practicing new languages intensively in my dreams, and this greatly benefited my efforts to learn Mohawk (though I am not sure this a very relevant example of routine dream processing, since my first instructors were Mohawk shamans who lived 300 years before they walked into my dreams).

In Tibetan dream yoga, dream processing is valued not only for clearing up issues from our present life experience, but for clearing "karmic traces" inherited from the whole family of lives to which we are related.

SPICY PIZZA DREAMS

A radio talkshow host once asked me whether it is true that dreams are caused by spicy pizza. There *are* "spicy pizza dreams," the bubbles of imagery that are very closely related to what we ingested the night before. That's all we need say about them here.

SCANNING DREAMS

Pioneering dream researchers Montague Ullman and Stanley Krippner noted that dreaming is *a vigilance operation.* While sleeping, we go through cycles of "heightened vigilance" during which dreams may reflect our scanning of the external environment.[4] We may literally be checking out that unsavory guy who's hanging out with a cell phone on the street corner, or that hotplate someone left on in the kitchen.

Our constant scanning encompasses benign and neutral phenomena, from the snoring of the cat to the lump in the pillow. Resulting dream imagery may incorporate both minor and major disturbances in our physical environment during sleep. For example: During a violent thunderstorm, I dreamed I was driving around wildly in a car playing "Night on Bald Mountain" at full volume on the stereo.

ENERGY DREAMS

Hal, an infrequent dream recaller, laughed as he recalled a dream from which he had woken at 3:00 A.M. He had to wake his wife up because it was so funny. All he could remember was that people were "throwing things up" from their cars—he couldn't say what. Yet as he shared this broken shard with her, they both started laughing. Even as he recounted the incident, more than a year later, everyone in the dream group started chuckling. Our energy rose notably. When Hal was able to speak coherently again, he told us, "It was laughter that got us through." Shortly after his dream, his wife fell gravely ill, and was "throwing up" all the time. We heard the echo: the people "throwing up" in the dream, the wife "throwing up" during her illness—but laughing her way through.

Night after night, while recycling our stuff, our dreams are also helping to *recharge* us. Hal's story is a simple and powerful example of how bringing the raw *energy* of dreams into our lives may be far more important than simply interpreting them. His dream scrap brought the healing power of laughter, which can literally drive away pain. We saw it in the group that night. It was being held at the dreary end of winter, with a freezing rain falling and the snow on the sidewalks turned the color of spat-out gum. People in the group had arrived coughing and hacking. Yet after we had finished laughing along with Hal, nobody remembered their physical complaints. A woman told me afterwards that she completely forgot about the extreme pain she had been feeling from an abscessed tooth until she got home and noticed she had scheduled a dental appointment for the following day.

Just as our bodies replenish and renew themselves during sleep, the *energy dream* can help restore our animal spirits, our vitality and even our sense of humor.

chapter ten

LEVEL TWO: DREAM MOVIEMAKING

Mirror, mirror on the wall, who is the fairest one of all?

—Snow White

George du Maurier was the author of *Trilby,* one of the best-selling novels of its day and the one that gave us the enduring character of Svengali. In another work of fiction, *Peter Ibbetson,* du Maurier gave us a brilliant description of how dream locales may be constructed from pictures and memories we have assembled or shared in waking life. His hero, in jail, has dream assignations with his lover. They meet in elaborately constructed locales in which every detail—the flowering trees, the weave of the carpets, the fold of the bedsheets—is drawn from what they have seen and experienced in waking life. They build a palace of love, brick by brick and pillow by pillow. When their dream environment begins to pall and grow tediously familiar, Peter's mistress travels the world so she can introduce new pictures and sensory impressions—a vista of snowcapped mountains in Canada, the smell of a Venetian canal.

We *do* have "Peter Ibbetson" dreams, in which our dream producer cunningly cobbles together images and impressions from waking life as the movie sets for our nightly dramas. The vital difference between our dream lives and those of George du Maurier's characters is that they are never able to go beyond what they have known in waking life, while our spectrum of dream experience (if we are awake to it) takes us far beyond what we have known, or can ever know, in physical reality. But our dream producers know what they are doing when they pull together bits and pieces from our past—the kitchen from that childhood home, plus that old flame, plus a picture window from a resort hotel, plus Bob Dylan and Peter Rabbit—to make a movie. Since the elements are drawn from our past, and the past is what we know, we are more likely to get the message, right? Well, maybe.

Our dream movies—like movies we watch on a screen—may simply be entertainment, pure and simple, a chance to laugh and cry and lust and relax. Better than the cinema, we can interact with the players, go to bed with the star, kill off the villains. Through all the fun and shivers, the special effects and film noir touches, the dream producers are also working with story ideas and scripts that are often tailored to one of three genres: the *mirror dream* that shows us how things really are, with us and around us; the *compensation dream* that shows us sides of ourselves and of life we have been trying to suppress or deny; and the *rehearsal dream* that show us what's likely to happen if we carry on as we are doing.

MIRROR DREAMS

Mirror dreams reflect the state of our relationships and our emotional, mental and spiritual health, often as flawlessly as somatic dreams reflect our physical condition.

Sometimes they get our attention and bring us clarity by acting out a wildly dramatic or comic script. Often they take us into dreamscapes that are a mirror for the psyche: a dream house with subterranean levels, an island (I-land) or a headland.

To give a simple example: While I was working on this book, I dreamed an enormous dinner had just been delivered—prime sirloin steak, perfectly broiled. The problem was that there was no space to eat. Every surface in my dream kitchen was covered with paper plates and dirty dishes. I had to bustle about clearing a space in order to get to the meat while it was still hot. I woke up chuckling, recognizing the very close analogy between the state of my dream kitchen (often, in my dreams, the center of creative activity—the place where things get "cooked up") and the condition of my study, where every surface was covered with teetering piles of books and papers. I spent the early hours of the morning sweeping my desk clean, to make plenty of room to get to the "meat" of my new book while it was still hot.

Sometimes it takes longer to recognize ourselves and our situations in the "magic mirror" of our dreams, because they show us ourselves and the worlds we inhabit in unfamiliar and sometimes uncomfortable ways. They show us the whole picture—including how other people see us.

Jungian analyst James Hall wisely observes that the great value of spontaneous sleep dreams—the dreams we do *not* ask for and may not want!—is their objectivity. "They present images that are not consciously constructed but arise spontaneously. Therefore, a dream has an objectivity in the sense that a laboratory blood specimen has objectivity; it comes from the patient and reflects the internal state of his functioning."[1]

Here is an example of how a man learned about his need to master his rage through the dream looking glass. In his dream, he encountered a savage dog on a commercial street. The dog was blue-black, built like a stocky boxer, with an amazing set of teeth, which were bared as it snarled. The dreamer froze, putting out his hand for the dog to sniff. The dog did not bite, but still looked poised for attack. The man seized the opportunity to slip into the nearest open store.

I encouraged the dreamer to go back inside his dream. After he relaxed enough to get back inside, he reported that the that the locales seemed flimsy, "like a stage set cobbled together for a one-night production, already being disassembled before the show is over." Much of the set seemed to have been cobbled together from his waking-life experiences, giving it the quality of a "Peter Ibbetson dream."

I urged the dreamer to take a closer look at the dog. He reported: "I took a rolled-up newspaper, just in case. For the briefest moment, I saw a huge Anubis-like shadow spring up behind the dog. Then the dog shrink in size, became shaggier, and trotted at my side like a faithful pet. This confirmed for me that the dog was an aspect of myself—my *mirror*—maybe reflecting how I seem to others when I bark and snarl, as I was doing in the store sequences."

He conceded that his sometimes violent temper had caused many unpleasant situations in his life, including business problems (remember the "commercial street") and now felt that the black dog personified his rage.

The two aspects of the dream I found most revealing were the transformations of the black dog and the made-up, movie quality of the dreamscape. The black dog figures in many mythologies as a guide and friend of the soul; for it to appear in a dream as an adversary is a clear warning that something is off, a message underscored by the fact that the dreamer owned a black dog! The "Peter Ibbetson" elements in the dream could be seized on by a certain kind of dream analyst as confirmation of a boringly predictable pattern of dream creation. But it struck me that, when we look more closely at some of our dream movie sets, we may actually find ourselves stepping beyond the processing models.

What the "black dog" dreamer perceived around him was conditioned and possibly generated by his previous experience and perceptions. But is waking reality fundamentally different? If the dream is a product of the creative reworking of impressions from waking life, might it not also be an analog for the creation of our waking realities?

COMPENSATION DREAMS

Compensation dreams show us aspects of ourselves and our potential that we tend to repress in waking life and can direct us towards balance and wholeness. Thus someone committed to a chaste religious discipline may have many highly sexual dreams, like poor St. Augustine (who gave thanks that God did not hold him responsible for his dreams). Jung maintained that compensation, in this sense, is "absolutely necessary for balanced action." He observed that "dreams contribute to the self-regulation of the psyche by automatically bringing up everything that is repressed or neglected or unknown."[2]

As long as we repress or deny vital aspects of ourselves, we are in danger of encountering our shadow side in the projections we throw onto others. What we most immediately dislike in another person (to take a very familiar example) may be a quality we fail to recognize in ourselves. Dreams help us to move beyond the shadow-play. This can extend to soul recovery: reclaiming a vital aspect of ourselves that was lost along the road of life.

REHEARSAL DREAMS

Rehearsal dreams prepare us for life passages and tests, and show us the natural outcome of our present actions and attitudes.

At the crossroads of our lives, dreams show us the consequences of the choices we are about to make. If we are deaf and blind to our dreams, we may rush ahead along the wrong path without even pausing to weigh our options wisely. In our mad dash, we may even fail to notice that we actually have a choice.

We can miss these messages because we cling to limited, ego-driven definitions of our issues. Many years ago, my dreams rehearsed me for the consequences of entering into a business partnership I was actively considering at that time. In one memorable dream, I was sitting down to dinner at an elegant restaurant with my prospective partner and a famous tycoon (who was a mutual friend in waking life). The sumptuous appointments and lavish menu looked very promising; chateaubriand—one of my favorite dishes—was being served as the main course. There was just one problem. I couldn't stomach the first course, which was *snake stone soup.* In the dream, I recalled that I had had a most unpleasant previous experience with "snake stone soup."

There was a clear warning in my dream of the cost of the rewards my venture seemed to promise. The old children's tale of "stone soup" is about trickery and deception. Add "snake" to the mix and you might get the sense of cold venom, even coiled menace. Yet in my little waking mind, I dwelled on the juicy chateaubriand, not the snake soup, telling myself the projected partnership would prosper. It took me five full months of largely wasted time and effort before I recognized that I had been badly deceived in the whole venture, and that the worst of the deceit had been my own self-deception. I abandoned that venture, and since then I have tried to be more alert to what kind of nourishment seems to come with different projects and partnerships in my dreams. Some time after the snake soup dream, a friend proposed a joint writing project. I considered this sympathetically until I dreamed I attended a party where my friend had arranged for an elaborate, multi-course meal. The problem here was that I did not like *any* of the dishes; I told people at the dream party I would rather order in pizza. When I thought over that dream, I decided not to pursue the writing collaboration.

As we work with our dreams over time, we get to recognize the personal ways in which they present our issues to us.

Dreams can also rehearse us in very literal and specific ways for tests we are about to face. As a student, both in high school and at university, I benefited from dreams that encouraged me to bone up on certain topics on the eve of exams. Almost always, I found that exam questions related to these exact themes. Brian Inglis recounts the story of a young Englishman who was anxious to qualify as a registered nurse and was preparing for his exams. Colin dreamed that his father—a naval surgeon who had died many years before—appeared in a brilliant white gown, looking about his own age. His father said distinctly, "The thyroid gland." Colin was so struck by the dream that he read up on the thyroid before leaving the next morning to take his exams at the Royal West Sussex Hospital. One of the questions on his exam paper was on the thyroid; he answered it with confidence.[3]

Dreams rehearse us for challenges in the workplace and in home or social environments, sometimes by showing us the hidden springs of other people's actions. A woman office worker dreamed the boss got mad at her, throwing a temper tantrum in which he spilled coffee over his desk and drove her to tears. In the dream, it was clear that his rage was not really directed at her, but at another person. She was merely a convenient outlet. Two days later, when the dreamer's boss blew his stack in the office, she was able to contain her own emotions—and even to intercept the coffee mug before it spilled on the desk. Later that afternoon, her boss brought her flowers along with an apology, and confided that his anger had actually been directed at someone else, as she had dreamed.

chapter eleven

LEVEL THREE: DREAMING WITH THE BODY

Grant me the measure of health my body requires to serve the purposes of the soul.

—PRAYER TO ASKLEPIOS BY AELIUS ARISTIDES

Every dreamer has a personal physician available who will make house calls at any hour, prefers to heal without surgery or pharmaceuticals—and does not charge a penny. We would spend a lot less time and energy on visits to doctors' offices, clinics and medications if we only listened to our personal dream doctors.

Every night, if we pay attention, we find that our dreams are giving us an impeccable readout on our physical, emotional and spiritual health. Our dreams rehearse us for possible health problems long before we develop physical symptoms. If we are willing to listen to these prodromic dreams and *take appropriate action,* we may be able to avoid manifesting those physical symptoms of disease.

When treatment is required, our dreams advise us on where to go—and where *not* to go—for help.

Dreams also show us the hidden causes of illness, taking us into realms that are only grudgingly acknowledged (when acknowledged at all) by mainstream medicine and psychology. They show us how we may have lost vital energy—pieces of soul—through pain or abuse or negative behavior, and how we can get it back. They show us where we may have suffered psychic intrusion, or be burdened by negative attachments that are stealing our energy and clarity. They direct us to establish healthy boundaries between ourselves and other people, including the departed.

The power of imagery to remold our physical bodies in the direction of health is now widely accepted. Our bodies do not seem to differentiate between mental, emotional and physical events providing the events engage our full belief and vigor. Just as we can make ourselves ill by dwelling on stress and fearful images, we can use healing imagery to make ourselves well. Dreams are the best source of this healing imagery, which emerges fresh, spontaneous and *personal* from our night journeys.

Beyond all this, in *big* dreams, we may benefit from spontaneous healing. Sometimes this comes as the gift of a dream guide who appears in the midst of a desperate crisis, when we are finally willing to ask for help and have opened a space within ourselves where the healing power can operate.

Dreams give us access to the wisdom of the body, as well as the realms of soul and spirit. The body knows what it needs to stay well, and it tells us through dream images. It had its own kind of knowledge about the future, which may be far more extensive than most of us imagine.

THE WHITE QUEEN GAMBIT

Remember the White Queen in Alice's adventures *Through the Looking-Glass?* She screams *before* she pricks her finger. When her brooch-pin subsequently flies open and she *does* prick her finger, she doesn't need to squeal. She got over her reactions before the event that explains them took place. "I've done all the screaming already," says the Queen. "What would be the good of having it all over again?"[1]

The body not only knows what is going on inside it now; it seems to know about future situations that will affect its health and well-being. It's as if the body, or the energy field that surrounds and permeates the body, has its own intricate antennae, constantly scanning for changes that will affect the nervous system. Most of us have experienced this in waking life. We experience a sense of elation or oppression, a lifting of the heart or a knot in the stomach, that has no rational explanation until a subsequent event takes place. The effect on the body and the emotions appears to precede the cause. This is sometimes called presentiment. Recent laboratory research confirms that it is a frequent, if not constant, phenomenon.

Let's look briefly at two series of experiments that suggest that, like the White Queen, we may squeal before we prick our finger (even if we have been missing the connection).

The Paint Chip Experiment

Swedish psychologist Holger Klintman ran a test that consisted of showing people a patch of color—red, green, blue or yellow—followed by the name of a color, and measuring the time it took them to (a) name the color they saw and then (b) read aloud the word that followed. As he expected, when the color they saw matched the subsequent word, people could respond quickly and accurately. If the color patch and the subsequent word were mismatched—for example, if a yellow patch was followed by the word "red"—people had quite a hard time naming both of them quickly and accurately.

What came up was randomly determined. Klintman's initial interest was in seeing how long it took for people to say the words that followed the glimpses of color. Then he decided to measure reaction times to the first stimulus (the color patch) to give himself a baseline. This is when he got something he had not bargained for—and a rather humdrum experiment turned into something very interesting indeed. Klintman discovered that his subjects' initial reaction times were significantly faster when the color they saw matched the word *they had not seen yet,* and slower when the color and the word did not match up.

Was it possible that on some level his subjects "knew" data that had not yet been presented to them (and whose content was also unknown to the experimenter)? Were their reactions conditioned by events that had not yet taken place? Further experiments convinced Klintman that this was exactly what was going on. He described it as "time-reversed interference." His volunteers' reactions were being affected by their *future* perceptions, picked up by the "unconscious nervous system," which is perhaps more conscious than we generally notice.[2]

The Porno Photo Tests

Las Vegas is a pretty good place to study the odds on anything, and it was in his Consciousness Research Laboratory at the University of Nevada, Las Vegas that Dean Radin devised a series of experiments involving presentiment that were rather more exciting than staring at a series of paint chips.

Like Klintman and many other scientific pathfinders, Radin made a big discovery while looking for something else. He thought he was studying Pavlovian reflexes: the psychophysical changes, sometimes called the "orienting response," experienced by humans in "fight or flight" situations described by Pavlov in the 1920s. The classic pattern includes: altered brain waves, dilation of the pupils, rise in sweat gland activity, a change in heartbeat, and a blanching of the extremities. These bodily changes sharpen perception, increase strength, reduce the risk of bleeding and promote fast decision-making.

You can produce Pavlovian reflexes by showing a person an emotionally provocative photograph. In his tests, Radin selected color photos for their shock value—sexually graphic photos and pictures of autopsies were favorites. The shocking photos were interspersed with "calm" pictures of nature scenes, cheerful people and so on. Subjects wired up to electrodes to monitor heartbeat and electrodermal activity were seated at a computer. Each time they clicked the mouse, the computer randomly selected a photo from the pool and brought it up on the screen.

You don't need a Ph.D. to guess that Radin's subjects got sweatier and breathed harder when they looked at porno shots than when they were shown scenes of country life. The unexpected discovery—the one that shifted the experiment and the researcher's sense of the ruling paradigm—was the subjects reacted to the shocking photos a second or two *before* they saw them. "Before the emotional pictures were seen, the participants 'pre-reacted' to their own future emotional states." *Their bodies seemed to know what was coming.*[3]

The importance of these twin series of experiments is that they give us objective, replicable evidence of the workings of the White Queen Gambit. We squeal, or at least feel like squealing, before we prick our fingers. We do this because on some level our body knows what is going to happen to it, not only through internal processes but as a result of external events. The paint chip and porno picture experiments show us presentiment or "time-reversed interference" working at micro-levels. To get to the macro-level, we need to look at how our body communicates with us through images as well as sensations, especially in dreams.

X-RAY DREAMS

In Paula's dream, she examined three X-rays of herself. The first showed her bones. As she looked at it, a disembodied voice told her she needed to take a calcium supplement. The second X-ray revealed a tiny fetus. Both these images were very small, no larger than slides. The third image was huge, more like a glossy photograph than an X-ray. When Paula looked at it, she saw herself, but in a way she had never seen herself in physical reality.

> I look at myself from the neck up, and I marvel at the beauty and radiance of my face. When I look down, I see my body is sheathed in a creamy-colored garment, possibly soft deerskin, that is covered in mysterious pictographs.

Paula's dream of her three X-rays is a fascinating example of how dreams give us a nightly readout on the state of our body, mind and spirit. The image of the bones focused Paula's attention on potential bone loss; following the guidance of the disembodied voice, she decided she would explore the potential benefits of including additional calcium supplements in her diet. The X-ray of the fetus took her self-examination to a different level. Already the mother of three, Paula was unable to have more babies. She guessed that the picture of the unborn child was showing her that something was gestating inside her in a different sense: a new creative project, an opening to new possibilities in her life. The big picture was the most exciting. She felt the photo—or was it a mirror?—of her radiant self was an opening to connect with her Higher Self, her larger spiritual identity. To honor this part of the dream, she decided to draw the pictographs, research their meanings, and incorporate some of them into her artistic work.

In Paula's dream, we see three levels of diagnosis, with body, soul and spirit all contributing.

The X-ray function of dreams was recognized and highly respected by the earliest physicians. Galen, one of the greatest of Greek physicians, maintained that the "vision in sleep" (*enhypnion*) was a reliable guide to "the dispositions of the body." Dream symbols might reflect the play of the four humors he considered fundamental to human health and illness; thus a patient who dreamed of smoke or mist might be troubled by "black bile" while a dream of snow and ice would denote "cold phlegm." Dreams provide clues to the progression of disease. Speculating about the origin of diagnostic dreams, Galen suggested that "in sleep the soul, having gone into the depths of the body and retreated from the external perceptions, perceives the dispositions throughout the body and forms an impression of all that it reaches out to, as though these things were already present."[4]

Most relevant for us, Galen observed that dreams anticipate physical symptoms before those symptoms become apparent to a doctor. Galen quotes the case of a man who dreamed that one of his legs had turned to stone. "Many of those clever about such matters"—the dream interpreters—"judged that the dream pertained to his slaves." But the man became paralyzed in the leg he had seen turned to stone, "although none of us expected that."[5]

Here is the answer to those of us who might wonder why we need X-ray dreams when we have X-ray machines. As Galen observed, dreams show us problems that may be developing in our bodies *before* we develop symptoms that can be detected by even the most sophisticated medical scanners. We may be given previews of this kind many years before symptoms manifest.

The state of our house or car in dreams (*and* in physical reality) very often mirrors the state of the body, as the house or vehicle of the soul. A Canadian woman dreamed there was furnace oddly situated on an upper level of her house, with tubes or pipes around it that were leaking into her bedroom. In dreams, she found herself confronted over and over with a problem furnace with leaky tubes attached until she went to her doctor, who detected a leaky valve in the lower left chamber of her heart. She was still puzzled by the fact that the problem furnace was sometimes in the attic at the top of her dream house. Then she learned that misalignments in her spine might have affected neural messages between her brain and her heart. She had felt desperately fearful after the "leaky tubes" dreams; she felt calm and confident as medical treatments began. Her dreams showed her how to support her healing through imagery and alternative medicine. In a big dream that followed, her problem house had changed into a dream temple, where she learned how to travel to higher levels of reality from the heart center.

Dream diagnosis has been central to traditional Tibetan medicine, which addresses body, mind and spirit simultaneously. Tibetan doctors—often also monks or shamans, since no strong dividing line was drawn between medicine and religion—believed that dream awareness travels, quite literally, through different parts of the body during sleep, and reports back from them. For example, according to a seventeenth-century treatise entitled *Blue Beryl,* compiled by Sangye Giatso, if our dream awareness roves through the lower parts of the body, it transmits images of moving through deep gorges and forests.[6]

Bodytalk dreams show us the possible long-term effects of current habits and attitudes. The pioneer sleep researcher Dr. William Dement describes how he was a two-packs-a-day cigarette smoker until he had an extremely vivid and realistic dream in which doctors told him he had inoperable cancer of the lung. Like Paula, he was shown an X-ray. As he looked at the ominous shadow in the chest area, he realized that his whole right lung was infiltrated. He experienced deep anguish and remorse at the realization that he would never see his children grow up—and that he might have avoided premature death had he quit smoking when he first learned of the carcinogenic potential of cigarettes. For Dr. Dement, waking up that morning was pure joy. To our benefit, as well as that of his family, instead of dismissing his dream as "only" a dream, he acted on it by immediately giving up smoking.[7]

Dement's dream warning about the possible long-terms effects of lifestyle on the body gave him very realistic, indeed clinical, imagery. The message may be couched in symbolic, but no less effective language. I once dreamed I was driving wildly and erratically all over a commercial road lined with fast food joints. Careening out of control, my car finally came to a safe stop—in what might have been a smash-up, but wasn't—at the door of a Chinese health food store. I noticed a very clear message to slow down and to watch my eating habits.

An older gay man attributes the fact that he is still HIV negative to dream warnings that began long before AIDS became a household term. In these early dreams, he repeatedly found himself in gay clubs and bathhouses "preaching like a Jesus freak" about a devastating virus that would kill all of them unless they practiced safe sex. The men in his dreams all laughed at him, as did many of the men in his waking life when he acted on his dreams by radically changing his habits. "Most of those people died," he says, "while I walked through the fire and came out unscathed, because of my dreams."

Night after night, bodytalk dreams show us what our bodies need to stay *well.* As a successful middle-aged executive, Don was getting very little physical exercise. He spend most of his day cooped up in his office. But in his dreams, night after night, he found himself running. "It felt like a real physical workout," he recalled. "Fairly soon I was running harder and faster in my dreams that I had ever run in my life, even when I was young and fit." With the dream runs came an endorphin rush that carried over into his waking body. "I felt fitter and stronger, as if I had had a complete workout." He decided his dreams might be telling him he would feel even better if he took up running in his waking life—and he did.

ANIMAL GUIDES TO THE BODY AND ITS HEALING

In dreams of animals, we learn how to follow the natural path of our energy and how we need to feed our "animal spirits." The condition of dream animals is often a direct commentary on the state of our bodies and our physical health. If you dream of a sick cat, you may need to ask what part of you—perhaps what physical organ—is becoming sick like the cat. If you dream of a bear with an injured paw, you may need to ask whether you have lost your ability to choose the right foods or the right medicines, and what you should do to get this back. (The bear, the great medicine animal of North America, is observed picking out roots and herbs quite carefully with its paw.)

Wendy dreamed a deer jumped into her car and settled down in the back seat. It was an unsettled night in which she woke up and went back to sleep repeatedly. Each time she went back, the deer was there on the back seat of her car. Eventually they were able to communicate. The deer told her it had been waiting for her and wanted to go with her.

Not long afterwards, Wendy developed the symptoms of Lyme disease, which is carried by deer ticks. Had her dream encounter with the deer anticipated this problem? A new dream of the deer mirrored her condition—and the conditions for healing—while she was struggling with the flu-like symptoms and a 104 degree fever. In the new dream, Wendy walked along a path in the woods and found a deer stretched out on the ground. At first she thought it was dead, but then she saw it struggling to get up. She held it in her arms and cut away an electrical cord that was wrapped round its neck. Released from the cord, the deer got up and gamboled around her. Wendy's woman companion told her that the deer was older and wiser than she had realized. The deer accompanied her as she walked towards a cottage in the woods. When she woke up her fever had broken.

Wendy was especially interested in the metaphor of the cord. Her husband asked, "What kind of cord?" She started laughing when she realized it was an *extension* cord. "The wisdom of the deer," she concluded, "is that if I wanted to recover quickly, I could not overextend myself." She worked with the dream messenger to accelerate her healing and recovery, reminding herself to put her energy into the most important things and avoid overextending herself.

Wendy's dreams remind me of a wisdom tale from modern Greek folk lore, in which the Mother of Animals is also the Sender of Dreams. She sews up dream messages in the skins of different animals. If the dreamer won't listen to the message brought by one animal, she'll put it in a different skin and try again. The container may be rather small, as in the next dream.

A middle-aged woman dreamed of a mouse that was barbecued and afterwards drawn and quartered. Her dream anticipated a health crisis in which her temperature shot up to 105 degrees and she came close to death. But the dream contained guidance beyond the immediate health challenge, and the key to it, surely, was the mouse. "If it were my dream," I suggested, "it might be telling me that I can't go on playing the mouse and hiding my light and my talents. The mouse is going to get barbecued. I need to claim my power and show my light." This brought strong recognition from the dreamer. Soon afterward she found a new job where she felt she would be able to develop and display her own gifts. She joked, "Maybe I'll dream of Mighty Mouse now!"

Called by the Bear

For Native Americans, the bear is the great medicine animal, and it is not surprising that it plays a central role in many dreams that involve health and healing. Terry was scared for years of bears that approached her in dreams. Once she tried to shoot the bear, but her gun would not fire. Another time she called the cops and they opened fire with rifles. But the bear kept coming back.

Finally she decided she would try to go back inside her dream, brave up to the bear and ask it why it kept pursuing her. She chose her birthday for this experiment. As she entered a conscious dream state, she found herself rushing through a kind of tunnel. When she came out, she found a baby bear. The baby bear chewed and sucked at her hand. The sensations were vitally real. Then came a squeal—from the baby bear or the woman herself—and the mother bear popped up. Terry was terrified, but kept telling herself, *I can't run. I asked for this. I cannot run.* The huge mother bear stood over her on all fours while Terry lay on her back. Fighting to control her fear, Terry stammered, "What are you? What do you really mean?" As she watched, she thought she could see the bear's mouth move. The response came clearly: *I represent the flow of life. You resist the flow of life.*

She came to recognize that the bear was a vital aspect of herself, and her power of self-healing. As she said later, "I came to realize that I was being called on to *become* the bear."

The approach of the bear in dreams may herald illness, but it almost always brings the promise of healing.

A woman in Roberta Ossana's dream-sharing group had a nightmare about a ferocious bear. She woke terrified and trembling. She drew the bear on a big piece of paper, brought it to the dream group and put it up on the wall. Her bear became a member of the dream circle for that evening. As the group worked with her fearful dream, it became clear that the bear had brought her a warning related to her health. She went to her doctor and discovered she had a life-threatening disease. The doctor actually told her that her condition was terminal. The dreams that followed revealed both the deeper causes of her disease and its possible cure. The dream group focused its energies on helping her work with these dreams. Following dream guidance, she made tough and intelligent choices, recovered from her illness—and was very much alive, healthy and productive years after the doctor had told her she would be dead.[8]

BODYTALK DREAMS GUIDE HEALING AND RECOVERY

Bodytalk dreams not only show us what might go wrong; they open paths to self-healing. What follows is a brief account of one woman's successful effort to use her dreams for guidance through her recovery from ovarian cancer. I have chosen Susan's story, from among many I have collected, because it is such a clear and practical example of the benefits of giving dreamwork a central role in integrative medicine. There are no miracles, cures or overnight remissions in this story. Susan underwent invasive surgery and chemotherapy. But she was able to use her dreams to hasten her recovery and to give her a vital "second opinion" on all the medical choices that confronted her and her doctors. Her experience demonstrates how we can use dream information to become active participants in our healing, and help our doctors to help us better. The creative play of imagery in these dreams—centering (with brilliant accuracy and a certain degree of humor) on a "chicken coop"—is quite fascinating.

Rebuilding the Chicken Coop

On a Friday evening, Susan was deep in conversation when she suddenly became aware she was dreaming. She recalls, "I also realized I was panicked out of my gourd. I knew, from prior experience, that I can't run from anything in dreamland. To cope with my fear, I bracketed the experience, stating: *Let this be of God. Let wherever I am going be of God.* Right away I was whisked away on a journey.

"I ended up with a man who was reaching inside my pelvic area, left side, and peeling a blob away from the back of the pelvic wall. The blob was ovoid and looked maybe 3½ inches by 1½ inches. The peeling of the blob reminded me of peeling blobs of chicken fat off chicken pieces. As he pealed the blob away, he said, *We have to take this out.*"

When Susan woke up, she realized that the operation had not been completed. The man in her dream had not finished peeling the "blob" from inside her body.

As Susan brooded over the possible meaning of her dream, it hit her that it might be both an X-ray and a rehearsal. Previous tests had failed to detect a tumor, but she was convinced by her dream that she must get new tests. While she was interested in alternative approaches to medicine, the dream also seemed to be directing her to a traditional Western doctor. As she observed, "They are good at cutting things out."

That weekend, she went into an emergency clinic. After initial tests, the doctor told her, "You've got something bigger than a Texas grapefruit in there." After further tests, she had surgery one week after the dream. All her female organs were removed. As in her dream, the left ovary was most diseased, although the cancer had also spread to her right ovary.

Four days after her *first* chemotherapy session, Susan dreamed of going to the clinic for her *third* session. In her dream, her assigned doctor was on vacation; she saw his partner instead. When the results of her blood test came back, she learned that her white blood cell count had been compromised. She refused chemotherapy, that day, insisting they must wait for at least another week. The substitute doctor "threw a fit." She told him, "You don't live in my body." With steady determination, she washed up and put her clothes back on. As she was leaving the clinic, her regular doctor appeared. He sympathized with her stand and managed to calm down the other doctor.

The next night, Susan's dreams took her into different territory. She dreamed she was inside a big chicken coop.

> The chickens have been cooped up too long, unattended. There are lots of dead bodies that need clearing out. I'm grossed out about picking up dead bodies. And there is chicken shit everywhere. *Maybe I shouldn't keep chickens,* I think. Even some of the chicks are dead. The dead bodies are toxic to the live chickens. I have to teach grown-up people something about this. It's getting dark and I'm running out of time. Who will help me get the chickens back where they belong? The walls of the old shed, which has many rooms, are broken down. Some of the hens don't want to go in. I have to clear out the dead bodies and clean up the coop, with fresh food and water. Long-term survival depends on this.

As she worked with these dreams, Susan realized they had given her a powerful warning about the possible effects of following the chemotherapy schedule. The symbolic dream of the filthy chicken coop gave her a dramatic portrayal of what was going on inside her body. As a result of the chemotherapy, there were dead cells in her body, like the dead chicks in the coop, and they could be toxic to new life. Just as the walls of the chicken house were broken, body tissues that were meant to separate functions were in disrepair, needing to be rebuilt. Susan reflected that she needed to do a major cleanup before she underwent another bout of chemotherapy, which was killing both wanted and unwanted cells.

Susan's *literal* dream had rehearsed her for breaking this decision to her doctors on the day scheduled for her third chemotherapy. Although waking events did not follow the dream script exactly, her dream accurately forecast the results of her blood test that day.

Her regular doctor was on duty. He was surprised that Susan had dreamed things about his partner that she would have had no way of knowing under ordinary circumstances. When she shared her dreams, he advised against postponing the chemotherapy treatment, but said he would go by what the white blood count said. As in Susan's dream, her white blood cell count was low—too low (her doctor now readily agreed) to risk chemotherapy. The session was postponed for two weeks.

After that session, Susan dreamed she had moved to a new home. The chicken house, though old, was clean and sound. There were only four chickens, old but healthy.

> I am scoping out where to build a new chicken house and how to do it so the dust won't bother our living space. A gate at the front is in need of repair. Chickens are slipping out and we have to shoo them back. It's time to get new chicks.

In the same dream, she took a trip to "back country." She found this was burned out, and badly charred.

Susan regarded this as another X-ray dream, bringing her up to date on what was going on in her body. The dream reassured her that the cleanup was well under way; the dead chicks (or cells) were gone. Some repairs were still needed, but only in one spot. But she was down to limited resources. Huge areas had been charred. She needed to get new "chicks" in the coop soon.

She paid special attention to the four hens in her dream. She received subsequent guidance to limit the chemotherapy sessions to four, rather than the usual six.

On her first day back at work, after ending chemotherapy, Susan had a powerful dream that confirmed and reinforced her recovery. At the start of the dream, she has a moment of fear. She is walking home at night and feels she is being followed by a car. So she runs across the yard to the chicken house to hide. Everything has been beautifully rebuilt. The coop is full of plump hens and fuzzy new chicks. She has a proper home for them. As the dream unfolds, it seems the coop is right in the middle of her house. A male authority figure, "sort of a John Wayne type," turns up at one point, disapproving. She speaks with him from the heart, "You have had your dream, now let me have mine." He smiles at her out of "beautiful blue eyes" and gives her his blessing.

As it turned out, this dream was another accurate X-ray of developments in her body: she had lots of healthy cells, both young "chicks" and full-grown "hens." Beyond this confirmation, the dream gave Susan the assurance that she would be supported and validated even by the "old guard" as she followed her deep resolution to "live life lovingly anew."

Susan's story is a beautiful example of how dreams can guide and strengthen us when our bodies require conventional medical treatment. As Susan's case shows, if we will only listen, our bodies will show us through dreams what symptoms we may develop and what treatments (and how much or how little of them) we may require. Doctors, as well as patients, can learn greatly from such dreams. I believe Susan's doctor learned from her.

REHEARSING FOR CHILDBIRTH

Dreams rehearse mothers (and other family members) for childbirth, and there is evidence that mothers who have extensive dream recall of labor and delivery may have an easier time when it comes to the event.[9] Pregnancy dreams are regularly discussed as "somatic" dreams in which the mother is intimately in touch with her own body and the physiology of the developing fetus. But there are even more interesting possibilities, as Janet's story suggests.

Look Who's Talking

Janet was quite convinced her second child, like her first, would be a girl. She was one of nine sisters and very much wanted another daughter. In the nineteenth week of her pregnancy, she asked for dream guidance. Her dream showed her something unexpected.

In Janet's dream, she had just given birth. Her newborn baby was lying naked on her belly. When she picked the baby up, she saw a penis and yelled, "Oh my God, it's a *boy!*" She was shocked.

She looked at her baby son and said, "This is not at all what I expected."

The baby looked back at her and replied, "We didn't communicate very well at the start."

She realized she needed to take care of her child, to keep him warm. She wrapped him in a soft towel. She wanted to call a friend to give her the news, but was unsure of the baby's birth weight and recalled that this is the first question everyone asks. She asked her husband to help her weigh the child. Her husband remarked, "I was only seven pounds. They didn't know if I would make it."

She took the baby home, still shocked that he was a boy. Again she realized the need to take care of him. She put him to her breast, and was amazed at how easily he took to nursing. As she watched him, she felt a great tenderness growing between them. *He may be a boy,* she reflected, *but he's kind of sweet.*

A friend showed up with a book of baby names. The friend opened the book to the "C" section and pointed to a very complicated word. Janet told her, loudly and adamantly, "Absolutely not!"

Janet notes that she derived a wealth of practical information from this dream. "It not only told me I was having a boy. It addressed other personal concerns about what to expect: whether I could adequately love and care for a boy after only having experience with girls; whether or not I should try to breastfeed; and whether to try for a vaginal delivery this time, or have a C-section as I did with my daughter. I had fears about both and was indecisive about what I wanted."

Ten days after the dream, Janet had an ultrasound which confirmed that she was carrying a boy. Her son was born four weeks early and weighed exactly seven pounds. During labor there were serious complications, and the doctor would have recommended a C-section but for the anterior position of the placenta. Janet's husband overheard one of the nurses say later that they didn't know for a while if the baby would make it. But in the end it was a successful vaginal delivery, and the mother made a much easier recovery than she had after her daughter's birth by C-section. Janet chose to breastfeed her baby and he latched on immediately.

Janet felt her dream had rehearsed her for every stage of this process. It prepared her for the delivery complications and reassured her that everything would be fine. It gave her a very vivid foretaste of bonding with her son, including the surprisingly pleasurable experience of breastfeeding. It showed her that the more she nurtured her son, the more connected they became—as proved to be the case after his birth.

Janet felt her son introduced himself in that dream. A question that often arises with pregnancy dreams is whether the information is coming from the mother's own body or from the new life within it. My impression is that the most significant pregnancy dreams are very frequently *babytalk* dreams, in which the baby is communicating with the mother—and quite often also with the father and other family members, if they are receptive. It is fascinating that Janet's unborn child tells her, nineteen weeks into the pregnancy, "We didn't communicate very well at the start." This statement had deep personal resonance for her. She now realized that, since she had been so definite about having a *girl,* she might have been blocking communication with her boy, and missing the wonderful opportunity to rehearse for his coming.

As in Janet's case, the fifth month of pregnancy is often a time of vital and revealing dream communication between mothers and the children they are carrying. Five months into her pregnancy, my wife Marcia came down in the middle of the night to the room where I was working and said, "If it's a girl, don't you think we should call her Sophie?" She had just woken from a dream in which our unborn baby not only revealed her gender but told us the name by which she wished to be known. This was quite specific: Sophie, *not* Sophia.

Around this stage of the pregnancy, moving into the third trimester, huge physiological changes are taking place. It is the belief of many religious traditions that equally decisive *spiritual* changes are taking place simultaneously: that this is the time the incoming spirit takes up definitive residency in the body of the unborn child. This may be the true explanation of the clarity and power of babytalk dreams during—and after—the fifth month. While the mother may see her baby as it looks inside the womb, or as it will look after birth or in infancy, the baby may speak in dreams like a mature person, or even an older and wiser intelligence. In some dreams from this stage of pregnancy, the incoming spirit seems to convey some of its personal and multidimensional history, sharing scenes from other lifetimes.

As we observed earlier, in the last months of pregnancy, the unborn child can be said to be dreaming nonstop. Unless we can actually remember our own experience inside the womb, or transfer our consciousness back inside that state (a rare but not impossible feat, as explained in Part III) we cannot say much with certainty about the content of these dreams. But I suspect the unborn baby is rehearsing constantly for its imminent transition into embodiment in the physical world—rehearsing its first breath, its first steps, its first speech. And the unborn baby is trying to communicate with us and rehearse us to recognize its identity and attend to its needs.

The unborn child communicates not only with its mother, but with receptive people in its environment who may find themselves cast in the role of interpreters or message-carriers. Linda dreamed her daughter-in-law had a baby boy. He looked about two years old, but he spoke clearly and distinctly, telling her that he was her grandson and his name was Jim. Linda was puzzled by this dream for two reasons. First of all, her son and daughter-in-law did not have a child and the last time they had spoken about this subject Linda had received the impression they intended to wait at least another year before starting their own family. Second, the baby boy in the dream was called Jim, which was the name of Linda's husband. Linda's family was Jewish, and Jewish tradition is to name children after departed, rather than living, members of the family. After puzzling for a while, Linda phoned her daughter-in-law and told her the dream. Linda's daughter-in-law was astonished. Unknown to Linda, she and her husband had decided to try to have a child, but did not know that the baby had already been conceived. They had also agreed to call their child Jim if he was a boy. Linda's husband Jim grew increasingly uncomfortable about this when it was subsequently confirmed that their grandchild was going to be a boy, and when he was born the parents decided to give him a different name. Linda felt that her dream might not only reflect telepathy with her daughter, but dream communication with the consciousness of her grandson-to-be. Was it possible that in another life, or in another dimension, his name was "Jim"?

Among Australian Aborigines, it is held that unborn children require spiritual, as well as biological parents. Specifically, there should be someone in the family—or available to the family—whose role is to communicate with the incoming spirit and guide it from its previous home into the body of the unborn child. Sometimes this role is assigned to the father. Sometimes it is assumed by a family elder or a "spirit man," a shaman. In the context of our everyday lives, many of us may be called on to play soul-helpers in this way. A dear friend of mine confided in me that she was deeply troubled by problems in her daughter's pregnancy. Her daughter was carrying twins, and they had arranged themselves in the womb in such a way that one was receiving most of the nutrition. There was a serious and growing risk that the less fortunate child, starved of nutrients, would arrive stillborn unless the doctors forced a very early and therefore highly dangerous delivery. I suggested to my friend—an avid dreamer and a highly intuitive woman—that she might take on the role of soul-helper by *talking* to the unborn twins about the problem and suggesting that they should try to adjust their position in the womb so a more equable feeding pattern was established. My friend agreed to do this. She spoke to the twins in her daughter's bedroom, leaning her head against the mother's stomach, and she spoke to them again in conscious dreaming. Within a few days, the doctors were surprised and delighted to discover that the twins had shifted their positions inside the womb quite dramatically, so a proper feeding flow had been restored. The twins were born normally, one significantly underweight, but otherwise quite healthy.

The soul-helper's role as interpreter has many facets. The unborn child may need help in dealing with toxins in the mother's body or environment to which the mother herself is indifferent. Another grandmother-to-be had a series of horrific dreams, full of rape and mutilation. She realized after a time that her perspective in these dreams was odd. It was as if she was viewing these repulsive images from somewhere down near the floor. The content of the dreams did not feel like personal material. Though she woke feeling nauseous, the experience was rather like watching a series of horror movies. When I asked her about the locale of these dreams, she told me she had the sense that all of this was somehow unfolding in her daughter's living room. I suggested that she should go over to her daughter's house and run a reality check. She found her very pregnant daughter slouched on the sofa watching the extremely violent movie *Seven.* A bunch of other rented videos atop the VCR had similar content. The dreamer believes—as I do—that her unborn grandchild flashed her an alert to change the program.

STALKED BY THE HEALER

Polly dreamed she was being stalked by a man who walked with a limp. She approached a policeman to ask for help. As she described her stalker, she spotted him walking towards her across the lobby. The stalker came right up to her, took her left hand, and asked her to let him know when an apartment became available in her building. Nervous and uncomfortable, Polly agreed. She glanced at the cop, wondering why he was doing nothing to help while the stalker kept his grip on her hand. The cop said softly, "I don't think this man is a stalker."

At that moment, Polly realized she knew the man with the limp. She had met him in a previous dream and he had told her his name was Chiron.

Chiron is one of the most famous names in the history and mythology of healing. He is the centaur—half-man, half-beast—who was teacher to Asklepios, the Greek god of medicine and dream healing. Chiron is also the model of the wounded healer. He has a wound that he cannot treat. He tends to walk with a limp.

Like Polly, most of us have found ourselves retreating from a dream "stalker" who may prove to be the healer. We tend to run away fast when the dream message may herald disease or something equally unpleasant. When we do this, we reject the gifts of healing and foresight, which are intimately connected in the ancient understanding of dream healing.

chapter twelve

LEVEL FOUR: PSYCHIC DREAMING

This much is certain, under particular conditions the antennae of our souls are able to reach out beyond their physical limitations.

—GOETHE, LETTER TO A SCIENTIST (JULY 23, 1820)

In psychic dreams, we have access to information about things at a distance from us in time or space to which we do not have access in a state of normal awareness.

Dreaming is at once an intimately personal and a highly social activity. Dreaming, we go places, meet people, do things. We connect, and we are connected.

Dreams help us to survive and flourish, not only as individuals, but as communities, and species, and perhaps even as families, of souls whose membership is not confined to a single era or dimension. I suspect that these factors underlie the phenomenon of psychic dreaming.

In a report on their celebrated work at Maimonides in the 1970s, Ullman and Krippner noted that dreams are oriented to the future more than the past. "The orientation of the sleeping subject is not primarily to his own past, but to the kind of immediate future situation to which he may awaken." This statement gave a 180 degree twist to the classical psychoanalytical method of connecting dreams to the subject's past. Ullman and Krippner also concluded that psychic dreaming serves a vital survival function because it identifies new resources that can support our lives. Our nocturnal scanning and scouting across time and space extends the range of options, people and opportunities available to us.[1]

More recently Ullman has speculated that psychic dreaming is concerned not only with individual or community survival, but with the survival and well-being of the species as a whole.[2]

TWO IN THREE PEOPLE REMEMBER DREAMING THE FUTURE

How common is psychic dreaming? Clinical psychologist David Ryback tried to answer that question in the 1980s by surveying 433 undergraduates at a college in Georgia. To his surprise, 70 per cent of the students responded that they remembered having experienced dreams about actual future events or simultaneous distant events outside the range of their knowledge. When Ryback pored over the dream reports, he rejected many of them because they were too vague or may have reflected waking preoccupations. For example, Ryback rejected a woman's dream of her husband falling from the roof before his actual fall on the grounds that the dreamer's husband had been working on the roof earlier in the week and her dream might simply have dramatized her waking anxieties. After much weeding and sifting, Ryback concluded from his survey that *one person in twelve* in the general population has psychic dreams that contain specific and verifiable information about future or distant events. Interestingly, when his writing partner, Letitia Sweitzer, conducted her own informal poll of people encountered in everyday environments, she found that two people in three report having experienced psychic dreams and *one person in three* can describe a psychic dream in specific and convincing detail.[3]

A skeptic might argue that any survey of this kind is suspect because—however carefully screened—the findings depend on the veracity of the subjects. How can we know that they did not edit their dream memories to fit subsequent events? Sometimes we *can* know, because the dreamer shared the dream with another person before the dreamed event was enacted, or because the dreamer kept an exact record. Of course, the skeptic might then object that the witness may have improved her memory too, and that journals can be edited. The only proof of these things that is likely to impress the hardheads is the registration of possible psychic dreams with an objective assessment center *before* the dreamed events transpire. There have been several (creditable) attempts over the years to develop a recording and verifying process of this kind, notably by the Central Premonitions Bureau and the Freiberg Institute of Parapsychology. One of the problems is that because dreams are deeply personal—and powerful—many of us would be quite reluctant to share our nightly "take" with outsiders on a regular basis. This would mean opening our journals to the world. For those who are interested in both proof and privacy, the method adopted for several years by Hugh Lynn Cayce (the celebrated psychic Edgar Cayce's son) may seem more attractive. Cayce showed his dream journal entry to a friend each day and had it formally witnessed. Yet, in the cyber-age, a way of documenting and verifying dream precognition on a vast scale is at hand. Around the clock, dreamers from all over the world are sharing their nightly experiences with remarkable openness and boldness on newsgroups, bulletin boards and other forums in cyberspace. At sites where dream reports are archived, it should be a fairly simple matter to ask dreamers to send in follow-up reports of subsequent events that seem to correspond to their dreams. And since most of the people who operate websites concerned with dreaming are extraordinarily generous about sharing resources and information, we might see the rapid emergence of a "psychic dream central" in cyberspace that would coordinate, sift and evaluate these match-ups.

NATURAL AND SUPERNORMAL

The great Victorian explorer of the psyche, F.W.H. Myers, coined many of the terms we use today to describe psi phenomena. He gave us the term *telepathy,* which he defined as "the communication of impressions of any kind from one mind to another, independently of the recognized channels of sense."[4] He also coined the term *supernormal.* Myers was extremely dissatisfied, quite rightly, with the widespread misuse of the word "supernatural" to describe psychic experiences that may be entirely natural, although they may transcend ordinary ability or understanding. He observed that "there is no reason to suppose that psychical phenomena are less a part of nature, or less subject to fixed and definite law, that any other phenomena." He came up with the word *supernormal* to describe "a faculty or phenomenon which goes beyond the level of ordinary experience, in the direction of evolution, or as pertaining to a transcendental world." He noted when we use the word "normal" we are usually talking about one of two things: what is average, or what conforms to normal expectations or standards. But humans are constantly evolving. What is considered "normal" today—in either sense—could look very different tomorrow. As Myers beautifully observed, "To assign a fixed norm to a changing species is to shoot point-blank at a flying bird."

> By a supernormal phenomenon I mean, not one which *overrides* natural laws, for I believe no such phenomenon to exist, but one which exhibits the action of laws higher, in a psychical aspect, than are discerned in action in everyday life.[5]

Stanley Krippner agrees that psychic dreaming is an entirely natural phenomenon. According to Krippner, our ability to tune in to things remote from us in time or space suggests that "there exists in the universe a dimension that is ignored, unacknowledged and virtually unexplored. This dimension of existence could teach us more than we know about time and space. It could expand our development of intellect, emotion, intuition, and creativity. It might even demonstrate that human beings do not end at the boundaries of the skin, but exist as part of a network of consciousness which connects one person to another person distant in space and time."[6]

Within the psychic internet, we connect and transceive in many interesting ways. Let's look more closely at five types of psychic dreaming.

Telepathic Dreams

If you are having a telepathic experience, you are picking up thoughts, feelings or physical sensations from a distance. In telepathic dreams and waking intuitive flashes, you may actually seem to slip inside another person's perspective and see things through their eyes. Telepathy may be possible because on the level of mind, there are really no boundaries, and we can intercommunicate by a process that the novelist Upton

Sinclair (whose wife was a gifted clairvoyant) called "mental radio." If we think of someone, waking or sleeping, in a sense we may reach out and touch that person.

Telepathy is especially strong when there is a psychic link between two people. Hawaiian kahunas say there is a psychic cord that links us to anyone who has touched our lives in any way. Thoughts, feelings and psychic energy traveling along these cords—for good or bad—unless they are cut. Another explanation for dream telepathy is that consciousness travels beyond the body in dreams.

There is considerable scientific evidence of dream telepathy. Even Sigmund Freud, who adamantly opposed the idea of precognition and was generally hostile to the discussion of so-called "occult" phenomena, accepted that there is a powerful case for telepathy. Though he professed never to have experienced telepathy himself, Freud wrote two major papers on the subject, one of which was published only after his death. In his 1921 paper, "Dreams and Telepathy," Freud noted that it an "incontestable fact that sleep creates favorable conditions for telepathy." He later conjectured that telepathy may be "the original archaic method by which individuals understood each other," pushed into the background with the development of language skills.

The Maimonides researchers used a strict experimental method in which the "normal" dreams of ordinary humans were studied with the help of electrophysiology. Subjects were brought to the laboratory in the evening, shown around, and put to bed with electrodes fastened to their scalps. When rapid eye movements and brain wave changes suggested the subject was dreaming, he was wakened. He told his dream and any associations that immediately came to him. In the telepathy experiments, an experimenter behind three closed doors had been trying to "send" a randomly chosen image to the dreamer. The content of the dreams was later compared to the content of the target image. A significant relationship, far above what could be attributed to chance, was found between what was sent and what was received.[7]

Though the dream laboratory was closed in 1979, other groups have continued this work under rigorous scientific protocols; for example, a dream telepathy experiment is a popular and important feature of the annual conferences of the Association for the Study of Dreams, the world's premier gathering of dream researchers.

In everyday life, the tug of telepathy—an emotional attunement to someone at a distance—can pull us into a full-fledged dream journey and/or out-of-body experience in which we enter their situation. Here is an example contributed by a woman dreamer:

Called to Help a Friend

"I went to bed feeling kind of agitated, and an out-of-body experience began.

"I felt as if I was being pulled! I started moving very quickly, and I received a message that said a close friend needed me.

"When my astral vision became clear, I was in a bedroom. My friend was lying in a bed and was crying. I asked her what was wrong and she wouldn't tell me, but I knew that she was going through something very difficult. She asked me if I would stay with her for awhile, and I told her of course I would. I wavered between floating over her and landing next to her. This lasted for what seemed like a long time. I could tell that she was glad I was there.

"Then she looked at me and I suddenly realized she was all right, and I woke up, it was 3:00 A.M.

"After this experience I just knew that something had been going on with my friend. I wanted to pick up the phone and call her right away, but after all, it was 3:00 A.M. in the morning! I went back to sleep and when I woke up I called her at work.

"She answered the phone and I immediately asked her, 'So what happened to you last night?' She told me that she had gotten into an emotionally wrenching argument with somebody she loved and had not been able to sleep until some kind of calm descended after 3:00 A.M. When I told her about my out-of-body experience she was surprised at the parallels in our realities at that time. She was feeling terrible, and it seems I got pulled out of my body to hang out with her until she felt better."

Clairvoyant Dreams

An Inuit name for the shaman is *elik,* "he who has eyes." The shaman's access to real power comes through gaining the shaman-light, *quamaneq,* a luminous fire that enables him to see with his eyes closed, into the future and into the secrets of others. The Selk'nam of Tierra del Fuego describe the shaman's power of seeing as an eye that extends beyond the shaman's body. The shaman may project consciousness like a "thread of gum" to his target. Distant viewing is seen as *elastic vision.* Apprentice shamans are tested by being made to describe objects at a distance.[8]

As shamans have always known, and U.S. government researchers reconfirmed,[9] remote viewing is a natural human ability that can be developed and refined through training. It is also a spontaneous feature of our night dreams as in the following story:

Fixing the Chimney

A friend renovated an old house in the Mohawk Valley of New York. When she first moved in, her family had trouble heating the upstairs rooms. The cold upstairs became a family joke. Then a carpenter who had done some repairs at the house but had never been consulted on the heating problem called my friend and asked if he could come over. He told her, "You are not getting heat upstairs and I had a dream that will fix that problem." My friend was quite surprised; she is quite certain she had never mentioned the heating problem to this man. When he came over to the house, he walked straight to an old wall register in the chimney area in the parlor. He asked if he could remove the register. He said he dreamed the problem was about three feet above the register. He removed the register, creating an opening so small that he had to twist his body sideways, flashlight in hand, to get a look up the chimney. Inside was a crudely soldered sheet of metal completely blocking the heat from traveling upstairs. It took considerable effort to pull it out. Subsequent investigation revealed that the previous owner of the house was a retired blacksmith. He and his wife had not slept upstairs in years and may have believed—erroneously—that they could direct more heat downstairs if they blocked the upstairs. Neither the helpful carpenter nor the lady of the house had any knowledge of this situation until his dream pinpointed the exact place that needed attention.

I think of the psychic faculty that was at work here as the *woodpecker sense.* For many Native Americans, the woodpecker is a very special bird. Shamans and medicine men of the Great Lakes often sported the feathers and even the dried heads of woodpeckers in their ritual headdresses. They admired the woodpecker's ability to reach into the unseen, to drill beneath the surface of the tree and pluck its food from inside. Our own "woodpecker sense" comes alive in dreams, often in highly practical ways, as in the carpenter's tale.

The carpenter had some connection with my friend, and the prospect of a job.

How can we account for the fact that we dream events at a distance that appear to have no connection with us? Some dreams of this kind involve major news events, in which we may be previewing what will be on TV or in the paper at a later date. But many of these dreams involve more obscure events.

If we look beneath the surface, we may find an unsuspected link. Jeannette, a Canadian singer, came up with an unusual explanation for some of her dream premonitions involving events that did not initially appear to have any connection with her.

Linked by Her CD

While living in another city, Jeannette dreamed of a terrible explosion in Montreal. In her dream, she saw people dousing the body of a homeless person with something like gasoline. Fearing an explosion, she started running away. She heard a loud boom behind her and felt the heat of flames. Smoke engulfed the whole street. Choking, the dreamer tried to help another woman who could not breathe and kept falling down. When she turned round, the fire was out. She saw a row of women in old-fashioned pink nightgowns. She thought of them as "virtuous women." Someone told her, "They died for us."

Jeannette had no strong associations with this dream, and was puzzled about its meaning until she read news reports from Montreal two days later. She learned that the day after her dream, a private contractor in Montreal had cut a gas line by mistake. There was a loud explosion, then lots of black smoke. There were efforts to get people out of a shelter for the homeless at the scene of the explosion. Two volunteers for the shelter—Grey Nuns—died in the tragedy.

There were strong correspondences between Jeannette's dream and the disaster the following day: a homeless person, an explosion, dense smoke, the "virtuous women" who died. But Jeannette wondered why she had "zoomed in" on this disaster rather than any of the others that go on in the world. When she shared her dream with a filmmaker friend, she came up with a possible explanation. She learned that the filmmaker had been doing the sound edit for a film just a few blocks from the homeless shelter. The sound edit included a song by Jeannette, from a CD she had recorded. Jeannette comments, "I wonder how often my premonitions are linked to people who play my CD. It's as if the energy of myself on the recording leads me to those places."

As in the next story, it is often hard to determine whether we are glimpsing something at a distance in space, or time—or both.

Reading the News Ahead of Time

Kathy dreamed she saw a long file card with the word "Amsterdam" printed on it in capital letters. A second card displayed a date, the date of the day when she woke and recorded the dream. In the same dream, she saw her son living a very different and dissatisfying life. He was struggling to break a drug habit. He looked different from the way he looked in waking life, and seemed quite desperate. Kathy had a strong feeling this was the way his life could have turned out if he had dropped out of school and stayed in the depressed area where he grew up instead of joining the military.

The following day, Kathy read a report of the arrest of her son's high school principal in the *Amsterdam Recorder.* She noticed that the lettering on the masthead of the paper was similar to the lettering on the card in her dream, and the date was the same. A high school principal had been jailed on charges of public indecency and being drunk and disorderly. Kathy recalled that she had been distressed, as a mother, by the obstructive role she believed this man had played when her son was scrambling to complete the last courses he needed for his high school diploma before leaving for boot camp. She felt her dream not only gave her a preview of the next day's news in the local paper, but played out the thoughts and associations she would have when she saw that news.

DISTANT ACTION DREAMS

"Thoughts are things," as Edgar Cayce, and many before and after him, have observed. If we think or feel about someone or something with any intensity, we reach out and touch that person or object. This is the basis of distant healing, just as it is the secret of the Aboriginal sorcerer's reputed ability to kill by "pointing the bone." I met an Aboriginal "clever man" in Sydney in 1998 who welcomed me as a long-lost brother and demonstrated his sincerity by taking me aside and showing me his bones: a pointed splinter of kangaroo bone, and a sharpened needle of mulgawood. He reminded me that they can be used either to heal or to harm at a distance.

We interact with other people and situations in our dreams. We may actually project an energy into their space, or receive a visitor in an energy body. This subject is explored more closely in the next chapter. Is it possible that we can actually cause physical effects through our dream actions? I think it is more than possible. Among indigenous peoples, dream hunters believed that, by marking and slaying an animal in their dreams, they brought about the event that followed in waking life. This world-view is reflected in the language of the Tzutujil Maya of Guatemala. The term they use for dreams is *tzikj,* which also means to call the animals or to influence the weather. The implication is that to work with dreams gives you the power to shape things in waking life.[10] An Amazulu hunter in South Africa dreamed of an easy kill. "I saw some buffaloes during the night. We were hunting them; they were just like cattle." He shared his dream with his friends and they agreed to go after water buffalo. They found their game in a valley very like the one the hunter had dreamed. Though the water buffalo can be a highly dangerous animal, "the buffaloes were just like cattle. We killed them and did not get so much as a scratch."[11] We may be after different game today—hopefully gifts of healing and connectedness and creative fulfillment—but the old way of the dream hunters may serve new purposes.

PRECOGNITIVE DREAMS

Precognition is knowledge of things to come that we cannot conceivably know about through ordinary channels. A precognitive dream contains specific data about a future event that is not available to you outside the dream. You receive confirmation of a precognitive dream when an event takes place that corresponds to your dream in specific ways.

Though the laboratory is not the most interesting place to test dream precognition, there is significant laboratory research in this area.

* At Maimonides, Stanley Krippner conducted precognitive dream experiments with a psychically gifted English subject, Malcolm Bessent. The experimenters woke Bessent from REM sleep repeatedly during the night and recorded his dreams. In the morning, they drew randomly selected "experience cards" to determine how he would spend the first part of his day. They then checked whether his dreams provided accurate previews of these activities. The experimenters found many close match-ups. One of the most striking was involved Bessent's dream of being taken to a cold white room with small blue objects and feeling very chilled. In the morning, the experimenters randomly selected an "experience card" that instructed them to take him to another room and drop ice cubes down his shirt while two blue fans blew cold air on him.[12]
* At the Stanford Research Institute, tests were conducted with another highly intuitive subject, former police officer Pat

Price, and others. Subjects were asked to track a "target" person who was to travel to a destination unknown to him (until he opened his instructions). In the course of the tests, it was discovered that talented remote viewers could spot the target's destination before he got to it—or even knew what it was.[13]

However, controlled experiments are unlikely to catch the *big,* one-of-a-kind experiences or most of those "trivial and silly" glimpses of things to come that provide delightful confirmation that dreaming the future is anything but "weird."

When I first led dream workshops at a community center in the old river town of Troy, New York, a young woman called Ellen asked me if I would like to read her dream journal. I was moved by her openness and generosity; a dream journal is a deeply personal document. I asked if she was sure she wanted me to read hers.

"No problem," she told me. She explained that the journal she wanted to share with me was one she had kept while she was working her way through school by waitressing at a popular local steakhouse. "There's not much going on in my dreams from that time," she commented. "I just kept dreaming what was going to happen the next day. You might be bored to death."

I wasn't. On one level, most of the journal entries were fairly mundane: a chronicle of generous or mean-spirited patrons, shift changes and kitchen gossip. A waiter calls in sick and Ellen is asked to take his shift. Someone forgets a bottle of wine left under the counter for a birthday present and has to go back to retrieve it. The manager loses his temper. A popular draft beer runs out in the middle of a banquet. The remarkable thing was that, again and again, Ellen dreamed and recorded the minute details of her working life *before* they were played out in physical reality, typically from one to four days before the corresponding event.

Every profession has its characteristic anxiety dreams. Professors and ministers of religion dream of standing up in public without their notes, or any recollection of what they were supposed to say. Waiters and waitresses dream about being the only server on duty, or having to work an area the size of a football field, or getting the orders horrendously mixed up. Ellen had dreams that might have been viewed, out of context, as generic "anxiety dreams." But the details were always entirely literal, never surreal, and the dreams very often proved to be quite accurate previews of situations that later developed in waking life.

Ellen's waitressing dreams are an excellent example that—contrary to widespread opinion—there is nothing "weird" about dreaming the future. The reason precognitive dreams so often escape us is because many of them are quite ordinary, even boring. Why bother to record that you dreamed a workmate had changed her hairstyle or that Joe called in sick again? Yet if we take the trouble to record *everything* we remember from our dreams, if only for a limited period of time, and compare all our dream reports with subsequent events, we may find, like Ellen, that we are dreaming what lies around the corner all the time.

Working with everyday dreamers, especially long-term dream journalists, explodes the notion that precognitive dreams are most likely to relate to events that will take place within a few hours or a few days.

Laura has been working with dreams since early childhood, and was encouraged to record and share her dreams by an interested family (a situation many of us might envy). She reports that she dreamed the death of a childhood friend's father, in specific detail, fourteen years before the dream was played out in physical reality:

Death in the Blue Car

My best friend, Kris, lived just down the road. During the summer of 1984, I had a strange dream about Kris's

> father. In the dream I could see him dead, sitting in the driver's seat of a blue car. The background was all whited out, so I could not accurately determine the location of the car. All I could tell was that it was parked on a gravel surface. I could not tell the make of the car; it looked different from the cars I had seen. The door to the driver's side was open. I was upset by this dream at the time, as my friend's father was undergoing open-heart surgery and everyone was afraid he was going to die. I told Kris about the dream, and regretted doing so. But her father survived the operation and the dream was almost forgotten.
>
> Fourteen years later, Kris's father picked up her mother from work in a blue car in the midst of a heavy snowstorm, almost a whiteout. On the way home, he began having chest pains. He died sitting in the driver's seat of the car in their driveway with the driver's side door open.

Laura believes this dream to be beyond coincidence, and I agree. The blue car had not even been manufactured yet in 1984 when Laura had the dream, and so many of the details are correct: the snow, the gravel driveway, where he was sitting, the position of the door. The fact Laura told Kris her dream in 1984, and Kris remembers it, confirms that Laura had the dream when she said she did, and did not make it up after the fact, or alter the details in retelling to match the events.

The Terrible and the Trivial

When the English writer J. B. Priestley was writing his important book *Man and Time,* he went on a late-night Sunday television program where the interviewer appealed to the viewing public to send in personal experiences that might challenge the conventional notion of time. Most of the hundreds of letters that streamed in contained precognitive dreams. As Priestley sifted these dreams about future events, he quickly noticed that most of them were concerned with either the terrible or the trivial, with death and disaster or with incidents that often seemed almost absurdly unimportant. Priestley speculated that this was because "both the terrible and the trivial are nearly always outside our control—the deaths and disasters because they are too big and fearful, the trivia because they are too small and unimportant." These possibilities are part of the future that will not be changed "either because they are out of reach of our will or beneath its attention and interest." By contrast, in that wide middle band of human experience from which precognitive dreams are less frequently reported, "there may so often be no determined future, only a confusion of possibilities still to be actualized."[14]

I'm not sure that Priestley is correct in making these distinctions, but I like his suggestion that at least in that "wide middle band" our future may be far from determined. This opens the vitally important distinction between precognitive dreams and warning dreams.

EARLY WARNING DREAMS

Early warning dreams show us events or situations in the future that we might be able to change. They reveal the *possible* future: what is likely to happen if no action is taken. If we see the probable future in a dream, and then take action to rescript coming events, we cannot say our dream was precognitive, because the event it anticipated never took place. A dream we can use in this way is *better* than precognitive. By giving us better information than may be available in ordinary reality, it helps us to make wiser choices in navigating the roads of life. Early warning dreams can even save our lives—when we remember and act on them. Remember how Wanda avoided the head-on collision with the red Honda on the bridge? This is a model for how to work with early warning dreams. We should carry them with us as travel advisories, roadmaps on the road of life.

The simple act of sharing a dream may change the future scenario the dream lays out. For example, if you tell your dream to someone who has a role in it, they may decide not to play that role. As Russell Targ observes, the fact that the scenario is changed does not mean that the dream gave you inaccurate information.[15] If a spy forewarns you that an enemy power is about to test a nuclear weapon and you act on the information by launching an airstrike to prevent this from happening, you do not judge the agent to be unreliable!

We see the possible future in dreams. We also learn about it—and about things that may be more important than anything that will happen in linear time—through encounters with beings who have wider or deeper knowledge than we do.

chapter thirteen

LEVEL FIVE: TRANSPERSONAL DREAMING

Some god has held his hand over me.
—King Priam of Troy, in Homer's *Odyssey*

INTERACTIVE DREAMS

We meet other people in our dreams, and many of them are just as real as the people with whom we share our waking lives. Some of our dream encounters are with other dreamers. Maybe you have already noticed that from time to time you have a dream that closely matches someone else's. This may be a shared or interactive dream in which you saw each other and did something together or it may be a dream in which you both experienced something very similar, or toured the same location, without necessarily being aware of each other's presence. If you journal your dreams over time, and share them with others, you may be surprised to find that these dream encounters are far from unusual. You can make a rendezvous with another dreamer to meet up in your dreams and go somewhere together—to a beach in Hawaii, Aunt Thelma's porch, or the dark side of the moon. You can even learn to embark on group dream excursions.[1]

Interactive dreaming with a partner to whom you are emotionally attached happens quite easily and naturally in sleep dreams and is not difficult to develop as a conscious dream practice. Because of the bond between you, there is a psychic bridge—your thoughts, feelings and energy bodies will flow toward each other quite frequently unless you to decide to put up a "Do Not Disturb" sign. Where sex and romance are involved, the energy available for dream journeying (including intentional out-of-body experiences) is tremendous. While having fun on your dream dates, you can also hone your abilities as a dream tracker by scanning the environments you visit for details you can check up on in ordinary reality later on.

Interactive dreams facilitate communication with other people in our lives on deeper levels than may be possible in ordinary reality. Interactive dreaming is also a fundamental mode of teaching and healing.

INTERACTIVE DREAMS AS A KEY TO DEEPER COMMUNICATION

One vitally helpful aspect of social or interactive dreaming that will reward much closer attention is our ability in dreams to communicate with people who cannot otherwise communicate—because they are inhibited, tongue-tied or blocked, either emotionally or physically. You can't talk to the boss at work because he won't listen to anything new? Try talking to him in a dream; you may find you can contact a more open and generous aspect of his consciousness that may actually get through to him when he wakes up. Perhaps someone close to you is impaired by a stroke or by Alzheimer's or has even slipped into a coma. Ask for a dream—or ask them inside a conscious dream—what you can do to help, what they may need that they can't communicate. Marina tells how her gravely ill mother, unable to make her wishes known in an ordinary way, was able to communicate clearly in a dream.

Meeting Mom at the Mausoleum

> Mom was in the nursing home, unable to speak, when I dreamed I saw her at a small mausoleum in a cemetery I know. She had a stack of legal-sized envelopes, and told me it was important that I was aware of these and checked what was in them before everything was signed and sealed. Then she showed me a heap of ashes. I was surprised they were an orangish color. She made it very clear she wanted to be cremated, not buried, and that I should take care of this.

Marina woke feeling the dream was a wonderful gift. It inspired her to go round to the nursing home to see her mother the following evening, at a time when she would normally have been eating dinner at home. Because she arrived at this unusual time, she ran into her mother's attorney, who was going through the motions of formal consultation with a patient who was incommunicado. This gave Marina timely access to documents (in "legal-sized envelopes") involving the disposition of the house; she believes that except for this coincidence, her mother's house would have been sold without consultation with her or her husband. She honored her mother's wishes about the disposal of her remains, as communicated in the dream. Though the family tradition was burial, Marina arranged for her mother to be cremated.

INTERACTIVE DREAMING IN TEACHING AND HEALING

Since I spend a good part of my waking life as a teacher, I am not surprised that I seem to appear quite frequently in the dreams of many people who study with me, or have simply read my books, in the guise of teacher or guide. In some of these dreams, I may personify the part of the dreamer that is the teacher. But many of these dream reports seem to describe interactive dream experiences, many of them quite spontaneous. Here are two recent examples:

Taking Notes at Robert's Lecture

> A woman therapist, who had attended one of my Esalen trainings, dreamed she came into a lecture room where I was speaking. I had written five key points on the blackboard that struck her as hugely important. Waking, she remembered the first three and wrote them down. The first was about practice—how you won't retain what you learn unless you practice. She then went back inside the dream to retrieve the missing points. When she sent me an account of this dream, I looked in my journal and found that around the same time (though not the same night) I instructed a large crowd in a lecture room on five key points about dreaming. The first was about the necessity of practice. I used words similar to Pliny's, quoted as the epigraph to an early chapter: "It is difficult to retain what you learn unless you practice." The

woman's first three points closely resembled mine. The last two used somewhat different language.

Deerskin Ties

When I woke on the morning of July 20, 1998, I wrote a rather detailed account of a dream encounter with a woman healer called Polly. In the dream, we discussed the nature and practice of dreaming itself. I led her through a healing meditation. A circle of animal guardians gathered to support the work, including the Deer, the Bear and the Panther. I took a deerskin medicine bundle from the Bear and gave it to Polly. I then took a second deerskin tie and fastened it around her wrist. Light blazed between us. I told her I had transferred a power of healing.

Shortly afterward, I received a letter from Polly—whom I knew only slightly at that time—dated July 21. She described a vivid dream experience in which she was approached by a man wearing deer antlers who fastened a magical object to her wrist. He offered her "a snake of white light." When she accepted, it became a blazing *sword* of white light. She was told she had been called into service. She returned from this experience deeply energized and certain of her calling.

Ann-Marie relates a moving story of how she feels she was able to bring healing and guidance to her mother through a conscious dream that was also an out-of-body experience. It begins with an encounter with a spiritual guide:

Helping Mom to Quit Smoking

I had a series of encounters with a being who resembled a living statue of a female Buddha. In the presence of this figure, I felt I was being "healed" in a spiritual sense. I floated and vibrated for a long time and felt as if I was being cleansed. One night I met this being, fully aware that I was traveling outside my body. She became highly animated, held my "astral hands," and started talking to me. She told me that I had graduated to the "third dimension"—whatever that means!

Her general message was one of support and I felt as if she knew me well and was looking out for me. I also had the distinct impression that it was difficult for her to communicate to me directly, she looked like she was sort of fading in and out (almost like a TV set that isn't getting good enough reception). I think that perhaps she exists on a higher vibratory level than me, which perhaps explains why usually when I see her she isn't animated and appears to look like a statue.

After this encounter, I saw my mother. I felt compelled to run my hands above her heart area for a while and try to draw out some energy muck. I received a message that told me that she wasn't able to process toxins like she used to and that I had to do this. I felt distinctly that my spiritual guide was helping me. I saw blue light around my mom and then I came back to my body.

I felt I wasn't finished but I woke up from a cramp in my shoulder. I asked that whatever I was doing on the astral plane could be completed even though I was awake. Luckily, my mom has an open mind. When I told her about this, she said she had been seriously considering quitting smoking. Early that morning, around the time I was with her in my dream, she had actually decided to quit. She had been a heavy smoker for 40 years and hasn't smoked since that night. I sure hope she keeps it up! I'm certainly not saying that I or my spirit guide made this happen, but isn't it possible that we somehow helped?

ENCOUNTERS WITH THE DEPARTED

Transpersonal dreaming is not confined to encounters with people who live in physical reality. Some of the most psychic dreamers I know—people who regularly produce reliable precognitive messages for others—tell me they make a strong association between the presence of the departed in dreams and precognitive content. On one level, this is easy enough to understand. If we can have authentic, transpersonal communication with the departed in our dreams, then we have access to people who are no longer tied to the body and the conventions of spacetime. The departed may then help the living by scanning the future and bringing knowledge from other dimensions. Of course, the departed do not become omniscient just because they are dead! Their messages have to be inspected just as judiciously as we would consider messages from our living family and friends. The departed, like the living, have a tendency to put a spin on things and see things from their own angles. They may miss the whole picture.

Nonetheless, the link between dreaming true and contact with the departed is widely recognized in dreaming tradition. This is reflected in the very language of the Hopi. The Hopi term for dream is *dimoki,* which also means "a bundle of the dead body prepared for burial."[2]

We have already seen that the presence of the departed in a dream is often a marker that the dream contains other psychic information, perhaps a clue to the future. In Part I, I described how a dream encounter with a departed Australian relative in March 1999 gave me a rather exact preview of the massacres in East Timor that began after the referendum in August. I learned a great deal about this subject in the year following my father's death in November 1987, when he repeatedly visited me—and another family member—in dreams with advice and information that was otherwise unavailable to us and that proved to be of immense practical help to the family.

What can be more natural than that our departed loved ones should want to look in on us from time to time and help us in our lives?

Sometimes, it seems they want an update from us, on how things are going in the world they left. Sometimes, they seem to give us an update on how *they* are faring in their new environments. A Memphis woman shared a wonderful dream in which she walked into her living room and found her mother, who had died years before, waiting for her. Her mother said she was "just visiting" and could not stay long. She looked about thirty years old, healthy and vibrant, with reddish tints in her hair. The dreamer asked, "Why are you here?" Her mother replied, "I just wanted to tell you I'm going to school and hope to get my Ph.D." Before her death, the dreamer's mother had been a woman of limited education and narrow views. In the dream, she appeared on a path of growth and learning.

What can be more reassuring—as we prepare for our own deaths—than the appearance of our departed as guides for the journey? One of the most stupid, as well as most cruel things our Western mainstream culture has said to us about dreams is that these visitations are impossible or unreal. They are not only entirely possible and very often entirely real; they are one of the main ways we learn about the larger reality.

Dream messages from the departed not only help us to see beyond linear time. They can lead us deeper into the understanding of time itself. Here is a pregnant example from my own journals, a lengthy dream communication that came to me from my favorite professor, long departed. The text will surprise those who maintain (quite incorrectly) that "reading" in dreams is difficult or impossible.

A TELEGRAM FROM THE PROFESSOR

I majored in history and briefly taught ancient history at my alma mater, the Australian National University (ANU). My favorite professor—and the one responsible for appointing me a lecturer at the precocious age of 21—was the celebrated and controversial Manning Clark. His political sympathies lay with the Left, and he flirted with the Soviets in ways that outraged conservatives; with his largely bald pate, his goatee and his gold-rimmed glasses, he looked a good deal like Lenin and enjoyed playing up the resemblance. Manning was also a man of *soul,* and I think he was far too interested in the individual to finally give over his imagination to collectivist solutions; his deepest interests lay in plumbing the wellsprings of human action and motivation. He pushed his students to read Dostoyevsky and Faulkner, Freud and Jung, even while they were writing papers on the Rum Rebellion or the trade union movement in early New South Wales. He reveled in the color and texture of words, and his speech and his magnum opus, a vast history of Australia, were peppered with locutions from the King James Bible. He urged me to make it my task to know "the ditch where a man is digged." At his often outrageous dinner parties, where we gathered round a vast table in the kitchen hung with pots and onions and cuckoo clocks, he slipped vodka in the soup to get his guests talking—his eyes glinting wickedly as a faculty wife revealed that she ate apples during sex with her husband to keep herself occupied—then wound the clocks noisily when he wanted us to go.

I was very fond of Manning, and grateful for the role he played as one of my first mentors. I had a couple of glimpses of him in dreams, including a dream shortly after his death in which he spoke to me in high excitement about some new research he was conducting. The setting reminded me of the library at the School of Advanced Studies at the ANU. But I had not thought much about Manning for many years until—a decade after his death—I dreamed that my old professor sent me a message.

In my dream:

> On returning to an office in the city where I work, I learn that a telegram from Manning Clark came while I was traveling. I never saw it, though I have been in and out of the office since it was received. I ask a pleasant female assistant to help me find it. She retrieves it from a pegboard near the water cooler. I point out that this is not the best place to leave a message for me; there's a pegboard in my own office where future messages could be placed.
>
> The message is tightly folded.
>
> When I unfold it, I read the following lines:
>
> *She underestimated the numbers,*
> *But not the quality, of God's gifts;*
> *The best is now to come:* indulgence.

The rhythm and beauty of these words brought me fully conscious inside the dream. I wanted to go on reading the telegram from my professor, but I was concerned the lines would slip away. I got up to write them down legibly, then set out to plunge back into the dream in hopes of retrieving the rest of the message.

In my dream reentry, I smoothed out the pages of the telegram and read, with gathering excitement, the following communication:

I did not expect the Other Side to be so hospitable. The colors are richer than I believed possible, from the palette of the Divine painter. There is an abounding sense of joy, the release from trouble.

The opportunity for research is astounding. I began, I confess, with a narrow agenda. I sought to find the material I needed in secret archives to silence my critics—those who contended my Australian histories were flimsy and partisan. But soon I found my interest in these old causes dwindling. I saw Australia herself diminishing into an island seen from a rocket ship under skeins of light cloud, in a blue ocean—dwindling and then gone.

I returned to studies that excited earlier and deeper passions: the quest for the wellsprings of man's doings, the search for *soul.*

Gogol and Dostoyevsky, they plumbed the dark deeps of man's being. I sought them out. I found collections of the works they gestated but never published. I found something better—the men themselves! Or their vital simulacra. What talks we had, over long breakfasts on the Ile St Louis (or what passes for it here). Thick coffee or *thé à la russe,* in glasses, aromatic cigarettes, flaky croissants and brioches—and a return to the sources of life!

Gogol was livelier than one might have expected. His drabber sides—the petty government official, the frightened mouse who ran back to hide in the Church—had both fallen away. He appeared sleek and light, even with a kind of radiance. There was a constant shimmering in the air above his high pate. I actually looked for a halo. I saw no halo, but the shimmer remained, and moved with him as he moved.

You may well ask: Is this truly Gogol? What is he doing in a counterpart France? I think for some of these

Russians, Paris was the mecca and apogee of civilization, even when their work was deeply rooted in their native soil. I had come to a heaven of Gogol, or a place recreated by a part of his consciousness. The Dostoyevsky here is 'his' Dostoyevsky (and naturally, mine also).

At this point, the telegram goes into considerable detail about the postmortem fate of various Russians whom Manning knew in his own time, with a description of a "heaven of dead spies." I won't include this passage here, because the details are unnecessary and the content might attract the conspiracy vultures who have already tried to make a meal out of Manning's bones.

The telegram goes on:

You had a glimpse of me in a library. I felt your presence and saw you leaving. I tried to speak to you, but you moved quickly, fading like a shadow. From our perspective, of course it is *you* who are insubstantial, though perceptions alter at different levels of vibration. Some of the locales here are quite solid and tangible. If I stub my toe, I feel the pain. I cannot walk through walls, unless I can manage a shift in awareness similar to the one you make when you leave your physical body. A great deal of *energy* is invested in some of these denser environments; some may actually be "heavier" that you are when you are traveling in your astral body, not to mention your Body of Light.

I am sending you this transmission from a locale on the higher ramparts of the astral realm. I am not sure I can give it a number. Things here are not as linear as Theosophists and Monroe-ites make them out to be, though they are quite orderly and uncluttered. I have entered a center of research and transmission where I work with colleagues who are deeply interested in the evolution of human ideas and the opening of human consciousness to the gifts of the transhuman. Our mentors have stepped down from higher dimensions. All have deep sympathy for man's conditions, though not all have had the experience of living in human bodies. In archangelic terms, this is the dominion of Raphael and Raziel.

I have been assigned to you because I was once your mentor and protector and there was deep affinity between us. But also as a test for me in my ability to communicate with earth levels and contribute something of value. I will help you to further your understanding of conditions on planes beyond the terrestrial, and to bring your knowledge to earth communities. Though our approaches and loyalties diverged during life on earth, we share the desire to further the cause of man. I will suggest ways for you to speak to those in your world who yearn for the opening to a deeper life.

What is a message without a return address? To contact me, think of me intently. You may also use the phrase I have improvised from the title of a little book I once wrote: "Meeting the More Than Human."

Remember to check for messages. Though my messages may sometimes come through when you are absent or not available to receive them, they can *always* be retrieved.

I found all of this quite fascinating. The telegram from the professor pushed me—as Manning had succeeded in doing in my student days—into intense, and intensely rewarding, research that led me down many unexpected paths. It drove me to reread those haunted Russian writers, Gogol and Dostoyevsky, and to reflect on the role of the psychic and spirit worlds in their books and their lives. It sent me hunting through the many volumes of Louis Ginzberg's *Legends of the Jews* and more obscure sources to try to fathom Manning's remark about Raphael and Raziel.

I knew something, of course about Raphael, and had sometimes asked for his protection. The archangel's name means "God has healed." He was first known in Chaldea and became renowned as an underworld guide and as a Healer. He features in the *Book of Tobit* (canonical only for the Catholic Church), where he acts as companion and guide to Tobit's son Tobias on a journey from Media to Nineveh. In the Book of Enoch, he is "one of the watchers" and a guide to the Underworld (*Sheol*). According to the Zohar, "Raphael is charged to heal the earth." He is sent to cure Jacob from the injury to his thigh after he wrestled with the dark angel at Peniel. This much I could confirm from the books. But I also knew things about Raphael that took me beyond the books. My primary source was a remarkably gifted and spiritual dreamer in my personal circle who had worked with the archangel Raphael, over many years, in guiding spirits of the departed who were lost or confused. By her account, Raphael is indeed an extraordinary guide to the Other Side, where she was grateful for his intervention to restrain and heal abusive personalities who had carried their habits and attitudes with them.[3]

Raziel, on the other hand, was a less familiar name. Back to the books. I found that Raziel is the Archangel of the Mysteries, and one who seeks to bring helpful knowledge to humans. The Library Angel guided me in my search for him. When I picked up *A Dictionary of Angels,* it fell open at a page towards the back where the name was reproduced from an old spellbook, in Roman letters and in cabalistic signs. The spell was for "the manufacture and use of a magic carpet." The carpet is to be woven of new wool, laid out facing east and west. You make a circle to enclose it and go round it calling on angelic powers (Raphael to the north, in this system) and raising up the four points of the rug. Turning again to the east, you invoke the Almighty and call for blessing and protection. Then you fold it up, for use on the night of a full or new moon, when you are supposed to inscribe the name of Raziel "on a strip of azure blue virgin parchment with the feather of a dove." You call on the power of God, and you go flying off into the dreamworld, on Raziel's magic carpet.[4]

Raziel's name, I learned, means "secret of God" and he is described as "angel of the secret regions and chief of the Supreme Mysteries." He is the supposed author of the *Sefer Raziel,* the Book of the Angel Raziel, "wherein all celestial and earthly knowledge is set down." Legend has it that he gave this book to Adam and that the other angels, out of jealousy, seized it and threw it into the sea. God ordered a primordial power of the deep to fish it out. Enoch later found it—or some part of it—by following a dream.

All good stuff, enough for a future book.

But was the telegram that put me onto it really from Manning? A skeptic (including the skeptic who lives quite comfortably in my own left brain) could argue that the whole text was a construct of my memory and imagination, and I have no particular quarrel with that. The whole thing was such fun, producing such creative energy and such wonderful research leads, that I am entirely happy for it to be attributed to my own imagination. Yet my sense that it was an objective, transpersonal message remains strong. The style of the telegram is redolent of Manning, who had a tendency towards purple prose. But my strong feeling that this is an authentic communication stems less from the style than from the depth of feeling it evoked in me. Quite literally, I was *surprised by grace.* With this message came my grateful realization that we really do have friends on the Other Side who take a keen interest in our greater good. And that they include people we knew in ordinary life—people with whom we may have had differences and struggles, but who are continuing to grow and evolve in the afterlife, and may return to us as helpers and teachers. Or may be assigned to us, as this Manning claims he was assigned to me.

I think of him fondly now, perhaps pursuing his research into "parallel lives" being lived in different places and times.

ENCOUNTERS WITH PARALLEL LIVES

In dreams, we find ourselves in contact with people who seem to be living *now,* and yet in a different time. Sometimes we find ourselves entering scenes from their lives again and again. Sometimes we remain observers; at other times we seem to slip inside their bodies and see the world through their eyes.

For as long as I can remember, I have had dreams of a Royal Air Force pilot who was shot down over Holland during World War II. He belonged to an esoteric order in Britain and was involved in the secret war against Nazi occultists. But he loved the thrill of the air and the challenge of a good fight and insisted on flying combat missions. After he was shot down, he survived for a time with the help of the Resistance, knew the love of a young Dutch woman, but was betrayed to the Gestapo by her Communist father (loyalties are not straightforward). Scenes from his life—a London street of brick terraces in the early fog, a woman's hair spread like a dark sunburst against a pillow—are as vivid to me as any memories of my own, as if we share the same holographic database. If I were a straightforward reincarnationist, I would say, *Well, there you are, and doesn't it explain a lot?* Like my nervousness, for much of my life, about going down (for example, on the escalator at the Bethesda Metro station) at a certain angle of descent, the one at which his plane began its nose-dive. Like "knowing" exact details of certain esoteric rituals without having been initiated into these things in this lifetime. Like having a reflex tendency—which I have had to labor constantly to master—to divide the world into good guys and bad guys (understandable enough in a young Brit fighting Hitler before the United States came into the war).

But when we step outside time, as we do in dreaming, our relationship with other life experiences becomes even more interesting. Is it possible we are connected—as the author of that telegram seems to believe—to a whole family of "parallel lives"? If so, that could well mean that our actions now influence, for good or ill, the lives of people *living now in their own times* (which is perfectly possible under the current laws of physics). We need to explore these things actively, and our dreams give us the entry codes. I believe there is a profound opportunity here both for healing and for deepening our understanding of time and of reality itself, to which we will return in Part III.

The mention of Raziel in the telegram from the professor brings us to the edge of an even deeper subject: the dreams that take us into realms of the sacred, and of absolute knowledge.

chapter fourteen

LEVEL SIX: SACRED DREAMING

The duty that the Supreme Being has assigned to you cannot be avoided.

—Ashante saying

I get all kinds of requests for help with dreams. I got one by e-mail while I was writing this chapter that had me doubled over, gasping with laughter. My correspondent told me he would like to devote himself to astral travel and dream exploration, but he did not have time. "I was wondering if you could go get the lottery (Florida lotto) numbers for me. Cuz then I wouldn't have to worry about time . . . Please let me know if you can help me out with the lotto. It would mean a lot to me cuz you can't get very spiritually developed at work. Thanks."

I promise I have not edited or "improved" this communication.

It inspires me to say something I believe to be quite crucial about our dream lives, and the agendas we carry into them.

One of the most important things that goes on in dreaming—and there may be nothing more important in our lives—is that the little self, the "daily trivial mind," is reintroduced to the *big* self. The big self has many names in different traditions: the Higher Self, the "soul of the soul," the God with whom you can have conversations. By any name, this entity is not very interested in who gets the winning lotto numbers!

Dreaming the future is understood in many world traditions to be a vital tool for divination, but "divination," in its original meaning, is a far cry from guessing the numbers. To "divine" is to seek to know the will of God, the deeper purpose and meaning of the things we experience. In ancient Egypt, as Robert Brier observes, "the dream state was not a psychological phenomenon. It was a . . . condition in which is was possible for man, for a brief period, to come directly in contact with the gods."[1]

The question, "Why do we dream?" is answered beautifully in a Navajo teaching story: Close to the beginning of the world, the Hero Twins traveled the earth slaying monsters. When they attacked the demon of Fatigue, he begged them, "Don't kill me! If you kill me, people won't get tired. And if they don't get tired, they won't sleep. And if they don't sleep, they won't dream. And if they don't dream, how will they stay in contact with the spiritual world?" So the Hero Twins let Fatigue live—so people would sleep, and dream, and return in dreams to the deeper dimensions of reality where the events of our waking lives have their source.

DREAMS BRING US TO THE BEATING HEART OF RELIGIONS

A young, secular New York Jewish media executive dreamed that an elderly man with a long beard and a tall black hat showed him a specific way of bobbing his head—twice to the right, twice to the left, then up and down and so forth—as a meditation practice. When he shared his dream with a friend who was studying Kabbala, the friend at once said, "Abulafia," referring to the medieval kabbalist Abraham Abulafia, who combined special patterns of head-bobbing, or *davening,* with meditation on sacred numbers and letters. This connection sent the young New Yorker off on a path of study and experiential exploration of the spiritual practices of his forebears.

An Italian-American woman was transported by a dream to a site in ancient Italy. On different levels, firmly divided from each other, different activities were being played out. Women were decorating a primal image of the Goddess—a raw, rough-hewn figure of stone and clay—in a cavernous alcove. On another level, men were celebrating a kind of communion; they wore animal masks or strange caps, and their libations included bull's blood. The dreamer could move between the two scenes. You might say she was moving between different aspects of her psyche, her feminine and masculine sides (for a start) and you might be right. But her detailed description of the rituals in which she participated satisfied the former ancient history professor in me that she had also caught a good glimpse of what might well have gone on in the women's festivals of the Bona Dea and the men's mysteries of Mithras some two thousand years ago. She has gone back into that dream again and again, in conscious journeys, and has followed its trail to Italy in waking reality. She felt the dream opened spiritual traditions to her that had belonged to her ancestors long before the Church in which she had been raised had come into existence.

Sometimes sacred dreams help us reconcile the tension between different versions of religion or spirituality. A woman from India had been raised by Christian Fundamentalists. While Suvasini accepted Jesus as a personal teacher, she also felt a strong connection to the Goddess—especially the Black Kali of Dakineshwar—but the gods and goddesses of her native land were reviled by her church-going family. How could these things be reconciled? Suvasini had a *big* dream. In her dream, Kali came dancing, naked and erotic, into the arms of a handsome and willing Jesus. They indulged in prolonged and joyful lovemaking, arranging themselves in an inventive series of erotic positions. As a result of their tantric sex, Suvasini was conceived. She woke thrilled and elated. She could not share her dream with her Fundamentalist family—at any rate, not at that time!—but she had a deep inner certainty that the source of her dream had shown her that her own spiritual identity and fulfilment lay in the union of two world traditions, and the marriage of the God and the Goddess.

Sacred dreams can take us beyond drab and confining orthodoxies to the beating heart of a religious tradition, and educate us about the need to reclaim the vital experience of spirituality from the encrustations of bureaucracy and dogma. A woman graduate of a a famous divinity school shared a wonderful dream about this:

Saving the Vatican Jewels

> I am inside the Vatican, and the whole of the Vatican City is on fire. I am desperate to save priceless jewels that have been kept here. In order to save the jewels, I must release them from their settings, which are heavy and tarnished. As I prise more and more of the jewels free, I feel exhilarated. I know that, even if the rest of the place burns down, I am saving what matters.

And then there are sacred dreams that encourage us to reflect that the divine light shines in all of us, however deeply buried, and that we may all be gods or goddesses in hiding.

An initially shy and defensive woman who came to one of my workshops took our breath away when she shared a waking dream.

The Opening to the Goddess

> I'm walking through the neighborhood. There are guys on the street with racing forms. A kind of shimmer comes into the air. I have to sit down on a park bench; I don't want the guys to notice I'm shaken up and am acting weird. Through the shimmer, I see a kind of opening. It's shaped like the Ace of Spades in a deck of cards. I flow forward, into the opening. I stay there for a long time. The shimmer is all around me, but I am filled with fear. Through the entrance is a deep cave. There are jewels on the floor and a magnificent woven cloth—an offering—on the wall. In the depths of the cave, I see the Goddess. She is bare-breasted, with her hands upraised in a commanding, formal posture, like those figures from Crete. I go towards her, but I'm still afraid. A huge serpent coils around her body. It rears its head above her head, expanding it like a cobra. I can see both heads at once. I want to apologize, to explain about my failures and addictions. The Goddess tells me I am *all right*: that I will be able to do everything required of me when I overcome my fear.

We did not *interpret* this dream; the whole circle felt the urgent need to honor it and help Bertha to claim the Goddess energy as her own. So we asked her permission to turn that dream into spontaneous dream theatre—and to dream it onward. She chose the people in the room who would play the different roles, including those of Bertha herself, the Goddess and the snake. Bertha sobbed with joy and gratitude as she watched her alter ego move through the gateway, into the embrace of the Goddess and the serpent. In the "finished" performance, the woman playing Bertha's dream self was very definite about *returning* through the gateway, bringing power back into the ordinary world.

I suggested to Bertha that she now needed to step into her own dream theatre and dream it onward, claiming the Goddess energy and the serpent power that belonged to *her.* She went through the entrance, shaking, and faced the Goddess/Serpent, while I shook a rattle. When she stepped into their embrace, she felt herself being *swallowed* by the Snake Goddess and coming out like a newborn child.

APPROACHING THE SOURCE

In sacred dreams, we approach the deepest Source of our knowing and our personal truth. When we ask for dream guidance, we can ask explicitly for this connection. Two of my favorite ways of asking come from two active dreamers. One of them, surprisingly, was an early Christian bishop; the other a medieval Persian mystic. Let's briefly explore how they understood dreaming, and then learn how they invited sacred dreams.

The Bishop of Dreams

Synesius of Cyrene (365–414) insisted that dreams should be valued and used as a personal "oracle"—the most reliable of all oracles. Born to a wealthy Greek family in Libya, he was a student of Hypatia—the great woman scientist and Neoplatonist philosopher—at Alexandria. He was a "philosopher" in the original (and best) Greek sense of the word: a "lover of wisdom" who aspired to direct experience of the sacred Mysteries. Though his mind and his heart were most at home in the world of Plato and Asklepios, Christianity was now the official religion of the Roman Empire. Making influential friends in Christian and pagan circles, Synesius applied himself to building bridges between their camps. Remarkably—since he had never been ordained and may not even have been baptized, though he had married a Christian woman—Synesius was appointed bishop of Ptolemais around 410.

About that time, on an incandescent night, he was inspired to write a book about dreams. "This work was completed, the whole of it, in a single night, or rather, at the end of a night, which also brought me the vision enjoining me to write it." He sent the manuscript to Hypatia, his "most sacred teacher": "After myself you will be the first of the Greeks to have access to the work."[2]

Hypatia was murdered five years later by a fanatical Christian mob egged on by a crazed monk who was supported by Cyril, the intolerant new Patriarch of Alexandria. Not content with killing her, the mob stripped the flesh from her bones with clamshells.

We do not know what Hypatia—a martyr of women's rights, and one of the brightest stars in the shining intellectual culture that was once Alexandria—made of Synesius' work. The Church in the West buried it, not because it is a difficult read (which it is) but because it urges people to seek their own truth—not only about the future but about the divine will—not from priests and middlemen, but from personal experience through dreams.

"Dreams are prophets," Synesius says flatly, and knowledge of the future through dreams is accessible to everyone. "This branch of knowledge is within us and is the special possession of the soul of each of us." In order to practice the art of dream divination, "it is enough to wash one's hands, to keep a holy silence, and to sleep." It might be helpful to incubate a dream by invoking divine help. "We shall pray for a dream, even as

Homer, perchance, prayed." Beyond this, dreaming is open to anyone, regardless of race or station. The gifts of dreaming come at the right time, in the right way—unlike lower forms of magic or theurgy which try "to set God moving by pressure and leverage."[3]

Synesius refers to his own precognitive dreams. This unusual bishop loved hunting, and he credits his dreams with guiding him to the quarry and showing him where to lay traps. Another dream warned him of a plot being hatched by his enemies.

Like many active dreamers, Synesius noted the distinction between clear dreams, which do not require interpretation, and symbolic or "enigmatic" dreams, which do. Some dreams are "more divine, and are either quite clear and obvious, or nearly so, and in no wise stand in need of the diviner's science." Such dreams are often out-of-body experiences in which the dreamer can travel across time and space and "soar above the eagles."

Like tribal shamans, Bishop Synesius contends that one reason we can see the future in dreams is that, dreaming, we are not confined to the body or its laws. A second reason is "advanced waves of things not yet present" appear in dreams before events are manifested in physical reality. In dreams, we glimpse what is gestating in a subtler order of reality and may appear as an event or situation in ordinary life—unless something is done to avoid that consequence. Such glimpses of a gestating future are "shadowed"; "the symbols are not as clear as in the case of already existing things. Nevertheless they are wonderful . . . in that they have come into existence from things that have not yet existed."[4]

Wonderful, also, because such dreams provide an opportunity to enact or avoid the future that is foreseen. While dreams of a happy future "prolong our pleasure by seizing joy beforehand," dreams that portend misfortune "inform against the worst so as to guard against it and repel it beforehand." The ability to recognize and work with these messages will grow by keeping a "night book," a dream journal. The North African bishop issues a rousing invitation to keep a dream journal whose wisdom echoes down the centuries. We lead "two lives," waking and sleeping, and we should pay ourselves the "compliment" of writing a narrative of both. As we work with our dream journals, we will improve "the observation by which the art [of dream divination] is developed."[5]

The most important gift of dreaming for Synesius, as for many dreamers before and after him, was the chance of a deepening encounter with the personal guardian, the Higher Self. He wrote a beautiful invocation to open the way for contact with the "soul's captain" that I sometimes use on going to bed, or when entering meditation, or when leading dream circles on journeys for higher guidance:

> CALL FOR THE SOUL'S CAPTAIN
> Give me a companion, O King, a sacred messenger of sacred power, a messenger of prayer illumined by the divine light, a friend, a dispenser of noble gifts, a guard of my soul, a guard of my life, a guard over prayers, a guard over deeds.[6]

Suhrawardi's Call to the Guardian Angel

The great medieval Persian philosopher and dream traveler Suhrawardi mapped out an amazingly detailed geography of the Imaginal Realm, and explained how we can go there, in conscious dream journeys, for contacts with spiritual teachers. He also bequeathed us a lovely invocation of the Guide that I have freely adapted from the original translation:

> PRAYER TO THE GUARDIAN ANGEL
> *You, my most holy angel, my precious spiritual being*
> *You are the Spirit who gave birth to me*

And you are the child who is born of my Spirit.
Show yourself to me in the highest of epiphanies.
Show me the radiance of your dazzling face.
Be my mediator between the worlds.
Lift the veils of darkness from my heart.[7]

Recite this prayer—or better still, improvise and reshape it with your own words and intentions—on going to bed, or on entering meditation, and what follows may fill you with awe and deep gratitude. A prayer like this opens a pathway home. So do dreams we haven't asked for, at least not on the level of the little everyday mind, the one that thinks that winning the lottery could change anything important. I would like to share a personal story about this, one that still gives me shivers.

A Conversation with Shams

I was taking a summer break in a cabin on North Hero Island in Vermont that looked eastward over Lake Champlain.

I dreamed that a very old friend had invited me to lunch with a pair of foreigners at a stylish but rather anonymous restaurant. Our lunch was pleasant, but after the food I thought it was time to go. My friend came hurrying after me, in high agitation. "Don't you *remember?*" he all but roared at me. "This is *top priority.* You must record everything they say!" I was confused. He demanded to know if I had read the briefing papers he had given me. I stammered that I had not had time.

I woke up puzzled, and yet strongly drawn by this dream. Why was my old friend—an early mentor I had not seen in fifteen years or more—so insistent? Who were the mysterious strangers? What was so important that I needed to record every word?

It was 3:00 A.M., and after a long drive the day before, I could have simply rolled over and tried to get some more rest. But the energy of the dream stayed with me, almost palpable, like a rainbow shimmer in the air. I knew what I had to do. I had to go back inside the dream. The answer to my questions lay there.

I lay back on my bed in the dark, with a yellow legal pad on my lap and a pen in my fist, and let myself slide back into the dream. This was not especially hard, since I was still strongly connected with the dream, with the energy as well as the images. I brought up a picture of the dream restaurant—its plush banquettes and chandeliers, the oily obsequious waiter who called us "Excellencies" or "Highnesses"—and noticed that the place was completely deserted except for our party and the staff, and that heavy drapes were closed against the outside world.

I wondered about the papers my friend had mentioned. I found a large manila envelope containing three documents. The first was a handwritten note from my friend stressing the importance of the meeting. The second was a newspaper clip from a paper called the *Teheran Times*. The headline read: "THE PRINCE AND PRINCESS OF FARS ARE TRAVELING ABROAD." This gave me shivers, though I did not yet know why. I was vaguely aware that "Fars" was an old name for the Persian heartland. I turned to the third document. It was a neatly typed list of twenty questions. The list began

1. What is the nature of exile?
2. What are the conditions for return?

These questions plucked at my heart. They filled me with a yearning as deep as my life. I hurried back to the table, praying that the mysterious couple would still be there. To my gratitude, they had waited for me. The Prince was handsome, with a smooth oval face, beautifully dressed in a tailored gray suit with a bluegray shirt with a white banded collar. His consort was veiled in the manner of a high priestess.

In my conscious dream state, scribbling notes in the dark, I read through the list of questions, and the Prince answered them one by one. I knew now that his name was Shams. Here I need share only his answers to the first two questions:

1. *What is the nature of exile?*
   To be an exile is to be separated unwillingly from your homeland. This is the condition of the soul when it comes into the body. It is the condition of the higher man when he is separated from the Higher Self.
2. *What are the conditions for return?*
   The return requires courage, the willingness to deny the ways of the world. It is always a journey to the Mountain . . . There are tests and obstacles along the way, also distractions and temptations. But Home reaches out to guide the returning exile. *There is always a guide.* The appearances of the guide are almost always unexpected. The face may be that of a familiar friend, or a stranger.

The conversation lasted more than two hours, until the first light was breaking. Exhausted but exhilarated, I crept from the cabin and lay on a floating dock to watch the changing light on the lake. A silver streak on the water near the horizon grew larger and larger. A rosy blush spread over it, cloudlike against the silver, until the water looked more like the sky than the sky itself. Fish broke the surface. A kingfisher plunged after them.

More had been given to me in this one dream, I felt, than in thousands of books I had read. And at the same time the dream gave me the key to unlock the most challenging of those books. I am still working on the insights from that night with Shams. These are some of the lessons:

* The dream guide sometimes puts on the mask of a familiar face, as the goddess Athena puts on the masks of mortals to

approach dreamers in the *Odyssey.* Be watchful of those "old friends" who turn up in dreams. They may be, quite literally, be old friends—or people who resemble them who will step into your life. The "old friend" may also be *the* Friend, the companion of your soul.

* We generally don't remember a fraction of what goes on in our dreams until we learn to go back inside them. This, by the way, is one of the easiest and most natural ways you learn to become a *conscious* dreamer.
* Truth comes with goosebumps.

chapter fifteen

LEVEL SEVEN: DREAMBRINGING

Clasping one another tight,
Holding one another fast,
We may finish our roads together.
That this may be, I add to your breath now.
To this end:
May my Father bless you with life
May your road reach to Dawn Lake
May your road be fulfilled.

—ZUNI PRAYER FOR THE NOVICE AT THE TIME OF INITIATION

We meet a stranger for the first time, or simply rub shoulders with him on the subway or in the supermarket line, and we *know* things about him before we know that we know. A sudden change in our mood, a dip or rise in our energy, the surfacing of an image (maybe a remembered dream, maybe one of our own life memories): these may all be telling us something about the stranger. Because we are in a hurry, we often miss the moment to read these signals. It's fascinating what can happen when we pause to look more closely at what may be coming through.

I was waiting in the green room of a television studio, sipping coffee and chatting to a couple of other guests who were going on the show, men who were previously unknown to me. I found a memory from my own life rising up so strongly that I felt a compelling desire to share it with one of these strangers.

The episode that had come to mind was not the material for light banter. It involved counseling I had once done for a young man who had been abused, at age eleven, by a Catholic priest. The violation had caused him enduring shame and guilt and confusion about his own identity. Its effect had gone deeper, resulting in what shamans call soul-loss. A part of him had been literally driven from his body by the pain and shame. Lacking this vital energy, he seemed to have lost his ability to know joy and share deep emotion. He had tried to fill the gaping hole in himself with whatever came to hand. To assist in his healing, I had to find a way to help him to reclaim his eleven-year-old self. I entered a conscious dream and went looking for it. My dream journey was not pleasant or short. I was required to travel into a very dark realm on the other side of death, and robe myself in darkness to come and go safely. I found the missing soul in a terrifying environment, a place of utter darkness inhabited by criminal souls—apparently including the priest—who appeared to be using the naked, shivering boy as an astral sex slave. To get him back, I had to take him by force. But when the energy of the boy-soul was brought back to the man, and placed in his heart, his whole being seemed to come vibrantly alive. The returning brightness in his eyes was beautiful. He told us, "I feel whole, for the first time in all these years. I can begin to live from my whole self."

As I say, this is hardly the material for casual conversation, in a TV studio or anywhere else. And although our society is changing fast, shamanic soul retrieval is not exactly a mainstream topic. After I had shared this story, a silence fell in the green room. I found myself shocked that I had spoken so freely about such a troubling and sensitive episode with a total stranger.

"I'm sorry," I told him. "I don't know why I told you that story—"

"*I* know," he cut me off. "You have just told me the story of my life." He proceeded to tell me that *he* had been abused at age eleven by his Catholic priest, who had since died, and that he, too, had known long periods in his life when he was consumed by shame and guilt and found joy was wholly absent. He was very interested in the possibility that when we lose our joy, and our ability to share love and trust, it may be because the part of us that can love and feel joy is somewhere else, lost or stolen. He told me that he was very active in helping victims of childhood abuse, and that he felt that my story of soul recovery might offer clues for many of them, on how and where to search for lost soul, and how to open paths for its return.

He said, "You have brought me a dream that I can bring to others."

DREAM TRANSFER

We can do this for each other: we can sit quietly with someone who has lost their joy or their way, and maybe a chunk of soul, and *dream for them.*

The dream we bring them may be one of our own life memories, the returning memory of a personal dream, an intuitive flash, or a series of images born fresh as we focus on the other person. It may be something we simply "make up," or an inspiring story we remember from a book or a movie or a TV show.

If the dream involves challenging or disturbing content, we always go through this and beyond it, opening paths to resolution and healing. We allow the dream to develop into a vivid scene and explore it with all our inner senses. Then we share the dream we have found and invite the other person to step inside it and explore its scenery. The dream beneficiary now tells the dream as her own dream, and claims its landscapes and its energy. This process has proven to be deeply healing and rewarding in many situations.

Sometimes the role of the dreambringer is to validate another person's dream, or life vision, and show them how it connects with a bigger story and how it can take root in the world.

Sometimes, as dreambringers, we are called on to work with people who are so crushed or depressed or soul-gone that we must begin simply by *seeing* them and helping them to see themselves as an individual, an embodied soul, someone who might deserve a dream.

I See You: Kindling Life Visions

Tina, a black woman who teaches elementary school in Los Angeles, told me how she starts her first class of the day. With one exception, every kid in her class comes from a single-parent home. The fathers of nine of the kids died from gunshot wounds. Most of the children have not had any breakfast when they arrive for school; many have no money for lunch. Precious few of them have been held, or loved, or even acknowledged by anyone in their world that morning.

"I got a full-length mirror and I stood it up just inside my classroom door," Tina said. "When each kid comes in, I get them to stop and look at themselves in the mirror. When they're good and ready, I get them to say to themselves, *I see you,* because they come from a place where they're not seen. Maybe we'll get to the point where they can say, *I love you.*"

You Dream Like Dante: Bringing People to Their Bigger Story

Here's another story about a dreambringer in the schoolroom.

Jane White-Lewis is a gifted and compassionate Jungian analyst and dream therapist who took the brave decision to take dreamwork to kids in tough neighborhoods by offering a course at a public high school in New Haven, Connecticut. The class had its bumps and grinds, but there came a luminous moment of breakthrough when a boy called Rick shared a dream that reminded Jane vividly of the opening of Dante's *Divine Comedy*:

> *Nel mezzo del camin di nostra vita*
> *Me ritrovai per una selva oscura*
> In the midst of the journey of this life
> I found myself in a dark wood[1]

The echo was so strong that Jane took the inspired step of bringing a translation of the *Divine Comedy* to school the next day. The only Dante anyone in the class had heard of was an Italian-American kid in another class. As Jane recalls, "It was a marvelous moment (especially for Rick) when I read his dream and then the beginning of Dante's poem, and the class recognized the connection between the two, between our dreams and great literature. They *got* it—the fact that creative possibilities lie within each of us, in our dreams."[2]

This is one of the vital forms of dreambringing: to help others connect to the larger story of their lives, to discover the mythic dimension that provides courage and juice for the journey. Rick's dream spoke to him out of that depth. But he needed the help of the dreambringer to confirm and unfold its power.

Dream Release From Guilt and Shame

We may need to help the other person move beyond the guilt and shame that are binding and blocking them. Carolyn Myss wisely observes that "by far the strongest poison to the human spirit is the inability to forgive oneself or another person."[3] Traditional healers in Hawaii operate from the understanding that guilt opens the door to disease and psychic intrusions. The release of guilt and shame helps us to recall our energy from past events and entanglements, and from fear and denial. We don't have to go on draining ourselves by trying to keep the lid on disturbing memories, or rehearsing self-justifications.

As dreambringers, we can help others to accomplish this. We can hear their confessions, with compassion and without judgment. We can show them a path to self-absolution. The path might be a guided dream or meditation. Here is a dream script I like:

Guided Dream: From the Ashes of Guilt

Pull up your memories of the shameful things, the guilty things, the things you've tried to keep hidden that are haunting you. Be honest about this. Catch them all. Name them all. You don't need to share this with anyone except the One who is always with you, the One who watches over your soul.

Now, gather these things together. See the garbage, the pain, the chains, all gathered together into a pile. See the pain, the hate, the self-loathing, those things you don't want to name out loud. Can you see them?

Now answer this: *Are you ready to accept forgiveness? Are you ready to be released?*

Answer with your heart. If you can answer *Yes* from the beating heart of your life, you will call down the fire from heaven that can cleanse and free you.

Let the fire of Love come on your heap of pain and shame. See the Fire from a Higher Source ignite the garbage. The flames rise higher and higher. They are bright and hot. The fire encompasses the entire heap and all of the garbage is burning . . . burning . . . b*urning.* Open your mouth and breathe out into the fire. Release all of it, all the heaviness and guilt that has lived inside you. There are only embers now. Breathe on the embers.

The embers are cooling now. They are cooling . . . cooling . . . all that is left now is ash. Begin to gather the ashes. You might need something to put them in. Scoop them up. Gather the ashes.

Bring them to fertile ground and spread them around. Scatter the ashes. Stir them in, mixing them with the earth making the soil even more fertile. Now scatter seeds and watch them grow in this rich soil. The sun is shining brightly. It might not be easy at first, but then, the little tendrils poke up through the earth, growing, growing, growing. Flowers begin to bloom. Can you see them?

This garden will continue to grow. This is rich soil. The sun will shine and the rains will water it. This garden will need tending. Who knows what might grow!

Transplanting Sunflowers: Dreaming the Soul Back Home

I looked into the large round face of a mature woman who had come to me for help because she had felt for many years that a vital part of her was missing. A dream was born in that instant, among the dust motes floating in a shaft of sunlight. I saw a circle of faces around her, eager and smiling. Each of them looked as she might have looked at an earlier age—at four, or seven, or nineteen, or at the time of her divorce. They swayed and beamed like great sunflowers bobbing their heads.

When I told the woman my dream of the circle of sunflower faces, she beamed too. The picture took hold, and she shivered with delight and anticipation. We both *knew* at once that we had opened a way home for several parts of her vital energy that had gone missing at different stages of her life, because of abuse and heartbreak and addiction. I asked her to make a welcoming space for these younger selves in her heart. When the energy flowed back, her eyes shone bright. She wanted to dance and skip. She looked fifteen years younger. Her nights were filled with sparkling dreams, and she filled her living room with sunflowers.

Dreaming is all about soul, and soul recovery is a special gift of dreambringers. The dream journey to bring back lost soul may be hard and long, but there are always helping powers and the rewards are tremendous. The path for returning soul is opened by dreams. It's best when we find it, for ourselves, in our own dreams—perhaps in the kind of dream in which you see a mysterious five-year-old who just might be your five-year-old self, or the one in which you keep going back again and again to your former home, maybe because there's something there you need to bring back. But when soul-loss goes deep, it may have taken away the part of us that dreams true. Then we need the dreambringer who can transplant a dream that can grow in us like a sunflower.

Sharing the Killer Shark: Seeding Dream Images for Healing

I was looking at a brave, intelligent, beautiful woman whose face and body were now bloated by the drugs she was being given in the aftermath of chemotherapy. I had no idea what, if anything, I could do to help her in her struggle with cancer. I simply closed my eyes and asked for a dream image that might provide guidance for both of us.

I saw her again as a beautiful big cat, turned a sickly green by the disease, stuck in murky waters. The big cat looked half-starved. I wanted to feed it. In my waking dream, I offered it milk and fish. It lapped at the milk hungrily, but only sniffed at the fish. I saw then that the cat was being distracted by something in the water. Ferocious piranhas, all snapping teeth, were mauling and savaging her body.

I felt an urgent need to pull her out of that foul river. One of my own dream animals was with me, but I did not want to send him into that river. I felt more and more nervous and agitated, not wanting to leave this painful and disturbing scene without some resolution.

I saw new movement in the murky river. An elegant silver-gray shark came gliding through the waters. Its message seemed to be, *Leave this to me.* The shark started gobbling up the piranhas like popcorn. I continued my mental dialog with it, asking, *Won't they tear up your insides?* The message came back, *They're no problem for me.* I wondered how the shark would finally dispose of the piranhas. *I'll excrete what is left quite cleanly, thank you.*

I came out of the dream and asked the woman I had seen as a big cat if I might share it with her. Her face brightened as she listened to my story. I knew we were on the same page when she told me that under her dietary regimen, she had been denied milk and fish, but that she had been feeling she needed to have them again, and that she had always felt very close to the cat family. Now I took her hand and gently led her deeper inside the dream dwelling on the fluid, graceful movements of the shark, inviting her to make my dream *her* dream and claim the shark as her helper. She was quite excited about this. We didn't spend any time discussing how well the piranhas might represent the cancer cells in her body. She told me that when she went home, she would dream with the shark, using a shark's tooth as a focusing device, and let it do its work inside her body.

I realized, after this incident, that the shark had come to me in previous dreams, both sleeping and waking. In a night dream months before, I was swimming in the murky waters of a public indoor pool when an elegant silver-gray shark came gliding by, dragging a huge sheet of newsprint that was crumpled into the shape of a woman's body. Intrigued, I swam after it. The shark guided me out of the murky waters into a tropical lagoon, a place of fecund, burgeoning new life. One of the oddities of this dream—the newsprint shaped like a woman—had clued me into the fact that it contained "news." Now the shark had showed itself again in a waking dream, I shared the previous dream with the cancer patient. We plunged deep into the tropical lagoon, and found beautiful pink geysers spurting and pumping beneath the waters. This seemed like a very good place to hang out and encourage the regrowth of healthy cells ravaged by chemo treatments.

This is a very simple example of how we can transfer dream images for healing. Our bodies *believe* our images, and will adjust to them *as if they are physical events,* if those images are empowered by the full force of our feelings and intentions. It is increasingly widely understood that this is a vital key to self-healing. Through dream transplant, we can go a step further: we can bring the healing images to others. This won't work if it is just some cute prefabricated visualization. It can and does work when we grow the dream out of a direct, authentic and individual encounter, bring the beneficiary inside it and help her to inhabit the dream with all of her senses and claim its raw energy and power.

Call this suggestion if you like. As Holger Kalweit, a leading researcher of shamanic healing, observes, "since there are no limits to suggestion, there is nothing of which shamans are not capable."[4] If dream transfer is a form of suggestion, it is an exceptionally powerful one, whose potential for healing has barely begun to be plumbed in our modern society. It is also a *real* exchange of energy, as well as imagery. As Lawrence LeShan wrote in *Alternate Realities,* "A reality is real to you when you act in terms of it . . . It is a valid reality when, using it, you can accomplish the goals acceptable to it."

Hole in One: Dreaming Paths to the Next World

Dream transfer is something we can practice in almost any environment, even with people who might run a mile from any mention of dreams. We don't have to call what we are bringing them a "dream"; we can call it a movie, a picture, a fantasy, whatever. Real dreambringers know how to adjust to their audience, and to circumstances.

I once got on a plane bound for Cincinnati, where I was to lead a retreat on death and dying. I found an elderly man sitting in my seat on the aisle. He moved to the window seat as I approached. I had a hunch there might be some kind of connection between us, since he had been warming my seat.

When we struck up a desultory conversation, I realized that under his tanned, outdoorsman's face, and merchant seaman's cap festooned with golf badges, he was carrying a great deal of pain. "There was a crimp in my life," he tells me. He worked on the railroad, like his father before him. There was never much money. He married twice, and both times his wife left him. His second wife had walked out a couple of years before, and this had left him deeply embittered.

I realized, as my neighbor warmed to his theme, that I might be facing two hours of a draining conversation about the disappointments of life. I decided to see if I could turn this around.

"I see you're a golfer," I said, looking at the badges on his cap. "I don't know much about golf. Why don't you tell me about the happiest day you ever spent on a golf course?"

He brightened immediately.

"I hit a hole in one," he announced proudly.

I asked him to tell me about the weather, the flight of the ball—to take me there.

"It was a fine sunny day," he recalled. "I watched the ball fly, and come down neatly into the hole, like a bird that was aiming for it."

"And I'll bet you were flying with that ball."

"Ah yes," he beamed. "I was flying all right." Then his face fell. "But there was no witness. Nobody saw me get that hole in one."

"What happens when you get a hole in one and there is no witness?"

"If you report it, they take your name and they put it in a barrel down in the Carolinas. They pick one winner out of the barrel. If your name comes up, they send you to Scotland to play golf there."

"But your name didn't come up."

"I told you, there's a crimp in my life."

The sun shone through the cabin window, over the tops of scudding clouds, making a lightburst around his head. I found myself *dreaming* his life, a life he never quite had in this reality—yet could now be a pathway into a deeper reality.

"As I listen to you," I told him, "I find I'm watching a movie of your life. Do you mind if I tell it to you?"

He leaned in closer, puzzled but excited.

"I see you hitting that hole in one. The light glancing off the links, the plunk as the ball drops in, the view of the mountains. I feel your spirit lift with that ball. Then I see them dropping your name in that barrel down there in the Carolinas. They spin the barrel, and your name is the one that comes up.

"So now you are riding first-class on a plane to Edinburgh. And you're sipping that single malt you wouldn't normally have, because this is a special occasion.

"I see you stepping out onto the links at St Andrews. It's a glorious day, and you are in rare form. You play a couple of holes, then you meet a beautiful woman who is also playing golf. She has finespun reddish hair."

"A *redhead?*" he snorted. "Never had any luck with redheads!"

"Bear with me," I carried on. "She has fine red hair, and she brushes a few strands off her face as she considers her next shot. She plays well, and you enjoy her company. Now she takes your hand, and she leads you to—the Library of the University of Edinburgh. She sits you down at a big reading table. She brings you stacks of books, books on subjects that always fascinated you but you never had a chance to study."

He gasped and grinned broadly. One of the great regrets of his life, he confided, was that he never went to college. He didn't finish high school. We discussed the subjects he would be studying now, with the redhaired woman as his friend and mentor—history, biology, science, philosophy.

He asked me to describe their meeting again, and the way she took his hand.

He was entering deeper into the dream I had brought him.

We spent two hours talking on that plane, in the air and on the ground. By the end of the flight, he had agreed it would be good to move beyond his regrets and his bitterness towards the last woman who left him. He promised he would think about sending her a letter, maybe just a postcard telling her he would love to play one last game of golf with her before they both popped off.

"Tell me about Scotland again," he urged me. "Tell me about that library. I'd like to go there."

I did not explain what we might actually be doing—which was to open a path into the next world. I just rambled on about my "movie" of his life. But I felt sure that, as he got deeper into the dream movie I had brought him, sailing aloft with the ball, smelling the dew on the grass, he was finding his path beyond stale regrets into a new dimension of possibility on the other side of physical death.

This is one of the easiest forms of dream transfer, when the mood and the space are right: to build on a life memory that has energy and movement. When synchronicity comes into play—as in this "chance" encounter on a plane—the transfer can become quite effortless.

DREAM AMBASSADORS

It is not enough to be able to drop your body as easily as a bathrobe, take flight like the eagle, enter the hollow hills, talk with angels, and dance among the stars. We must make the return. We must live in this world and be gardeners for the dreams that want to take root in it.

When we look around, we notice that people everywhere are hungry for a dream. Some of them have forgotten that there are worlds beyond the surface physical world, even though they have come from them and will return to them after death. Some of them know that important things happen in dreams but suffer from the aching divide between dreams and waking reality.

In the last stages of writing this book, I asked for dream guidance. It came to me at once, in a vivid scene that unfolded in a conscious dream in the hypnagogic zone. I found myself looking at a sparkling blue frame. It was electric blue; the sparkles were silver and very bright. I zoomed in on a scene beyond the frame. Now I was looking across an alley or narrow city street into the window of an apartment, maybe in the projects. A slim black woman was there with her three kids. I knew that she was a single mother, that her budget was tight and things were tough. She *wanted* to believe in dreaming her dream, but she would take some convincing. She knew that we dream the future, that spirits are real and that the departed talk to us. She needed no convincing on that. What she needed to know was how to put such knowledge to use, to better her life and save her kids from being swallowed up by the rage and addiction around them. The future events she dreams are often dark and menacing; the departed who speak to her and trouble her kids are sometimes ghosts of men who died by violence or hooked on drugs.

She needs a dream conductor who can help her get on the right track. I hope this book will speak to her.

I have had other guidance, in visions of the possible future of the Earth itself, ravaged by the wanton human destruction of life-forms and the daily erosion of the ecosphere, and of the creation of latter-day Frankensteins through the arrogant exploitation of biotechnology, especially cloning.

The Seventh Dreamer, say the Beaver Indians, is one who combines the knowledge of seven levels of reality, and brings it to work in the life of the community.

Dreambringers must dream with the Earth and all forms of consciousness that share life on it. They will make bridges between the dreamworlds and the world of clocks and commutes and crackheads. Their influence will be subversive of consensual beliefs and consensual realities. Where others find blank walls, they will see openings and step through. When others say things (or people) will never change, they will say, "Just watch." As more and more of us experience the separate reality they inhabit, and alter our definition of reality, reality itself will change. Dream ambassadors are among us, encouraging us to leave our stuck places and dream our dream. Where that can take us, and our world, is the theme of Part III.

part three

DEEPER DREAMING

The significant problems we face cannot be solved at the same level of thinking that created them.

—Albert Einstein

chapter sixteen

DREAM HUNTERS AND DREAM HEALERS

Hunters nearly always say that a successful hunt has been preceded by a dream. . . . The dream brings an event into being from the multitudinous events of possibility.

—Robin Ridington, "Beaver Dreaming and Singing"

In Paleolithic times—and in the lives of some indigenous peoples up to the present day—the ability to dream in the way Harriet Tubman dreamed for escaping slaves may have been, quite literally, how people stayed alive.

When I moved to upstate New York in the mid-1980s, I started dreaming in a language I did not know, which I eventually found to be an archaic form of Mohawk. My dreams set me learning assignments. The people who seemed to be communicating with me in these dreams—an old woman healer and a warrior shaman of long ago—were most insistent that I should stretch my understanding in order to be ready to grasp what they wanted to share with me. So I studied the Mohawk language, and spent great amounts of time among old books and documents reading what records survive on the dream practices of the First Peoples of North America at the time of first contact with the colonists from Europe. My researches, both in dreams and among the library stacks, led me deeper and deeper into the lives and visions of peoples for whom the dream world is the real world, and the physical world is only the shadow or surface world.

In the starving times of Midwinter, with supplies running low and game animals hard to find, the peoples of Northeast America sent their dream hunters out to locate food for their survival. Like Harriet Tubman, the dream hunters took flight—sometimes on the wings of a hawk or an owl—and ranged over the frozen landscape until they located the deer. When they returned from their dream flights, the village gathered around to listen. The skilled trackers asked questions to clarify which places the dream hunters had visited. Was the lightning-blasted oak the one on this side of the river, or the other side? When the details of the dream were clarified, hunting parties were sent out to follow an exact itinerary. There was not much leeway for wishful thinking or improving the story here. The dream information had to produce results. If the dream information was wrong, the *ratetshents* (the Mohawk term for a shaman or medicine man simply means, "one who dreams") lost respect, and might even be driven out of the village by public ridicule. Peoples on the edge of survival, like escaping slaves, do not have the luxury of playing with New Age soap bubbles.

Here are some early stories of dream hunters in the American Northeast, drawn from the *Jesuit Relations,* a vast compendium of reports from the blackrobe missionaries that is an unequalled source on the traditional dream practices of the Iroquois and their neighbors:

* An Oneida woman respected as a strong dreamer told her community she had dreamed that a war-party of Susquehannocks would attempt a surprise attack on the village. She named and described the leader of the raiding party and the route the enemy would take. She said she also dreamed that the Oneida warriors would rout the enemy and burn their leader to death. The Oneida elders acted on her dream by sending out war parties in exact accordance with her instructions. They were so confident of the fulfillment of the dream that the women started preparing the victory feast immediately.[1]
* A warrior dreamed of a moose that said, "Come to me." The moose showed him an unusual stone inside its body. Guided by his dream, the warrior embarked on a hunting expedition. He found the location he had seen in his dream, and the moose was there. When he killed the moose and cut open its body, he found a stone in its gallbladder like the one he had dreamed.[2]
* The Jesuit LeJeune, wintering among the Montagnais in 1634, summarized the way many of the Woodland Indians dreamed the hunt through encounters with the "elder," or group-soul, of a particular species. "They say that animals, of every species, have an elder brother who is, as it were, the source and origin of all individuals, and is wonderfully great and powerful. If anyone, when asleep, sees the elder or progenitor of some animals, he will have a fortunate chase. If he sees the elder of the beavers, he will take beavers. If he sees the elder of the elks, he will take elks, possessing the juniors through the favor of their senior whom he has seen in the dream."[3]

It is important to remember that these stories come from peoples who were struggling for survival, caught up in bloody wars, ravaged by imported disease, and often on the edge of starvation in the depths of winter. They turned to their dreams to direct the hunt and even military strategy because they found that dream precognition *worked.*

A more recent Native American tale of the dream hunt comes from the Blackfoot:

Weasel Tail, a Blackfoot, rode out with a raiding party in search of wild horses. While they camped overnight, he dreamed an old man came to him and said, "You are to see a coyote. Watch the animal, notice the direction his nose is pointing and go that way, and you will find horses." He shared his dream with his companions in the morning, but they dismissed it. But while they were still eating breakfast, a coyote appeared on a nearby rise. Always pointing towards the south, the coyote raised its quavering yelp. It howled four times—a sacred number for Native Americans—then trotted off towards the south. The Blackfoot hunters immediately changed their opinion about Weasel Tail's dream. The raiders rode south, and found their horses.[4]

The dream hunt, and the ability and responsibility of gifted dreamers to provide accurate dream guidance for the community, are central to traditional dreaming cultures. Among the Ngoni of Malawi, "those who dream of an event directly are very much respected" and people are regarded as having an obligation to share dream "omens," especially if the dreams involve animals or glimpses of accidents or misfortune for other members of the community.[5]

THE SECRET HISTORY OF THE WORLD

The role of dreaming in human history and evolution runs underground—more like a river than a railroad—beneath the chronicles of events and discussions of cause and effect that we suffer in school. There is a secret history here that is yet to be written. It is a story of all peoples and all times, but it has countless permutations. It concerns the secret springs of decisions and events that have shaped world history. It involves humankind's ability to survive the most terrible adversity and keep the flame of spirit alive. It is urgently relevant, I believe, to our ability to rise to meet the twin challenges of the new millennium, which are (a) to achieve an expansion of consciousness to match our accelerating technological revolution and ensure it serves human ends and (b) to achieve a level of active compassion and connectedness—a human internet—that can overcome the forces that strive atavistically to hurl us back into the nightmare of tribal hatred and bigotry.

I do not intend to offer the "secret history" here, only a few portholes into what we may learn from it.

Here are a few quick history lessons, involving some fairly well-known episodes whose deeper significance is often missed:

When We Don't Trust Our Dreams

The ultimate skeptic, perhaps, is the one who refuses to trust his own experience. A character in Robert Heinlein's novel *Glory Road* speaks for this type when he says, "I'm not going to believe the impossible simply because I was there."

The great orator and statesman Cicero (106-43 BCE), one of the towering figures of the late Roman republic, was skeptical about divination through dreams. He wrote that "obscure messages by means of dreams are utterly inconsistent with the dignity of the gods." He observed that dreamers "cannot by any means understand" their dreams, and heaped scorn on the dream interpreters who purported to explain them by "conjecture."

> Let us reject this divination of dreams . . . For, to speak truly, that superstition has . . . oppressed the intellectual

> energies of all men, and has betrayed them into countless imbecilities. [*De divinatione*]

The distinguished, highly literate and somewhat snobbish Cicero was no doubt turned off by the vulgar fortune-tellers and dream-readers who proliferated in his time.

Yet his views on this subject must have been shaken in his later years, when a powerful dream introduced him to a boy he had not yet met, and suggested that this youth had an extraordinary destiny. In Cicero's dream, someone invited the sons of the senators to the Capitol because the top god, Jupiter, was going to appoint one of them to be ruler of Rome. The boys in their purple-edged togas walked to the temple, while a big crowd gathered around. The temple doors opened, and one by one the boys filed in, to be inspected by the god. To their disappointment, they were all dismissed. Then another youth was brought into the god's presence. Jupiter stretched out his hand and announced, "Romans, you shall have an end of civil wars, when this boy becomes your ruler."

Cicero woke with a vivid impression of the boy's appearance.

Next day, Cicero was astonished when he recognized the boy from his dream among a crowd of youths who had been playing games on the Field of Mars. When he made inquiries, he was told the boy had the same name as his father Octavius, "who was not a person of great importance," and that his mother was Julius Caesar's niece.

Despite his views on dreams, Cicero took a keen interest in the boy he had met in his dream. Plutarch reports that "after this, Cicero was always careful to take some notice of the young man whenever they met, and he on his side welcomed these kind attentions."[6] The boy from Cicero's dream became famous in history as the Emperor Augustus, the founder of the Roman Empire.

Cicero's dream may have guided him in his decision to lean towards Octavius in the civil strife that grew fiercer after the murder of the young man's great-uncle, Julius Caesar. However, he apparently reverted to his original opinions about dreams. If he received forewarnings in his dreams about the circumstances that led to his most unpleasant death, he seems to have ignored them. As a grown man, the boy Cicero had cultivated struck a deal with his bitter enemy, Mark Antony, and a plot was hatched to remove Cicero from the political scene by assassination. The killers who were sent to murder Cicero at his country estate cut his throat, then hacked off his head and hands.

We can't know whether his dream might have saved him had he only paid attention. But history does record the stories of other prominent men who owed their lives to dream warnings. One of them was a young Austrian known to history as Adolf Hitler. He was a corporal in the bloody trench warfare along the Somme in 1917. He had a terrifying dream of being trapped below a massive pile of earth and molten metal. Gasping for breath, Hitler tore himself from sleep and rushed out into the chill night air. A French shell landed on the bunker he had just fled, killing all the men inside. Hitler later claimed that his dream was an act of divine intervention to save his life so he could save the Fatherland.[7]

It's a pity that Hitler listened to his dreams and Cicero did not.

When We Fail to Act on Our Dreams

One of the most famous dreams in American history was the one in which Abraham Lincoln foresaw his own death. The episode raises fascinating questions about whether it might have been possible to use the dream information to avoid the foreseen event.

Unlike Cicero, Lincoln believed strongly in intuition and dream precognition. He told his friend and biographer, Ward

Lamon, that shortly after the 1860 election he looked in a mirror and saw a double image of himself. He took this to mean that he would be elected for a second term and would die before he completed it.

A month before his assassination, President Lincoln had a dream that anticipated his death in a more specific way.

Lincoln dreamed he heard people weeping "as if their hearts would break." He followed the sound of the unseen mourners through the White House until he came to the East Room. "There," he told Lamon, "was a sickening surprise. Before me was a catafalque on which rested a corpse wrapped in funeral vestments. Around it were stationed soldiers who were acting as guards." When Lincoln asked the guards, "Who is dead in the White House?" they told him, "The president, he was killed by an assassin."

Lincoln dreamed this scene in March, 1865. In April, he was shot and killed by John Wilkes Booth in Ford's Theatre in Washington. We know that Lincoln took his warning dream very seriously; he shared it with his wife and several close friends. Might he have been able to avoid his assassination had he been able to gain further information from his dream—such as the date and cause of his apparent death?

Though we might dismiss such questions as impossible to answer, it is fascinating to recall that the life of a *future* president, Ulysses S. Grant, may have been saved from death on that same night at Ford's Theatre by his wife's intuition. General Grant was the hero of the hour; he had recently accepted the unconditional surrender of Confederate General Robert E. Lee. Grant and his wife Julia were scheduled to accompany the President and the First Lady to Ford's Theatre and to be toasted by the town. But on the day of the play, Mrs Grant woke with a sense of a desperate need to go home to New Jersey. We do not know from the documents whether she remembered a specific dream related to her urgent desire to leave the capital, but she kept on at the general all day long until he finally agreed to cancel their evening with the President. When they reached Philadelphia, a courier brought them the news that President Lincoln had been assassinated. They would have been sitting in the same box. Grant later learned that he was on John Wilkes Booth's hit list.

Lincoln's dream, as reported by Lamon, did not give him the details he would have needed to escape his rendezvous with the assassin in Ford's Theatre. Might he have obtained the vital missing details had he been able to go back inside his dream and gather more information? Or if he had asked for a new dream to provide guidance on the exact circumstances of his death?[8]

Of course, historians cannot answer these questions. What we *do* know, from studies of early warning or precognitive dreams of people connected with other tragedies, like the sinking of the *Titanic,* is that they were frequently able to escape disaster provided (a) that their dream warnings were sufficiently specific and (b) that they were willing to take appropriate action (e.g., giving up a berth on the *Titanic*).

When We Can't Get the Message Through

History is also full of the stories of gifted dreamers who produced accurate warnings for others but could not get a hearing. Sometimes, like Cassandra or Caesar's wife, the people they needed to reach did not want to listen—because they did not like the news, or because they did not believe in dreams. Calpurnia had two dreams the night before Julius Caesar was killed. In the first, she saw blood flowing from his statue. In the second, she saw his body fall under the knives of his killers. For ancient dream interpreters, the repetition of the same dream or dream theme in the course of the same night was widely regarded as a sign of a "true" dream that must be taken very seriously. Here, the same action was played out twice, symbolically and realistically. Yet, as every schoolkid knows (or used to know) Caesar insisted on making his public appearance, and down he went.

Sometimes it was impossible to get the dream warning through to the person who needed it because of practical circumstances. A Catholic bishop dreamed of the assassination of the Austrian Archduke in Sarajevo—the event that triggered the First World War—in such detail and vividness that he tried desperately to get a message to the Archduke not to visit that city. He was unable to contact the Archduke before he reached Sarajevo. We cannot know whether the Archduke would have been influenced by a dream, even the dream of a Catholic bishop, but it is interesting to speculate whether the course of the twentieth century would have been changed if that dream had reached its intended recipient.

ANCIENT WAYS OF SETTING UP DREAMING

Unlike some of the most ebullient modern dreamworkers, traditional dreaming peoples do not believe that all dreams are "good" dreams. It is recognized, for a start, that where we travel in dreams will be conditioned by our level of personal evolution, by our appetites and desires. In this sense, dreaming can be a bit like going out on Friday night. You can have a wonderful romantic encounter, write a chapter of a book, watch a horror movie, listen to a lecture by a French deconstructionist, or get stoned out of your mind and end up having anonymous sex with someone whose face you don't even remember.

Similarly, not all dream visitations are good visits. If your psychic doors are open, you might find you are entertaining distinctly and unpleasant invited guests. Some of them may be other dreamers who are traveling about in their denser energy bodies. Some of them may be departed people who are "earth-bound" because they are lost or confused and are clinging to you or the place where you live.

For these reasons, the ancient schools of dreaming—both Western and Eastern—recommend that if you want a *big* dream of guidance or healing for your life, you should start by cleaning up your act and getting your intentions very clear. And if you want to avoid undesirable dream visitors, you should spend some quality time cleaning your psychic space and establishing healthy psychic boundaries.

A few words on each of these parallel approaches:

Dream Incubation

Throughout the ancient world, and in many cultures today, people journeyed to sacred sites to seek guidance and healing through dreams. The journey might be hard, dangerous and expensive. Offerings might be required at the temples of healing. Preliminary rites of purification—cleansing by water, smudging with incense-laden smoke, being dressed in a simple new garment or shroud—were almost always required.

It was considered vitally important to do something to ensure that the seeker entered the place of sacred sleep with a clear mind. Over the outer gate of the precinct of Asklepios at Epidauros was an inscription that is often quoted in a famous translation:

> *Only the pure may enter the fragrant temple*
> *The pure is he who thinks only holy thoughts*

A more up-to-date version might go more like this: "Check your habits and your mind-set at the door. You are entering a different space, where all your pasts and futures are accessible now, and many things become possible."[9]

Ancient Celts went to sleep on the graves of their ancestors, hoping to draw on their knowledge.

An ancient Tibetan ritual for obtaining "dreams of enlightenment" and "dreams of power" involves sleeping on kusha grass and anointing the eyes with a special milk or ointment. The tradition of sleeping on kusha grass survives to the present day; the Dalai Lama hands it out at the week-long Kalachakra ceremony, advising those attending to place it under mattresses and pillows to produce "unmistaken, clear dreams." The use of an eye ointment is interesting. It underscores the Tibetan understanding that we do not "have" dreams; we "see" them.[10]

It was recognized by strong dreamers in ancient times, as it is today, that we do not have to go on a physical journey to reach the special place where we can receive true guidance and healing for dreams. Your own bed, even the side of the road (in an emergency) can be the temple. The real temple of dreams is *within* us, not out there.

We might find it helpful to conduct a simple personal ritual before going to bed, like lighting a candle or taking a cleansing bath. We might want to go over the events of the day, and our current preoccupations, and try to either resolve them or lay them aside so we can focus on the main intention for the night. We will certainly want to give careful thought to our intention: to framing the question or request we will put to our dreams, and the powers that speak through dreams.

"That dream is most sure," wrote the Renaissance magus Cornelius Agrippa, "which is concerning those things which one did meditate on, and revolve in his mind, when he goeth to bed."[11]

It's important to remember to ask in the right way.

"Give me next Wednesday's winning number" or "Fix my kidneys" or "Show me how to get a pay increase" are all questions I have been told that people have put to their dreams.

I don't know what is of most concern to you in your life right now, but try for a moment—if it's possible—to put yourself in the mind of the Angel of Dreams. (There *is* an Angel of Dreams, more correctly described as an Archangel. For Jews, Christians and Muslims, the Angel has the same name: Gabriel.)

If you were the Angel of Dreams, you would probably have been wearied by an unending succession of human requests, over the millennia.

Who is more likely to get your attention (or that of any of your reliable dreambringers): Someone who is moaning about a physical complaint or grasping for money, or someone who says something like:

"Show me the right path to take"; or

"I open myself to the knowledge of God"; or

"I open myself to my creative Source"; or

"Show me the radiance of Your dazzling face
Lift the veils of darkness from my heart"[12]

Your call. I plucked the last couplet—an invocation of the Higher Self—from a prayer of Suhrawardi, the great dream traveler from Persia, the land of flying carpets, whom we met in earlier chapters.

Keeping Out Unwanted Night Visitors

Most of us pay a fair amount of attention to physical security, especially if we live in crowded urban neighborhoods. By contrast, we are often fairly inattentive about psychic protection, and this can lead to a good deal of confusion, not only about the content of dreams, but in our energy levels, our feelings and even our physical symptoms.

Experiences that some people report as "bad" dreams or nightmares—as well as many of those formless but awful "night terrors"—are quite frequently *psychic intrusions.* Something is entering your space that does not belong there. This is both a dream and an energy event. When it is causing problems, you need to set up effective psychic screens or shields so that you are not endlessly being bothered.

This, for as long as we have records, has been a key element in dream science. Go back to the ancient dream "books" and inscriptions of the Egyptians and the Assyrians, and you will find the most detailed instructions on how to cast out an energy intrusion reflected in a night dream. You will blow the energy of the "bad" dream into fire, or into a lump of clay that will be dissolved or dispersed in a running stream, or something along these lines.[13]

Since I have written a good deal about psychic self-defense in *Dreamgates,* I would advise you to go to Part One of that book for more detailed advice on this area.

The Matter of Interpretation

There is another perennial problem in the history of dreaming true, and that is the question of when (and how) to interpret dreams and when *not* to interpret them. Harriet Tubman did not sit around interpreting her dreams. They were clear and accurate, and they required action, not analysis.

Throughout history, gifted psychic dreamers very often dream in this way, bringing back clear and realistic snapshots and maps of situations that will develop in the future. These dreams do not require interpretation, though sometimes they require clarification of telling details. Which barn is safe? Am I sure the car was a red Honda?

But dreams are often filled with symbolic language, and require a somewhat different approach. Pharaoh had a dream that contained the key to saving his countrymen from starvation in a long drought still seven years off. But he could not winkle out the meaning of his dream of the seven fat cows and the seven lean ones—even though the theme was repeated in a second dream the same night—until Joseph interpreted it for him.

Pharaoh's befuddlement is one we have all shared at some time, in trying to fathom our own dreams. There are things there we cannot grasp until someone else—sometimes a complete stranger—makes an association or latches on to a pun we missed.

But the history of dreaming contains strong cautions not to give dream interpreters *authority* over our dreams. Since rabbinical tradition values dream interpretation highly, it is interesting to note that there is a wonderful parable in an old Jewish *midrash* about the possible penalties for turning over our dreams to the dream interpreters.

In the story, a traveler crosses the desert to the city of Sodom, notorious for a number of things including a certain sexual proclivity and inhospitality to strangers. All he has is his broken-down mule and the Persian rug strapped across its back. The people of Sodom turn their backs on him. Then one Sodomite trader steals a peak at the Persian rug. It's a good one that would fetch a hefty price. He invites the dusty traveler to stay with him. After a couple of days later, the traveler is refreshed and ready to leave. But there is no sign of his Persian rug or the rope that tied it to the mule. When he asks his host about this, the Sodomite strokes his beard and smiles indulgently.

"What was the pattern of the rug?" he asks.

The traveler describes a pattern of rich orchards and flowering trees.

"And how long was the rope?"

The traveler spreads his arms as far as they will reach.

"Ah," the Sodomite reassures him, "this is an excellent dream. The rich orchards mean you will have great wealth and the long rope means you will enjoy long life."

"But it wasn't a dream!" the traveler protests when he realizes that the Sodomite has turned his Persian rug into a symbol.

Their disagreement grows so fierce that they take it to the court. The justices rule in favor of the Sodomite, because he is a celebrated dream interpreter who is never wrong. The moral of the story is that—like the unfortunate traveler—we may lose what is of greatest value when we allow our dreams to be interpreted rather than experienced and explored.[14]

A Persian rug is no ordinary carpet. It holds the promise of flight. And it was the people who remembered they could fly—in a beloved black American folktale inspired by the Underground Railroad—who found their way to the Promised Land.

THE RETURN OF THE DREAMER

Anthropologists have popularized the word "shaman"—borrowed from a Siberian language—to define a type of person that many indigenous cultures call simply a *dreamer.* With this in mind, let's look at what Thomas Berry has to say, in his beautiful essay "The Dream of the Earth," about the need for this kind of individual in our modern society: "More than any of the other human types concerned with the sacred, the shamanic personality journeys into the far regions of the human mystery and brings back the vision and the power needed by the human community at the most elementary level. The shamanic personality speaks and best understands the language of the various creatures of the earth."[15]

In an inspiring recent book on *Reinventing Medicine,* Larry Dossey proposes the creation of a National Dream Team of tested and certified dream athletes who would be asked to "dream collectively for the nation," providing intelligence on social, economic, military and foreign policy questions.[16] If this idea were adopted, it might herald the reappearance of the ancient dream hunter in modern dress, though Dossey prefers to make the comparison with the oracles of ancient Greece. It is worth recalling that the success of oracles like the famous one at Delphi depended on their independence from state or party control (and, some cynics might say, on the notorious ambiguity of the responses, which made it possible to claim that a prediction was accurate no matter what happened).

A National Dream Team would be a grand idea—if we could stop government agencies from distorting and even corrupting its work, and make sure these dream athletes would speak only the truth of their dreaming, which would probably include a great deal that governments would prefer not to hear but might very much need to be told. My own feeling is that, more than a national team, we need *community* dreamers who will promote the well-being of people where they live, in every section of society, and build bridges between them. And we need international networks of *Earth* dreamers who will put us in touch with the consciousness of the planet, the life-forms we share it with, and our way towards evolving together in peace and harmony.

We've had a couple of short history lessons in this chapter. Let's close it with one more, that speaks to the role that dreamers have played—and can play in the future—in bringing through positive change, the liberation of oppressed minorities, and the healing of our social wounds. In the nineteenth century, many, if not most, of the leading supporters of women's rights and the abolition of slavery were very active spiritual explorers. They were deeply involved in the birth of the Spiritualist movement, but above all in what independent-minded Quakers called "unbroken communication between the Infinite and all beings." Isaac and Amy Post, who ran a drugstore in Rochester, New York, were at the forefront of all of these movements. Frederick Douglass was a frequent guest in their house on Sophia Street, which was a very busy station on the Underground Railroad. In Harriet Tubman's heyday as a conductor, the Post family was frequently providing free room and board for a dozen or more fugitive slaves. These good people believed—as passionately as they believed in the cause of equal rights—that each of us has direct access to the sacred. It comes through communication with the departed, through dreams and visions, through the calm clear voice of the personal angel. Sometimes they spoke of the "spiritual telegraph."[17]

The story of the Spiritualist movement is too often discussed today as a chronicle of table-rappings and mediumistic seances, dubious or otherwise. The vital leadership role of the Spiritualists in the cause of freedom is still neglected, despite a ringing early endorsement by the leaders of the women's suffrage movement and a brilliant recent study by Ann Braude.[18] Writing in the 1880s, Elizabeth Cady Stanton and Susan B. Anthony declared that

> The only religious sect in the world . . . that has recognized the equality of woman is the Spiritualists . . . They have always assumed that woman may be a medium of communication from heaven to earth . . . that the spirits of the universe may breathe through her lips.[19]

But the early Spiritualists were very far from being a religious sect, and the understanding of their practice needs to go beyond discussions of the "rappings" produced by the Fox sisters (whose psychic experiences in a house near Rochester in 1848 helped give rise to the Spiritualist movement).

When we go deeper—as we recover more of the secret history of dreaming in history—I suspect we will find something of far greater contemporary importance and relevance. Many of the Americans who first rose to the clear understanding that we must judge people not by the color of their skin, or their gender, or their social circumstances, but by "the content of their character" were directed and sustained by their dreams and visions. They did not march in lockstep with anyone's agenda. Because they were visionaries and dreamers, they had a direct line to higher knowledge. They acted on their dreams, not to hunt but to heal, as we must today.

chapter seventeen

BECOMING A WAYMAKER

When the soul of a man falls into a great excess of any passion, it can be proved by experiment that it binds and alters things in the way it wants . . . Everyone can influence everything magically if he falls into a great excess . . . and he must do it at that hour when the excess befalls him and operate with the things which the soul prescribes.

—Albertus Magnus, *De mirabilibus mundi*

Ancient Polynesian navigators managed to sail thousands of miles across the Pacific without compasses or instruments of any kind. They voyaged from Tahiti to settle the islands of Hawaii. How did they do it? This was a vital question for a venturesome group that came together in Hawaii in the 1970s to build a big outrigger canoe in the hope of duplicating the ancient voyages. They brought an old-time navigator—a Waymaker—from Melanesia to train their crew in the old ways.

Over many days, he taught them how to listen to the waves, talk to the winds and follow the stars. But he led them through the master class on a single night. He gathered the Hawaiians on a point of land. He asked them to turn until they were facing their destination—the island of Tahiti, 2,500 miles away. When they were facing in the general direction of their destination, he told them to close their eyes and *see* the island. He coaxed them to use all their inner senses, to taste it, smell it, touch it. To be there. When the vision was vivid and wholly alive, he gave them this most important instruction: "Hold the vision in your mind, or else you will become lost."

This is the entire advanced course in Polynesian navigation. The Polynesians call it Waymaking. It is one of the most creative forms of dreaming: of dreaming your dream and bringing it into manifestation in the physical world. If you worry overmuch about all of the steps involved in getting from here to there, you may never reach your destination. You'll certainly risk getting lost in choppy seas, when you cannot see the stars. *Hold the vision,* says the Waymaker. In a curious, but entirely practical way, your vision exerts a certain magnetism. It draws your destination towards you. Those modern-day Hawaiian navigators got to Tahiti, and they did it without a compass.

How do we become Waymakers, in the context of our own lives?

There are three simple but all-important steps, which closely resemble the old Polynesian navigator's instructions:

1. *Turn in the direction of your true destination, your heart's desire.*
   What is your deepest dream? You need to think about this from the heart, not the head. So you might begin by sitting or lying down in a relaxed, comfortable position. Take a few deep, easy breaths. Put your hand on your heart. Feel your heart beating or fluttering in your chest. Ask yourself:

What is my heart's desire? You can be completely honest about this. You don't need to share this with another human soul, unless you choose to. What is your heart telling you? What do you *yearn* for? A child, a lover, a community of caring people? A home, a job, creative success, material rewards or spiritual fulfillment? The simple pleasure of a sandy beach? Wellness, release from pain or guilt or fear?

As your heart guides you towards your deepest desire, let an image form on your mental screen. Little by little, the picture grows stronger and more vivid. The picture shows you your complete fulfillment of your heart's desire. It may come to you at first as a floating image—a face, a postcard, a flickering glimpse of something like a TV screen. Or as a subtle sensation, like baby's breath or a soft wind rustling your hair, or fresh linen or the anticipation of a lover's kiss. It stengthens and deepens and becomes a whole scene.

2. *Be there.*

   Now you are stepping into the picture. As you enter the scene, all your senses become richly alive. You taste it, you smell it, you touch it. You hear sounds that belong to this place. You look about in all directions, taking everything in. You enjoy this scene richly. This scene shows you the complete satisfaction of your heart's desire. Explore and enjoy for as long as you wish.

3. *Hold the vision in your mind.*

   Now you are coming back into physical focus. As you do so, hold the vision in your mind. This is not a one-time visit you have made. You have traveled into an *attainable* future.Your creative task—your richest form of play—will now be to bring your destination, the complete fulfillment of your heart's desire, closer to you day by day.

Begin by deciding *now* on one small, specific action you can take and will take in your waking life over the next week that will demonstrate your commitment to fulfilling your heart's desire. Don't make this one of those New Year resolution kind of things that maybe you'll honor and maybe you won't. Make it easy, make it *small*—so small and easy that you are virtually bound to do it. As small and easy as writing a letter or sorting the garbage into recycling containers. Write down what you *will* do in the week ahead to bring your dream closer, and just do it.

This is how you begin to become the Waymaker of your life's dream.

Let's be real about this: There will be days when the contrast between your vision and the clutter and letdowns and bruises of everyday life seems so jarringly huge that you give up hope.

But this is not about hope. It's about vision, which is more substantial than hope. *Hold the vision in your mind,* however rough the seas turn out to be. If you can dream it, you can do it. Take a break from the clutter and occasional despair. Clear your mind, open your heart, and let your heart's longing carry you back inside the vision. Let the vision deepen and expand. If the scene includes your dream house, explore the additions and renovations that may have been made since you last came here. If you are well, strong and vital, in your vision, revel in those feelings until you sense them coming through to your body; if you trust your feelings, your body will believe you. If you are loved and supported in your dream, then trust in your (sometimes) invisible support and that it *will* be manifested in your physical world. Each time you come back, determine one more simple, specific action you will take to demonstrate your resolve to move decisively in the direction of your dream.

You'll do this over and over, returning to your vision, polishing it and refreshing it, and finding ways to honor it in your waking life. And as you do this, and rally the courage for greater leaps and longer journeys, you will find that the universe starts to believe you. People, resources and opportunities will appear in your life in unexpected ways to support your vision, and your vision will expand to make room for them. Day by day, the "I-land" across the vast ocean will draw closer.

chapter eighteen

BRINGING DREAMS INTO WAKING LIFE

I slept, and I dreamt that life was joy.
I woke, and I found that life was service.
I acted, and I found that service was joy.
—Rabindranath Tagore

We can dream our way to the Promised Land. Let's return to the powerful image of the underground railroad, this time as a dream metaphor. Again and again, in my dreams, I am riding trains or waiting to board a train, or trying to figure out how to get to a certain station or platform, or which line to take. Sometimes I pause between platforms to study maps and make mental notes of where I will need to change in order to get to my destination. Although I ride trains and subways from time to time in daily life, I ride the underground railroad of dreams far more often, and in far more important ways. As I have become more attuned to the vocabulary of my dreams, I notice there is wonderful guidance here. The line I am choosing may be a line of work. Change may be required of me, and in me, to get to where I want to go. Sometimes I need to wait for the right train. Sometimes I need to simplify my luggage, or detach myself from people who are holding me back. Riding the train may be a "training" I am going through, or need to go through. Detraining may be a process of "unlearning" old ways or habits, which is often required as we change and grow. Sometimes I'm glad to be traveling with other people; other times I want to get off and find my own way, on foot if need be. Occasionally, when conditions get tough—when there's a problem on the line or too many people or ticket collectors—I remember I can fly.

One way or another, you *can* get there from here, on the underground railroad of dreams.

FINDING YOUR DREAM PARTNER

An intelligent but rather melancholy man once confided, "I know thrilling romance in my dreams. I have sex beyond anything I've experienced in waking life, but it's not just the sex. The woman feels like my soulmate. We touch each other's hearts."

His sadness stemmed from the brutal contrast between his dream romance and his waking reality. He had gone through a messy divorce and was without a steady partner.

"If it were my dream," I told him, "I would look for specific ways in which I could bring that romance and passion from the dreamworld into my waking life."

"You mean find that woman?" he gaped at me. "But what if she doesn't exist?"

"What if she does? And what if she is dreaming of you?" I paused before adding, "You can only find her if you make room for her in this world." I suggested that this would mean following his dream—perhaps in the quite literal sense of taking a vacation in one of the dream locales where he had been with his dream lover—and jettisoning the excess baggage of habits and expectations.

I don't know whether he has found his dream partner, but I know, from many other stories that have been shared with me, that it can be done. And what do we have to lose by trying?

We fly, in our dreams, into the arms of a dream lover. Since dreamers all over the world are doing this every night, it is no surprise that the dream lover is a favorite motif in mythology and romantic adventures from every continent. Folklorists tag it "Falling in love with a person seen in a dream." In some versions, the hero or heroine succeeds in bringing the dream lover into this world and the tag becomes "Future husband (wife) revealed in dream." In other versions, the dream lover exists only in another dimension; our prince or princess fades when we wake up. Or we meet the dream lover in this reality but can't keep her/him here.

Our dream lovers may not only have physical bodies; they may be dreaming of us long before we meet in this reality, if we ever do meet.

We may still have to overcome great odds in order to come together. There is a Persian story about that. The hero and the king's daughter are dreaming of each other, and have fallen in love in their dreams. But the princess is under great pressure to choose a husband. Her father arranges a banquet to which all her suitors are invited, and fiercely commands her to choose from among those present. She bursts into tears when she fails to find the face of her dream lover in the crowd. "See, it was only a dream!" her father roars. He orders her to abandon her vain fancies and pick from what is on offer in the "real" world. Distraught, she rushes outside—and finds her dream lover at the gate. The dreamer must hold to her personal vision, her conviction that her dream is true, against crushing social pressure to conform to other people's beliefs and expectations until, finally, she is supported by a physical event that other people can see.[1]

Indian literature is filled with these tales. In one popular story, a king has a huge dream adventure in which he overcomes all sorts of obstacles in order to enter a city of armed women and make passionate love to a ravishingly beautiful girl who had shut herself away from the world of men. At the moment of climax, someone wakes the dreamer up. Frustrated, the king shares his dream with his closest friend. Instead of discussing symbols, his friend urges him to draw a detailed map of the dream city. The map becomes the key to finding the girl, who not only exists, but has been dreaming of making love to the king.[2]

If you go looking for your dream lover in waking life, it could be very helpful to have a map! Maybe it's even better to have a portrait.

A woman dreamer describes how she drew the face of a partner she saw in a dream long before she met him in waking life. She drew him more than once, as she saw him grow in her dreams from a boy to a gawky teenager to a robust adult. She observed him living in different houses and cities, and drew some of these landscapes too. When they eventually met and started dating, he took her to visit his childhood home and she found herself inside the landscape of one of her childhood dreams.

Another contemporary woman dreamer, Andrasda, tells the following story: "I drew the face of my dream lover from the time I saw him in a dream when I was eleven or twelve, until I was seventeen, when I fell in love with someone for real. He strongly resembled my dream lover except that the man in my drawings had a different haircut from the man I met in college. Later I found his old high school yearbook in his school library. The boy in the photo had the exact same haircut as the lover in my dreams."

There was further confirmation. In one of her dreams, the young Andrasda had seen her dream lover posing in front of a yellow vintage 1930s automobile. He told her, in a cavalier way, that he had come to defend her from soldiers who were invading her hometown. Years later, she found the whole scene—the yellow roadster, her dashing lover leaning against it—in a painting by a professional artist. In high excitement, she asked the artist if he had modeled his painting from life. He told her he had painted an actual car, but the man in the picture was a "composite."

These modern dream romances echo another ancient Indian tale from the *Yogavasistha,* a collection of stories and sacred teachings from Kashmir. A princess dreams she has a thrilling encounter with a perfect lover in a place she does not recognize in waking life. She surfaces from the dream excited and happy, her nerve endings tingling. The princess sends for a wise man who is said to be an authority on dreams. The intuitive listens attentively as the princess tells her dream. When she is finished, he offers no interpretation. Instead, he hands her the piece of paper on which he was doodling while the princess talked. She gasps when she recognizes the face of her dream lover. The message is clear: her dream lover does not exist only in her dreams. He can be seen by others, and if this is so, he might even be found in waking life.

The princess embarks on a journey. She comes to a place she has never seen before, in physical reality, and finds herself inside the landscape of her dream. This is further confirmation that the dream can be manifested. She renews her search with even greater ardor. She embarks on a journey, and reaches a city she recognizes from her dream. She finds the house of her dream lover. When she bursts into his bedroom, he is waking from a dream of her.

It's fun to draw faces, as well as landscapes, from our dreams. Sometimes they belong to a separate reality, sometimes they also belong to our future. When they do belong to our future, it's interesting to see how closely the pictures match. And isn't it remotely possible that by drawing the dream (or sculpting it, or dancing it)—by giving it form and texture in physical reality—we help bring it into the world?

There is a powerful magician and dreamworker, in other popular Indian tales, whose name is Citralekha, which means "Sketcher of Pitchers." Her pencil is her magic wand; every time she creates an image we find it is the reflection of someone who truly exists. The scholar Wendy Doniger O'Flaherty comments: "The artist, midway between the yogin and the ordinary person, receives the dream passively but learns to control it actively, to transform it into a material object that all of us can see and touch."[3]

So if you have not found your mate in waking life, but dream of a splendid partner, don't despair. Like the Indian sages and heroines, take down the details and see if they can show you a path in waking life that could lead you to your dream date. Make a map, draw your dream lover's face. And if you are happy in a stable relationship, try to bring some of the adventure and romance from the dream into your life with your partner. If you dream of making love to a heavenly being, find that radiance and divinity in the eyes and the body of your partner. It's there.

FINDING YOUR DREAM HOME

The house, in our dreams, can be many things. It might be the house of the psyche, with basements and tunnels leading deep down into the subconscious, hidden rooms and unsuspected spaces—sometimes whole floors of possibility—waiting to be opened and explored. The dream house might be an analog for the body: the state of its plumbing and wiring or the condition of its furnace a metaphor for how our physical systems are working or not working. An unfamiliar house, in our dreams, might be a place in a separate reality or a place we might visit in the future in ordinary life. It might be a house where we will live in the future. It might be a *soul home,* the place where we truly belong.

If we can dream it, we can get there.

A passionate dreamworker recalls, "For many years I dreamed of homes and places with natural wood, beginning with a dream I worked with in the early 1980s. It was very profound and is alive today. Now our summer place in the Adirondacks is here in physical reality with pine paneled rooms and a cherry hardwood floor. When the sun sets in late afternoon, the big front room shimmers as if on fire with the light filtered through the pines."

A Place on the Lake

Here is how Mary dreamed her way to her place on the lake in Ohio:

For many years, she had lived in the beautiful Finger Lakes region of upstate New York. When her job took her to New York City, she kept a little cottage on the lake. When her work obliged her to relocate to Cleveland, she was quite uncomfortable about the move, which would put her out of range of her refuge. After some prospecting in the Cleveland area, she had despaired of locating the kind of quiet, natural setting where she had been at home.

In the midst of her preparations for the move, she had a dream she did not understand. In her dream, she was knitting an intricate, multicolored bedspread. A German shepherd pounced on the bedspread and started ripping it up.

After waking, she could not figure out the message—until she decided to ask the dog. She put herself in a relaxed state and asked him, "Why are you ripping up my knitting?"

The dog told her, "This is your inner life. If you don't take care of it, I'll rip it up."

This made sense to Mary, but it did not solve her housing problem.

As the time for the move approached, she picked up a set of my *Dream Gates* tapes, planning to listen to them on the long drive to Cleveland. She liked the suggestions about looking for an animal guide and using drumming to enter a conscious dream state. When she played the drumming session on the tapes, the German shepherd appeared and took her at once to her beloved cottage on the lake. The dog told her firmly that it was okay to let go, and that she would find what she was looking for.

In Cleveland, she found a condo to rent but remained very nervous as she went over for her appointment. She arrived early. As she parked her car in the shade, she saw a beautiful young girl walking a German shepherd outside her condo. The dog was the same size and coloring as the one in her dream.

A wrong turn on the way back took her to Lake Erie. She found herself at a small, quiet park—so quiet and protected it seemed like private land. She went to walk there by the lake at the weekend, and found two more German shepherds, one of them only a puppy. The puppy jumped up on her lap. She felt protected and at peace; she was deeply convinced a dream animal had helped to steer her to her new place on the lake.

I described in my book *Conscious Dreaming* how two series of dreams—totaling 17 individual recorded dreams—guided my move from a farm to a house on the hill in an old Hudson River city. The dreams not only showed me my future home before I had ever set eyes on it (or even thought of moving) they guided all the important details of the business side of the move, including where to go for a loan and whom to employ as an attorney. My dreams then showed me the deeper reason for my move: which was to bring dreamwork to where people lived, instead of isolating myself on my country acres.

More recently, I have been dreaming of a house that is very close to nature, a place built on one level around a spreading tree, with a creek running through it and the sea a short walk away. When I return here in dreams—both conscious journeys and sleep dreams—I frequently notice changes in the locale. New technology has been brought into my office, for example. I was recently delighted to find a Courtyard of Animals, with lively, life-size bronze statues of animals that have shared my dreaming. I am not sure whether this is a home where I will ever live in ordinary reality, but I greatly enjoy hanging out there, relaxing in the pool, eating lunch on the terrace, playing with my kids and their friends, reading the books I haven't written yet. We need a soul home like this, and we can bring its magic into our physical space even if we never succeed in finding it as a place of brick or shingles.

But don't be shy about asking that too. If you need a new home—a place that will satisfy your soul—ask your dreams to take you there, and then to show you the steps you'll need to take to get there from here. Be open to surprises. A man who attended one of my workshops was looking for a new office space. He had fairly firm ideas about what he wanted. He asked for a dream to show him how to get there. In his dream, his guide was a large, avuncular black man who reminded him of James Earl Jones. The black "broker" escorted him to a number of spaces that fitted his waking conception of what he needed, but he soon found them unattractive and confining. He slipped into a dream-within-the-dream in which he was in a place like a meditation garden, by a pond. He was so happy here that when he returned from his dream he decided to revise not only his office plans but his whole approach to work, get off the commercial fast track he had been on, and make room for nature and soul.

TAKE YOUR DREAM VACATION TONIGHT

I have a woman friend who enjoyed a two-week vacation in the US Virgin Islands in one night. She came back from a delicious, vividly sensuous dream with memories that engaged all of her senses: the smell of the fish on the barbecue, the feel of the sand between her toes, the sound of the waves, the taste of her dream lover's kiss. And she did not have to pay thousands of dollars for her vacation or wait for her bags at the airport. I told part of her story in a previous book.[4] The sequel came after I wrote that book, about three years after my friend had her dream of two weeks in one night. When she decided to remarry, her husband-to-be proposed that they spend their honeymoon on St John. When they got to the island, she found herself right inside her dreamscape, down to the smell of the fish on the barbecue.

A young man shared a similar experience, in which he spent a three-day vacation in Cancun in a single night. He reports, "It started out the day before we left and I packed up and everything and the next day we got there. We didn't take an airplane or anything. We were just there. We spent a whole day there and we spent a long time in this really neat aquarium and we went on a boat ride on a lake or a bay. The next day we went out of the hotel and down to a pool where there were some ancient stairs beneath the water, it looked so real. Then I realized that I needed to get on my shorts because I was wearing pants and it was 100 degrees out. I don't know how I lived for three days in one night but it sure was fun!"

How is three days in one night possible? Because in dreaming, we step outside time. In his celebrated dream journey, escorted by Gabriel, the prophet Mohammed travels through all the heavens and receives the whole text of the Koran—in less time than it took for a beaker of water that was knocked over at the start of the adventure to finish spilling.

If you are longing for a *real* break, but can't fly off to the Caribbean or Hawaii tonight, consider asking for a dream vacation. You could use a photograph as your way in. Pick a good one—white sand, waving palms or whatever you hunger for. Study it closely. Close your eyes and try seeing it clear behind your closed eyelids. Let it become more and more real. Then let yourself flow into that scene with all of your senses, and allow adventures to unfold. If you do this just before you're ready for sleep, you can direct yourself into a dream vacation that may last all night.

DREAMING THE WAY FOR THE ORGANIZATION

Delia was a career facilitator, employed by a powerful federal agency in Washington D.C. She was asked by a new department boss to facilitate a "brainstorming" session. The department was grappling with major technical challenges, centered on moves towards higher levels of automation, and the atmosphere in the office was bad. Some of the employees seemed listless and demoralized, or embroiled in personality conflicts.

"That office needed healing," Delia recalled.

The problem with brainstorming sessions is that too frequently the people engaged in them are working with the same parts of the brain that harbor their everyday thinking and patterns of expectation: the parts that are most resistant to a radical shift in perception.

This was reflected during the first day of the retreat Delia arranged for the department staff. Nasty personality issues surfaced early in the day. By the end of it, many of the people at the gathering were yawning and fidgeting and looking at the clock. No one had come up with any creative ideas about the major issues on the agenda.

Then Delia took the plunge.

"Why don't we all relax, go home and dream on it?"

This brought raised eyebrows and bemused smiles. Was Delia making a joke?

She explained that dreaming has facilitated creative breakthroughs in many, many areas, from the invention of the sewing machine needle to the winning strategy in some of the world's decisive battles. Why not ask for dream guidance on the office problems?

"We've got nothing to lose," the department boss nodded thoughtfully.

Delia outlined the simple techniques for dream incubation that she had studied in my book *Conscious Dreaming:* write down your theme or question, put it under your pillow, and be ready, when you wake, to write down any dreams you remember and any feelings you have about them. Even if the dream at first seems to have nothing to do with the question, it will almost always prove to contain something helpful and relevant—and sometimes the solution that eluded your waking mind.

The staffers left the first day of the retreat with mixed feelings. Few of them had ever recorded dreams. Several professed *never* to have remembered dreams. Some had been scared by nightmares they did not care to revisit. To all of them, the idea of sharing dreams in the office environment was wildly exotic—and not altogether welcome.

The next morning, Delia asked everyone to gather in a circle and take turns to share dreams. The initial results were disappointing. "I don't remember my dreams" was a common contribution. Some staffers indicated they were not comfortable about sharing their dreams because the material was too "personal." Others reported dark, disturbing dreams and nightmares, some of which seemed to reflect the poor relations in the department—and a measure of performance anxiety.

The department boss surprised everyone by saying, "I have a dream I really want to share with all of you."

In the boss's dream, the department received the Chairman's Award for Excellence—the top honor in a vast and powerful federal agency—because of the way its staff had come together, as a team, to integrate new technology and improve human relations. The department chief proceeded to outline some specific new ideas for team performance that were also the gift of the dream.

"This dream galvanized the whole group," Delia reported with deserved satisfaction. "By the end of the day, everyone was pulling together and had gotten through an amazing amount of planning. It was as if they had all made that dream *their* dream."

As a result of the breakthrough made that day, the dream came true: nine months later the department received the Chairman's Award for Excellence.

Delia's story is a powerful example of how the dreamwork can be used to create (or *re*create) the future in many group environments, and to build more creative communities. You might consider sharing this example of what dreaming on a problem can accomplish with your own colleagues, and see what you can dream up together. Do you find it hard to imagine your employer sending you and your workmates home to dream a solution?

I have the sense that things are changing, and can be helped to change even faster, for the better.

It may not be as difficult as we tend to imagine to explain these things to people in places of influence in mainstream society. Every corporation, government agency and faculty I have ever come across would support the idea that fostering creativity is a good thing. However, they often fail to pay sufficient attention to the techniques that support creativity. Dreamwork and dream incubation are wonderful engines of creativity.

As we have discovered, dreams help us see things from new perspectives, bring different elements together and tap into a deeper source. They give us blueprints for better and attainable realities. I am quoting the phrase "attainable reality" from Anjali Hazarika Ph.D., the director of the National Petroleum Management Program in India, who has been leading seminars for top Indian business and government executives in creative dreamwork for years.[5]

BRINGING DREAMS TO THE WORKPLACE

In the workplace, we can use dream insights to handle colleagues and employers better. A woman friend of mine is the creative director at a powerful advertising agency. She's also the one who tends to be left holding the fort when her male bosses go off to play golf or dine at fancy restaurants with the top clients.

One of her male bosses decided to cut my friend's department by two people.

She asked for dream guidance.

She dreamed she was facing her employer with "pages and pages" of account information, as if she were head of the accounting department.

She decided to discuss her dream with the head of the accounting department, who told my friend that he, too, had trouble communicating with their employer. The accountant observed that the boss refused to pay attention to detail, and frequently got things wrong because he refused to go through "pages and pages" of information.

The dream message began to shine through.

With the accountant's help, my friend wrote a three line memo detailing the profits her department had achieved in the last two quarters, and the projected increase in profits that would result from keeping the two positions her boss had decided to eliminate.

The boss whipped through the memo, and told her, "No problem." She saved the two jobs.

The Woman Who Brought Her Wolf to Work

In one of my dream workshops, Gail met her wolf. This happened during a drumming session in which participants were invited to go on a conscious dream journey to connect with an animal guardian. It was a very vivid experience. Gail found herself reconnecting with a younger, vital version of herself, swirling into a primal dance around a campfire. A wolf's face loomed out of the shadows. She was nervous of the wolf to begin with, and pictured herself flying far away, high up above the world. But something told her, clearly and firmly, that she must accept the power of the wolf, and the part of herself that was like the wolf.

> I am shifting into wolf . . . In the wolf body, I feel a sense of muscle power and strength, running and rolling, leaping and smelling. I have never felt this kind of physical power in my body, either sleeping or waking. I am very excited about the physical power surge when I became the wolf. It makes me think that even if the body ages, I can experience youthful power in other ways.

She asked the wolf for guidance with a health issue. Her physician had just told her that symptoms she had developed might be a sign of Lupus. In her lupine form, she was quite certain this diagnosis was wrong, and that there was no serious problem.

> I see the wolf burrowing and snuggling down for a nap in the sun, already feeling healed . . . I become the

sleeping wolf, take a psychic nap and feel wonderful on awakening when the drum stops.

Gail's doctor told her the following week that the pathology report ruled out Lupus. He now assessed her symptoms as an "unspecified" allergic reaction, "nothing to worry about."

Throughout that week, Gail continued to feel very close to the wolf energy. She ran with the wolf along jogging paths, and enjoyed the sense of feeding the wolf when she ate meat. She took her wolf with her to the office, and this produced very interesting results. "Once you have not only met a wolf, but felt the raw power of movement and strength in running, and experienced the feel of grass on fur, and seen with new eyes, you develop a new perspective. The week following the workshop, I not only led our management meetings but dealt with in-house opponents in a no-nonsense manner." She had been having knock-down battles with an aggressive male, one of her superiors in the department. By week's end, she had noticed a major change in him. He was pleasant, complimented her on her work performance, and actually came seeking her advice. "I almost felt sorry for him," Gail commented. "He did not know with whom he was really dealing."

When we are in touch with our animal spirits, we do move differently and have extra sensors, and others sense the change even when they can't explain to themselves what they are picking up. If we are walking with the wolf or the tiger, people no longer see us as vulnerable. I think it is especially helpful for women, dealing with male assertiveness or aggression in the workplace—or anywhere else—to draw consciously on the energy and instincts of the dream animals. All of us benefit from this connection, and all of the animals have gifts for us. Sometimes it's good (especially for overblown egos) to connect with one of the small, burrowing animals that knows when to lay low and stay close to the earth.

BRINGING DREAMS INTO FAMILY LIFE

Children are naturals at dreaming true—until the adult world crushes them under the weight of mockery, denial or simple inattention. We are missing huge possibilities to build creative and highly *functional* families because we rarely make room for dream-sharing in our family lives. This is as sad for parents as for kids, because children (especially in the early years when they are very close to the dreamworld from which they have come) are wonderful teachers about the nature and possibilities of dreaming and they often bring us vital messages—if we will only listen.

Community dreamworker and consciousness explorer Jean Galliano had a childhood experience that is an object lesson. When she was twelve, Jean dreamed of the death of her maternal grandfather. Her dream was synchronous with his passing, and gave her foreknowledge of the phone call that would confirm his death. She woke everyone in the house, yelling, "Answer the phone! Pop's dead!"

She repeated these words, over and over, in a trancelike state.

Her parents splashed water in her face, trying to snap her out of it.

"Pop's *not* dead!" they insisted.

Then the phone rang. The call brought the news that Pop had died around the same time Jean had called out.

The other members of Jean's family were astonished. But it did not make them any more receptive to her gifts. Jean recalls, "They were so freaked out everyone went into denial." She had more dreams of Pop, and some of them seemed to contain important messages. Her mother told her, "You just want to see him. He's not there."

The collective pressure began to take its toll.

One night, when Jean received another dream visitation from her grandfather, she told Pop, "You're not here. *I can't see you.*"

This is a moving example of how the adult world—often for well-intentioned but misguided reasons—moves to crush the dream gifts of children. The theme reverberates through C.S. Lewis' visionary *Chronicles of Narnia.* As the children grow older, and conform more closely to the thinking and attitudes of the grown-up world, they cease to be able to see Aslan, the White Lion. When they finally catch sight of Aslan again, he at first appears like a wraith, transparent and insubstantial. They have to learn to adjust their senses (and their sense of reality) in order to reestablish contact with this most wonderful and powerful spiritual guardian.

Jean Galliano survived the widespread adult attempt to drill it into children that dreams are not real and that spirits do not speak to us; she has become an energetic dreamworker in the Philadelphia area. Many of our kids eventually buckle and bend under the pressure. Told again and again that what they see and experience is not "real" they end up by adjusting their sight until Aslan becomes invisible.

"I was a fine child," wrote Coleridge, "but they changed me."

How do we bring the gifts of dreaming into our family? As in any other context, we begin by creating a space where dreams can be safely shared, a space where we will pay attention. Ideally, we would do this at the breakfast table, but most of us parents have to rush to work and our kids have to get to school. So we can begin by making a little time in the evening or at weekends. It starts by asking, "What did you dream?" It continues with figuring out something to do with the dream.

BRINGING DREAMS TO SCHOOL

We need to bring dreams into our schools. Here are some of the reasons:

1. Sharing dreams builds tremendous communication skills and interpersonal gifts.
2. Recording and telling dreams builds the gifts of storytelling and storymaking.
3. Keeping a dream journal is a tremendous creative adventure that turns people effortlessly into writers and researchers.
4. Dream incubation (asking dreams for guidance) is a wonderful engine for creative breakthroughs in all fields.
5. Many important scientific and technical discoveries (from the invention of the sewing machine needle to Einstein's Special Theory of Relativity) have flowed directly from dreams or dreamlike states.
6. Through remembering and sharing dreams, we move beyond barriers of intolerance and prejudice. We come to understand other people's situations and viewpoints and build bridges between our communities.
7. Dreaming, we are constantly rehearsing for future situations. School kids can even use dreams to prepare for exams—I have seen many do it with excellent results!
8. By sharing dreams, we can safely talk about things it might be hard to communicate—or even recognize clearly—in a different way. This is often vitally helpful and liberating for kids who may need to communicate something about a family/authority/peergroup situation but don't feel they can speak out safely.

Could we "sell" the idea of dream centers in schools to educators in Western countries? Why not try? We certainly need them. In the school environment, a place to share dreams might be all of the following things:

* a place of gentle and effective counseling and nurturing;
* a center of personal growth and vocational guidance;
* a center for the creative arts;

* a hub of creative innovation in all areas—including science, technology, and social reform;
* a wonderful place to bring alive the study and appreciation of folklore and mythology;
* a place for building interpersonal and communications skills.

If we give kids a space where they can share and celebrate their dreams, we give them a place where they can also be helped to develop their personal vision of what the best they can do and be and give—and then find the tools to bring their dream into manifestation. This is very practical stuff. It gives us courage and energy and inner resources for the journey.

Where do we begin? How about encouraging projects of the role of dreams in scientific and creative discovery? How about giving kids materials on how dreams guided escaping slaves to safe stations along the Underground Railroad? I can't think of any more powerful and *practical* evidence that we can "dream our dream"—except what will come as each of us starts *doing* it.

There is a final, powerful reason for bringing dreaming into our schools. Its urgency has been brought home by the rage and frustration that has exploded into violent tragedy in several recent episodes in American schools. It was expressed to me very clearly by my youngest daughter when she was nine. I asked Sophie what she thought about bringing dream-sharing into schools.

Sophie wisely asked, "Why don't you ask kids what they think?"

"Fine," I responded. "Let's start with you."

She thought for a moment, then said, "I think if we gave kids a place to share dreams, we'd give them a safe place to tell their troubles."

Sophie is right. Our kids need that. And so do we.

chapter nineteen

DREAMING AND FUTURE SCIENCE

We need a new science to explore the objective side of human consciousness and the subjective side of matter: a science willing to embrace both objective and subjective avenues to discovery while recognizing the legitimacy of individual experience.

—WOLFGANG PAULI, NOBEL PRIZE–WINNING PHYSICIST

In physics, the nineteenth century was an age of increasingly confident materialism. As they made discoveries that rapidly expanded man's mastery of the physical world, physicists became more and more certain they were about to produce a Grand Unified Theory of Everything. All mysteries would be dispersed by their blazing spotlight; the innermost clockwork of the universe—with or without a Creator—would be laid bare.

Einstein exploded that bubble in 1905, starting a revolution in physics that has still not run its course. The physics of the twentieth century was a science of uncertainty, improvisation and wonder. It revealed that behind the seemingly solid surface of things is an incredible dance of energy, or pure consciousness. It showed us that time and space, as we experience them on the way to the office or to pick up the kids from school, are not conditions for any other kind of life in the universe, merely human conveniences (although they often seem more like inconveniences). By the end of the twentieth century, after other mathematicians and physicists had picked and pulled at Einstein's equations, the agreed "laws" of physics tell us the following:

* Time travel into the future is possible.
* Time travel into the past is not forbidden by the current laws of physics (although many scientists, like Einstein himself, flatly refuse to believe that it is possible for humans).
* Travel beyond the speed of light (contrary to one of Einstein's most tenacious beliefs) is possible.
* There is no firm separation between subject and object in the universe. The observer and the "outside world" he thinks he is observing are enmeshed together. Indeed, at subatomic levels, it is the act of observation that plucks events from a soup of possibilities.
* Humans have an innate ability to communicate and influence people and objects across a distance. This has been proven in laboratory tests, but probably goes on all the time.
* The mind is nonlocal. Consciousness acts outside the brain and outside spacetime.
* Any event that occurs in the universe is immediately available anywhere as information.
* Our experience of reality, like our experience of linear time, is a mental construct. Change the construct, and we change our world.

I stress that these are insights of twentieth-century physics. Other branches of science, over the past hundred years, seem to have inherited the pall of Victorian materialism. This is notably the case in biology, where a zeal worthy of the original Dr. Frankenstein still drives the effort to crack the code of life and character by gene-stripping and brain vivisection, and to play God through cloning and swapping organs around as if organs and bodies are only machines made of meat. The moving experience of my friend Claire Sylvia, an incandescent dancer whose body lives through the gift of the heart and lungs of an (initially) unknown donor, should give our modern Frankensteins pause. In her dreams, she discovered the source of her donated organs, and realized in the process that in some sense two souls are now sharing her body. She has honored this realization in many ways, reminding us that a mastery of body parts is no triumph, if detached from a relationship with soul.

To pick up the main thread: Twentieth-century physics showed us a universe that baffles common sense, a universe that operates along utterly different lines from one in which the commuter train from Grand Central leaves at 6:05 P.M. (if we're lucky). Yet the findings of leading-edge physics, over the century Einstein shook up, have brought us scientific confirmation of the worldview of shamans, mystics and dreamers, who have always known that there is a place beyond surface reality where all things are connected, a place beyond time where all times are accessible, and that consciousness generates worlds. Physicist David Bohm tells us about an "implicate order" within which all the events and circumstances of our "explicate" world lie "enfolded."[1] Bohm and his exegesists enthuse about a holographic model that compares our experienced world to a vast hologram projected from a deeper source. These are provocative and probing ideas that have helped to open many previously locked-up minds to the many levels or "frequency domains" (Karl Pribram) of the multidimensional universe. But let's not get trapped in the analogies. The comparison of the universe to something manufactured by human intelligence (holographic laser photography) has a flaw at its center, as obvious as an earlier era's comparison of the workings of the universe to the mechanism of a clock. Nothing made by man can encompass what is made by the Source that is his maker.

Twentieth-century physics gave us the atom bomb. However hard its equations are for the average brain to assimilate, however remote a quantum decision may seem from an action in everyday, human-sized life, this is a physics that works. It could yet destroy the world that produced it.

How do we bring all of this together with our lived experience, our human needs, and our hopes for world peace and a gentle upward evolution of our species?

Through dreaming.

Dreaming, we are at home in quantum reality, where the act of looking brings things into being. Dreaming, we discover the existence of alternate realities and parallel worlds—including dimensions that escape human conceptions of form—and can actively explore them. Dreaming, we very easily confirm that consciousness is never confined to the body and that we can reach people and objects at a distance. Dreaming, we are time jumpers, able to visit (and possibly influence) both past and future.

As dreamers, we can achieve experiential understanding of the multidimensional universe that science is discovering.

As active dreamers and dream journalists, we can also contribute in important ways to what will be—if we are lucky—the foremost contribution of the twenty-first century to science and evolution: the emergence of a true science of consciousness.

A MATHEMATICIAN'S CHALLENGE

Research mathematicians, like active dreamers, are often driven by the sense that there is a deeper logic to be discovered. In pure mathematics, as in dream exploration, you'll get nowhere of interest if you stick with existing theories. An unsolved problem in higher mathematics is like a mysterious dream; it must be approached on its own terms, and approaching it this way may take us far beyond previous levels of understanding. In an important article, mathematician Patrick Morton, a professor at Wellesley College, observes of both disciplines that "in the process of solving one problem, another whole avenue of investigation opens up and something beautiful falls into your lap." He adds that "the creative process of dream interpretation can lead to insights in a shared reality, just the way different mathematicians' insights and images and proofs combine to form the shared reality of mathematics."[2]

Morton asks a most provocative question: "In science we base our understanding of physical reality on mathematics. What would happen if we based our understanding of reality on our dreams instead?"

I would like to offer some responses. I offer these with unfeigned humility, because I am no scientist; any book that borders on "hard" science gives me a headache and I need physics-literate friends to interpret even the simpler ones. All the same, I am a rather active dreamer and I have been leading parties of dream explorers into the alternate realities that physicists and mathematicians speculate about for many years. We have experiences in perception that give us some first-hand clues as to what the holoverse is like when perceived from inside the fifth dimension, and possibly higher dimensions. I remember the thrill I experienced when I first noticed I was observing a whole room full of people from every angle at once, simultaneously, as if my awareness at that moment was at every point on the circumference of a sphere that contained the whole space. Some of us have the experience of perceiving a pulsing object we believe to be a tesseract—a "cube of a cube," as Mrs. Whatsit explains to the children in *A Wrinkle in Time*—not the kind of thing you see every day on the street with your eyes open. As in my dream with the Einstein figure, where the landscape could be folded so points normally separate in space and time were instantly connected, some of us have dreamed possibilities of traveling without moving through hyperspace.

Here are some examples of the contribution active dreamers can make, based on experiments and adventures I have been conducting in my workshops and dream circles over many years. Where appropriate, I have suggested guidelines for further projects, including several in which you can participate from your own home.

THE DREAM JOURNALIST'S CONTRIBUTION

The philosopher of science, Thomas Kuhn, observed that we get a paradigm shift when the accumulation of "anomalies" forces the abandonment of old scientific paradigms and the adoption of new ones. Dream journalists can contribute mightily to the emergence and understanding of new paradigms in science. Here are some of the things we can contribute:

* Case studies of interactive dreaming that will provide mutually confirming evidence that consciousness is never confined to the brain.
* Documented and witnessed reports of dream precognition, telepathy and other psi phenomena that will establish that these are entirely natural events and that our everyday expe-

rience is not the only engagement with time and space that is possible.

* Serial dreams in which we return to locales where we seem to be leading a continuous life as our present selves, but with some different elements in the scene. For example: we may be married to a different person, living in a different town, following a different line of work. Serial dreams of this type may provide strong experiential evidence for the "parallel universes" hypothesis.
* Serial dreams in which we enter the situation or perspective of people living in other times or dimensions who are clearly not our familiar selves. These experiences may be suggestive of our connectedness, in our multidimensional identity, with a vast family of consciousness in many time periods and frequency domains.

RESEARCH INSIDE DREAMS

More than studies *about* dreams, we need active, dedicated research *inside* the dreamstate. This will require training many more people in the core techniques of conscious dreaming and shamanic journeying, as well as in recording their dreams and working with their journals. We will need people prepared to journey deeper and deeper into the dream matrix (I do not mean "The Matrix" in the movie sense) where forms are generated, who can then study how these emerging forms and images in turn provide templates for physical events, including events inside our physical bodies. In group explorations I have been leading, we have been actively researching many possibilities, including these:

* Distant action and distant healing;
* Time travel;

* Changing the cellular memory of the body;
* Exploring different frequency domains and the conditions for travel between them;
* Parallel universes;
* The connectedness of the multidimensional self with other identities and experiences;
* Creating and re-creating realities from inside the dreamspace.

GROUP DREAM TRAVEL: THE POMPEII TRIP

To give you a more vivid sense of the possibilities, I will share a report from one evening meeting of my regular dream circle. We gathered in a pleasant space in a very ordinary-looking office building a few miles from my home in upstate New York. We agreed to go on a group excursion. We decided it might be fun to go to the Bay of Naples and take a look at Vesuvius and the ruins of Pompeii, which a friend of mine in another town had independently proposed as a good target location.[3] We were in the mood for play, and decided we would set ourselves no specific agenda except to go there—on a dream outing—take a look around, enjoy a mini-vacation, and share our travelogues.

There were twelve of us that evening. Everyone except me lay down on the floor in the dark—relieved only by a candle—after looking at some photographs of the general area. I sat up, drumming for the group for slightly less than 15 minutes.

Many members of the group reported flying or hovering over the Bay of Naples. More than half the group (a) had strong impressions of the density of the oil and other effluvia from shipping and human waste that appear to have made much of the Bay unswimmable and yet (b) were surprised by the green-blue color of the outlying waters. We had impressions of each other's movements and focus of interest as we fanned out to explore the sites and the volcano. Though time travel was not on our explicit agenda, most members of the group had strong experiences of traveling into the lives of people who may have lived near the volcano before and during the famous eruption of 79 AD, but also at other times. I observed a possible episode taking place at the time of the lesser eruption of 1944, during World War II. I also found myself drawn *forward* through time to the scene of a possible future eruption in 2023, with lava flowing into the sea.

I watched one member of our group focus intently on a particular house, studying something on its façade. I wondered whether Wanda would bring us back a detailed architectural report (both she and her husband are architectural historians). She brought back something more interesting. Here is how Wanda wrote up her report:

> Thursday, September 23, 1999, 9:00 P.M.
> Dream Group
>
> *Assignment:* Journey to Pompeii, Naples, Vesuvius and bring back images. Internet photos were passed around as an aid to journeying.
>
> *Report:* I immediately found myself in a mass of terrified running people who were fleeing the molten lava flowing over houses, streets, people, destroying everything in its path. A mass of people had made their way to a city gate, but either the gate was barred or the sheer mass and weight of the crowd made it impossible to open the gate. I focused on a mother with two children. She was being crushed by the crowd but was screaming because one of her children had fallen and had been trampled to death. She picked the second child up, a girl, and began

> to clamber over boulders that ran up along the gate. Other people found the same path. As she climbed I looked up beyond her to a small house, very small with a front door and so narrow there were no windows in the front facade. Above the door was a ram's head. I believe an elderly woman was still inside, sitting very still, very afraid. The house threw me for a moment back into a dream I had in the early 90s when I had seen a small house with a ram's head above the door.

We agreed that Wanda would check into whether there was archeological evidence of the house with the ram's head, and the possible significance of this symbol in Roman iconography—for example, in the popular cult of the Egyptian god Ammon, sometimes shown with the head or horns of a ram.

Rosemary also seemed to arrive in the midst of the eruption:

> As I landed on the tile floor, it started to pitch about. Soon I was joined by two children. As I looked about people were screaming and running about and buildings were collapsing. I asked what to do. The children and I jumped into the oven that you had a picture of. Inside there were many people standing around the circumference. In the center was a whirling cyclone of light and we were all holding hands and watching it.

Ann had the intriguing experience of entering an ancient circle of dreamers:

> I found myself at a courtyard that was tiled in the pattern of one of the pictures you passed around. The building was a large temple or official governmental building. There were several people there, the leader, an

> older male, and a group seated to his sides and behind him, mostly women. They welcomed me and invited me into the building, I was free to explore the rooms and gardens. I did this briefly but came back to the group and took a seat behind the leader. Our purpose there was to hear dreams that people from the community brought to us and we would then give our opinions and give guidance based on the dream. The dream brought before us was of a man who dreamed he was bitten by a horse. He was very concerned about the reality of the dream and wanted to know how to avoid this in waking life.

Sara, who had been to Pompeii, found herself following a more personal agenda, and used the group journey as an opportunity to take a dream vacation:

> My glimpses of Pompeii took a selfish turn during that journey. I started off at the church where my parents were married and then continued into the ruins. As I walked the surroundings came alive and I could see it as it was before the eruption. People were going about their business. I arrived at the market place and decided to check out the volcano. As I was cruising down into the mouth of the mountain I realized that I didn't know how much time I had and decided to pay a dream visit to the love of my life (and maybe many other life times). I felt safe since the rest of the group was on the same continent with me. I went and saw him sleeping, called to him and he joined me on the rest of the journey. We came back to the vicinity of Pompeii and Naples. We ended up walking wearing very formal 50s dinner wear. He wore a white tux and I had on this gold off-the-shoulder gown. We strolled under the palm trees

along one of the walkways of Amalfi. It was great and we caught up some of the 20 years we've missed. We came back to the foot of the volcano. I could see some of our group. He decided to go back before we got to them. Then the recall sounded. It was a good mini-vacation.

Group dream travel can be enormous fun and unlike package tours it does not cost a penny. You can share experiences with your fellow-travelers in fifteen minutes that you may never get to share in a week of ordinary travel, and you don't have to listen to them snoring in the next room.

Group dream travel is likely to play a critical role in the emergence of a true dream science. This kind of experiment—which Yeats would have called "mutual visioning"—can provide further evidence of the objective reality of dream experiences. One type of evidence comes from the interactive dreaming. Most of us in the group were satisfied we were able to travel to a specific location and bring back specific and mutually confirming impressions of the sites—and each other's movements—that had not been planted by suggestion. Yes, we used photographs as an initial focusing or direction-finding device. But the old, grainy black-and-white shots I passed around were evocative more than representational. The favorite image among members of the group was a photo of a black-and-white tiled floor, so artfully constructed that you might have sworn you were looking at an array of three-dimensional cubes. What group members saw and experienced took them far beyond any images they had previously viewed, including the memories of two group members who had visited Pompeii and Herculaneum many years before, in ordinary reality.

Further evidence of objective reality of these experiences can be found in the detail and specificity of individual reports, both in the "remote viewing" aspect and in the "historical discovery" department. Sightings and specific data could be checked by research encompassing history, geography, iconography and archeology—and vulcanology (on the chance of a twenty-first century eruption of Vesuvius). To verify my own sightings, for example, I needed to check out two names that came through to me quite distinctly, the names of a Roman landowner and of a German officer who was in Naples during World War II.

It's wonderful to be able to find corroboration and documentation of this kind. However, inside the experience itself, there comes a moment when we simply *know* this is real, and we are *there.* During the trip to Vesuvius, this moment came for me when I paused to look at a familiar but puzzling object that seemed to be hanging in a Roman house. Purplish in color, fleshy yet with stretch marks. It took me a long moment before I realized it was a large and appetizing fig. When I recognized the fig—so palpably and sensually *there*—I entered fully into the lives of the Roman landowner and the woman with dark ringlets in the room beyond.

All of this was great fun. If there is any science in it, that is the glaze on the fig. Don't we always get our best results when we enter into a state of creative play?

When we forget to have fun, it's often because we get snagged in guilt and regret over something in the past. Instead of moping about wishing we could change the past, we should practice "wishcraft" by using conscious dreaming techniques to see whether we actually *can* change the past. This has been the focus of some of my recent group experiments, and the findings to date are discussed in the next chapter.

chapter twenty

CHANGING THE PAST

If at first the idea is not absurd, then there is no hope for it.

—Albert Einstein

One of the most extraordinary claims made by Seth, the entity channeled by Jane Roberts, is that by changing our beliefs, we can change the past as well as the future. We are not at the mercy of the past, Seth insists, unless we believe that we are. When we alter our present beliefs, we actually reprogram our past. In *The Nature of Personal Reality,* Seth maintains that we can even alter the cellular memory of the body, and that this is the key to some cases of spontaneous healing.[1]

This flies in the face of our common understanding that the past is sealed and cannot be altered, that "all our tears" cannot wash out one word of it. I was born in a certain year, had chicken pox at seven, fell in love, got married and divorced, got hired and fired, and that's an end of it—right? If I could travel back to the past and start changing things, I would run up against the "Back to the Future" problem; my tampering could change something that would prevent me from being born. And if I am not born in the "future," how can I travel back to the "past"? This is known as the Grandfather Paradox among theorists. If I go back in time and kill my grandfather, I won't be born and consequently will not be able to go back in time, and so on. It makes sense, doesn't it?

Yet Seth's opinions—and even the idea of time travel into the past—are not in conflict with current science. Einstein's special theory of relativity allowed for travel into the future, but ruled out travel into the past. Then in 1949, Einstein's friend and protégé Kurt Gödel, one of the greatest mathematicians of his century, published solutions to Einstein's general relativity gravitational field equations that appear to suggest the possibility of time travel to the past. Since Gödel's remarkable theoretical findings, a number of reputable physicists, including Kip Thorne of Caltech and Igor Novikov of the Lebedev Institute in Moscow, have been working on the construction of actual time machines, taking a popular fantasy theme into the laboratory. Paul Nahin contends that "right now known physics doesn't forbid time travel" and the challenge for people who can't stand the idea is to discover the "new" physics that would rule it out.[2]

Personally, I remain skeptical about both the practicability and the potential benefits of traveling *physically* into the past. The notion conjures up dark fantasies of Nazi scientists trying to smuggle the secret of the A-bomb back to Hitler in 1939. What interests me is the possibility of changing the past, in an authentic and helpful way, through consciousness, including dream travel.

Fascinating recent laboratory research suggests that changing the past by exercising our mental powers today is indeed possible, at least on the level of micro-reality. For the big picture, we'll need to turn to dream travelers.

RETRO-CAUSALITY IN THE LAB

While graduate students at Caltech try to figure out the physics of a time machine, some other very interesting experiments are being conducted that suggest that—whether or not we can go back to the past, body and all—we may be able to influence the past through mental powers. The fancy names for this area of research are "retro-causality" and "retro-psychokinesis."

The Two-Way Clock

You are sitting in front of your personal computer, looking at a clock face on the screen. The clock looks homely enough, but it doesn't show time in the normal way. The minute hand swings backwards as well as forwards, at wildly varying speeds. When the minute hand moves forward, the clock hands are blue. When it swings backward, the clock hands turn red.

You are instructed to use your mental powers to make the minute hand move only clockwise. You are pleased when it swings forward to the quarter-past position. But then it jumps back and turns red. Gritting your teeth, you try again. As you stare at the clock, willing it to run clockwise, you are pleased to see the minute hand jump to the half-past position. You give a whoop when your glaring seems to drive it all the way round the clock face, and the hour hand moves forward.

The clock on the screen is a clever disguise for a "random" flow of data that is being fed into your computer by an electronic binary number generator that spews out sequences of ones and zeroes. The minute hand on the clock face advances with every "one" but ticks back with every "zero." The further the minute hand shifts, the further the data stream is departing from the statistically probable result of an equal number of ones and zeroes. Your effort to exert your mental power to shift the stream in one direction is a typical example of an experiment in psychokinesis.

What makes *this* experiment interesting is that you are trying to change something that has already happened. The data being fed into your computer was prerecorded, but not observed. By the rules of mainstream science, it is impossible to change that data. But researchers at the University of Kent in England claim to have demonstrated the impossible. Peter Moore and his fellow researchers at the "retro-psychokinesis project" conducted on-line experiments (like the "clock" experiment I tried) with more than 1,000 subjects. Moore believes that his findings offer compelling evidence that our present thoughts can influence the past—at least if the past is *unobserved.* He claims that the chance of his retro-psychokinesis results being produced by accident is one in 630 billion.[3]

The University of Kent project built on the work of German parapsychologist Helmut Schmidt in San Antonio in 1992. Schmidt used a group of martial arts students as his subjects. He showed them prerecorded random numbers via an electronic display. The numbers had been generated months before by an apparatus that monitored radioactive decay; readings acquired in this way are widely agreed to be as truly "random" as anything observable in nature. The martial arts students were instructed to use their "mental influence" to change the visual display, whose behavior was determined by the prerecorded numbers. In this way, they would supposedly be influencing the statistical distribution of the numbers themselves. A significant "bias" was found in the numbers' patterns at the end of the experiments, one that had a less than 1 in 1,000 probability of occurring by chance.

How are these things possible? One scientific theory involves "quantum superposition." According to this model, a radioactive atom—like those that generated the numbers in the San Antonio and University of Kent experiments—can exist in two states simultaneously. In one state, radioactive decay has occurred; in the second, it has not. The atom is forced into a single state only when the decay is observed by a human observer. That moment of resolution came about, in the experiments, when human viewers looked at the electronic displays.[4]

RELEASING ENERGY TRAPPED IN THE PAST

Let's go beyond the lab work into the science of *experience.* We can enter the past with our consciousness. We can revisit scenes from our earlier lives and bring back memories that are long buried. Sometimes, when we do this, we can achieve closure on important issues that have remained unresolved, and release energy that was wasted on denial or repression, as any sensitive therapist well understands. Sometimes we can go further. We can bring back a piece of our soul—a part of our vital energy that left us because of pain or grief or simply because we were living the wrong kind of life and something that was bright and good in us became disgusted and flew away. There is an old Persian story about a king who lost his radiant soul-energy, which the Persians call *xvarnah* and which belongs to a true king, because he told lies. Every time he told a lie, his radiant energy separated from him, like a falcon that flew from his heart, flapping its wings. Finally the winged brightness left him altogether; he sickened and lost his throne.

Many of us understand the inner meaning of this story.

A Canadian woman asked me for help because she felt she had lost the part of herself that could know joy and express love. I asked her to record her dreams for a week before we met, and to bring me what she could catch. When we met for our session, she was embarrassed because the only dream she had been able to recall was a tiny fragment. She was in a room—she wasn't sure where—looking at three Post-It notes on a table. The notes were large in size, and in different colors, but the writing was faded and she couldn't make it out.

I asked her to relax. We spent a while simply relaxing into the flow of the breath. Then I asked her to let the scene from her dream come up on her mental screen, and become strong. I helped her go back inside the dream, and suddenly she was *there.* She now realized she was inside the living room of a house where she had lived in Montreal twenty years before. As she walked around the room, she made an inventory of the furnishings. The room was stuffy. She had never liked it much; she said it was hard to breathe there. I asked her to go to the table and look at the Post-It notes. She now realized there was someone else in the room, her ex-husband. He was oblivious to her. She inspected the notes. The colors became brighter and the text leaped out in big letters. Now she could read the typed messages. The first read in bold capitals, "YOU CAN DO IT." They were all about living with heart, and trusting life.

She realized that she had left her ability to love and to trust in that airless room for twenty years. I asked her what she needed to do. She told me, "I need to bring my heart out of that room and put it back in my body." She gathered up the messages and made the motion of bringing them into her heart. As her hands crossed over the place of her heart, we both saw a sweet and gentle light shine out from her heart center. She trembled, eyes shining, and told me, "Something has just come back. Something that was missing for twenty years."

It was her dream that gave her the key. It showed her which room from her earlier life she needed to reenter. She changed the past by releasing something that belonged with her in the present. Her life has been richer and fuller since. She looks younger, and she listens to her heart.

CHANGING THE CELLULAR MEMORY OF THE BODY

What about that amazing and thrilling suggestion from Seth that we can actually change the cellular memory of our bodies? Is it really possible to achieve release from the gene code and the karma of this lifetime? Can the body be taught to "forget" the history of a disease, and with it the disease itself?

These questions call for active exploration rather than theoretical discussion. My hopes that the answer to all three may be "Yes!" is growing as I work with people who are willing to work with their personal dream images and embark on their own journeys of healing. This is the subject of a future book on dream healing, but I will share one provocative report here:

The Man with Blue Tattoos

Jackson had been battling liver cancer for two years. While he was still physically strong and looked quite healthy, his medications had produced no improvement in his condition. He embarked on a series of conscious dream journeys to seek ways in which he might be able to advance his own healing.

The first of these experiences was quite terrifying. In a place of the dead, he encountered his angry father, who had died still cursing him for his alternative lifestyle. Jackson's father slashed at him with an arm that had turned into a gigantic crab's claw. When Jackson thought about that horrific image, he remembered that the Latin word for crab is *cancer*. The dream encounter seemed to be telling him that his father's rage—and maybe his genetic inheritance—had contributed to his illness.

Deeply disturbed by the continuing conflict with his father, Jackson resolved to journey further back through his bloodlines, to get in touch with previous generations of his family and ascertain whether some form of healing was available there. In a highly vivid waking dream, Jackson found himself in a wild northern landscape he felt to be somewhere north of Hadrian's Wall. He was confronted by a hairy, muscular man who was almost naked. The man's skin was an intricate maze of blue tattoos. He spoke to Jackson sharply in a language the dreamer did not comprehend. Jackson wondered if the man was a Pict and if his speech was Pictish. With deep urgency, the wild man pointed at the images tattooed on his body. Was this about some ancient form of body-piercing?

Suddenly, the message broke through.

The tattooed man was showing Jackson a *blueprint* for the body. The images he was pointing out were ones Jackson could work with to repattern the energy template of his own body. Maybe this way he could program his body to "forget" its history of disease—and the possible genetic legacy from recent generations of his family—and conform to a new blueprint for health.

There was more than a message here. There was an *energy* that seemed to move from the dreamscape into Jackson's energy field and reached through it to touch the cells. Fantasy, some might say. But if "fantasy" works—if the body believes it and responds to it in positive ways—then it is more than fantasy.

Jackson decided to cease taking medication and take a leap of faith. To the surprise of his physicians, his body seems to have forgotten it had liver cancer. We will all die of something, if only old age, but it now seems unlikely he will die from the disease that was his adversary before he met the tattooed Pict.

VISITING YOUR YOUNGER SELF

When she was thirteen, Izabela had a shocking experience while lying in bed, in the twilight state between waking and sleep. She felt a surge of energy through her body, followed by powerful vibrations and rushing sounds in her ears. Then a vortex opened in midair. She found herself pulled out of her body and whirled along something like a tunnel. She landed with a thump on a large round bed. She had a clear vision of the flowered wallpaper, the cheval glass on the dresser, the bay window beyond it. But her attention was soon entirely focussed on the naked olive-skinned man who was preparing to have sex with her. As he caressed her body, she realized that it was no longer the body of a pubescent girl. She was a mature woman who enjoyed sex and had had a fair amount of experience of it. She knew, quite specifically, that she was now 37.

In the midst of this interesting scene, she found herself shooting back—with more bumps and grinds—into the body of a 13-year-old girl.

The sequel is fascinating. When she shared this story with me, Izabela was 37. She remembered her adolescent experience as her lover joined her on the round bed in the room she had visited in her curious journey nearly a quarter-century before. She had the sense of a vortex opening again, of a tunnel that could whirl her back into the life of her adolescent self. She decided not to go through that tunnel; there was a chance she might not be able to go back!

This experience may not be as exotic as it sounds. It may be that we check in on our younger (and older) selves quite frequently in our dreams, even if we do not understand what is going on. The mysterious same-sex companion who figures in many dreams sometimes proves to be our own older and wiser self. This is what Robert Monroe, the intrepid explorer of out-of-body travel, discovered after many years of research. He concluded that one of the mysterious guides who had frequently escorted him through non-ordinary reality was actually the self he had grown into, after he had gained the wisdom of experience. I have noticed the same phenomenon. Over the past couple of years, I have been experimenting with revisiting scenes from my past—in this as well as in other possible lifetimes—to see whether I can correct or heal those things I regret, and to determine whether I can function as a mentor and friend to the lost, lonely, desperately sick child that was me for most of my preadolescence. I am starting to find match-ups between my dream journeys now and dream reports I wrote many years ago of encounters with a mysterious same-sex companion, who played the role of friend and protector.

I am now encouraging others to experiment in these areas. Suppose you could drop in on your younger self at a time when you had to cope with immense challenge or pain or heartbreak—at a time when you most needed an unconditional friend and counsellor. Wouldn't it be interesting to see if you could play the role of elder sister or brother to your younger self, to be the one who could reassure that scared or despairing kid, "You'll make it. You'll survive. I guarantee it"? Here is one example of how this can play out:

Saving My Younger Self from the Giant

When she was nine, and living with her family at their old house in the Northeast, Toni had the following dream:

> I heard something huge coming down the street. I ran quickly to the window. I saw a giant man, maybe fifty feet tall. I ran frantically around my bedroom, trying to find a hiding place. I knew the giant was looking for me.
>
> I crawled under the bed, and lay face up, gripping the coils of the mattress.
>
> Next thing the giant was in my room, lifting the bed, looking at the floor. I was still lodged in the coils. The giant did not see me.

This became a recurring dream. Again and again, Toni found herself hiding from the male giant, "lodged in the coils." As a mature woman, living with her husband and children on the West Coast, she recalled that these recurring dreams coincided with a time when she discovered that the love of her family was "conditional" on her adapting in ways she felt would crush her own identity. "I made a decision in myself for it to be okay not to get love from them. It was not worth the cost of losing myself. I realize now what that decision has caused in my life."

Vivid memories of her childhood dreams of hiding from the giant returned to Toni during one of my workshops. These memories brought sadness, and shortness of breath; Toni *knew* there was something here that still needed to be resolved.

I suggested that she should try to go back inside the dream, with the support of a partner.

"Try to go back as your adult self and see if you can talk to your younger self and offer support and encouragement. Try to reassure your child self that, despite everything, she's going to get through. She is going to come out of hiding and shine."

The woman Toni had chosen as a partner had proven herself a gifted dream tracker in previous exercises. Toni did not *see* her partner during the dream reentry, but she felt her presence, holding the space. "I felt the protection and the security to do what I needed to do."

When she reentered the dreamscape, Toni found her younger self sitting on top of the bed. She sat down beside her and put her arm around her. She told her everything was going to be okay. "I then started to tell her who she was. I spoke about the love and the beauty of her essential self. She listened and remembered."

Toni took her younger self's hand and walked her over to the window. They watched the male giant approach—and walk by, without even glancing at the two Tonis in the window.

He began shrinking as he walked on down the street. There was no more fear.

At that moment, Toni saw a white lotus flower open. A fountain of white light streamed from its heart, and then turned into a spiraling tunnel of graywhite smoke. The two Tonis went flying up into it.

As she returned from her dream journey, Toni felt the smoke blowing through the depths of her body. "I blew it out and a deep cleansing went through me, especially at my throat center, which is often blocked."

Afterwards, Toni told me, "In the past when I have tried to see my younger self for healing, it troubled me that I could never see her. Through the dream reentry, I saw and felt her in the deepest and truest way. For my feelings when I told her who she was in her heart, I have no words. My adult self also remembered as I was telling her and I now feel more whole. This has been a profound experience that I will easily be able to go back to and remember. I have always had this dream in the back of my mind; now it is understood and transformed."

EXERCISE: JOURNEYING TO YOUR YOUNGER SELF

Here is a simple way you can go back to a scene from your earlier life and experiment with playing the role of mentor and friend to your younger self. As always, you need to begin by getting comfortable and relaxed in a quiet, protected space.

1. Picture yourself standing on the bank of a river. The water flows cool and dark and deep. This is the river of your life. If you travel upstream, you will move through scenes from your earlier life.
2. You lean towards the river. You push off lightly from the balls of your feet, and you are hovering above the water.
3. You begin to flow upstream, above the dark surface of the river. On either side of you, you glimpse faces and scenes

from your earlier life. You may pause to observe moments of challenge or decision, moments of joy or grief.

4. There is *one* scene that draws you strongly. In this scene, your younger self needs help and protection. You will enter this scene and explore it in depth. *Do not succumb to the emotions you felt at this moment in your life.* Remain a compassionate observer. Do not buy into the feelings your younger self is experiencing.
5. Try to offer love and reassurance, and also specific insights you can offer. You have made it through all the obstacles and land mines your younger self is struggling with. You can tell her, at the very least, that she is going to make it through—despite the evidence!
6. You may be drawn towards the waterfall, and the source of the river. Save this for a later expedition in which you may choose to journey back before your birth. Your focus for now is on healing what can be healed within this lifetime.
7. Gently return to physical focus, and decide on at least one thing you can do that would please and reward the younger self you visited. This may be as simple as eating a candy you haven't touched since you were five, or putting on an old Carole King album.

chapter twenty-one

DREAMING HUMANITY'S PATH IN THE NEW MILLENNIUM

Mankind utilizes the dream world as a preliminary working ground. Your wars are fought, lost or won in the dream world first of all, and your physical rendition of history follows the thin line of only one series of probabilities.

—Seth, in Jane Roberts'
The Nature of Personal Reality

On April 27, 1860, a small but sturdy black woman walked through a cold North wind towards the railroad station in Troy, New York, the city on the Hudson river where I lived when I wrote this book. She paused near the courthouse, where people were jostling and shoving. A runaway slave called Charles Nalle was being herded into the courthouse to be tried. Anger flared in Harriet Tubman when she saw an escaped slave about to be taken back into captivity. She led the charge to set him free, hurling herself at one of the policemen. Sympathizers followed her lead. Nalle broke free from his captors, and Harriet rammed her bonnet down over his head so he became invisible to the police when the friendly mob closed ranks around him. Harriet and Nalle had to lie low for a couple of days, sheltered by local people, before they could slip away to Schenectady and then to safety in Canada.[1]

I didn't know that Harriet Tubman had come to Troy until I was in the final phase of writing this book. My dreams had guided me to a home atop a hill in Troy. The books don't tell me whether Harriet's dreams also led her to Troy on her mission of mercy. But maybe her presence accounts for the odd glimpses I have been getting over the years—often in the twilight zone when I'm not yet asleep but not quite awake—of a small, determined black woman with a set jaw and a mark on her forehead that rarely shows, because she usually appears in a hat. Maybe this is what triggered the *big* dream in which I saw schoolchildren all over North America learning about the value of dreams—and becoming inspired to dream their own dreams—by the story of the dreams that steered the Underground Railroad.

I learned, while living in Troy, that dreaming is for the community, not just the individual. As I found myself teaching and traveling all over the world, I continued to conduct evening classes at the local arts center downtown, and was constantly inspired by the experiences shared by people of every conceivable background, and the light their dreams bring into their lives and the lives of those around them.

A local story: A woman I'll call Mindy dreamed there was a stone in the place of her heart. Mindy woke with a sense of cold and numbness, a numbness worse than actual pain, because at least pain lets you know you're alive. When she shared this dream, I asked her what she needed to do about it. She told us, "I need to find my heart."

I asked her to go back inside her dream to look for it.

When she reentered her dream, she met a luminous being she recognized as something like a guardian angel. She asked this being, "Will you help me find my heart?"

The radiant guide offered her a gift.

Her joy turned to bitter disappointment when she saw that the gift was a stone—a stone baby. She tried to give it back.

The guide told her, "You must raise this baby. You must nurture it."

When Mindy came back from this dream journey, she was sobbing. Other women in the group gave her hugs and brought her tissues. "It's okay," she assured them through her tears. "It's not what I hoped for, but it's something. I feel something *here*." She pulled on the fabric of her sweater, over her heart.

Mindy went home and dreamed some more. Next time, wreathed in smiles, she shared a *big* one that had come in the night. "My baby came to life. My baby is a glorious, dancing golden child. When I scooped her up in my arms, she came into my heart. Now she lives there. She gave me back my heart."

As she spoke, the light of her dream danced between us and tingled in the air. We didn't analyze her experience; we participated in it. In that moment, all of us relived the times we had suffered heartbreak and soul-loss, and basked in the warmth of returning soul energy. We celebrated together the resurrection of all our "stone babies" and the gift and beauty of returning to the path of heart.

This is what dreams offer us, and our species: a return to the path of heart.

This, beyond all other reasons, is why dreaming is so vital to finding humanity's path in the new millennium. Visionary dreamworker Roberta Ossana, the editor and publisher of *Dream Network*—one of the few publications in the world that is devoted to reporting dreamers' experiences, rather than theories and commentaries about them—gave us the wonderful phrase "dreaming humanity's path." This is the exact name for the endeavor our dreams are inviting us to undertake.

People ask me about prophecies and premonitions of the future—a generation, a century, a millennium from now. Will half of California vanish into the sea? Will New York and Sydney become sunken cities? Will we colonize other planets and establish tenable ecospheres on them before we burst the bubble of air that supports human life on Earth and exhaust our food and fossil fuel supplies? Will we fry each other, or actually learn to love each other across barriers of race, religion, skin color and lifestyle?

My own dreams have shown me glimpses of *alternative* possible long-range futures for humanity and the Earth itself. In one of these series, a possible future Earth seems to have a much smaller population than the six billion figure that was reached before the calendars flipped to 2000, or the nine billion projected for the mid-twenty-first century. On this possible Earth, areas that were previously woodland or farmland are whipped by harsh desert winds, and the sun is so fierce it seems to have come much closer to the Earth. Scientists and priestesses of a new world religion or spiritual order—nonauthoritarian and integrating the best of all traditions—labor to midwife a new society that will transcend the conflicts and stupidities of the past.

In another cycle of dreams and visions, I seem to tune into the debates of some kind of cosmic council that is monitoring the story of human life on the planet. Some members of the council recall the time the "Link" between higher intelligence and bioforms on Earth was made. Some councillors were always skeptical about whether the experiment would prosper.

Some are indifferent or actively hostile to humanity. Others champion human possibility and urge patience: humans may yet evolve into compassionate, connected, multidimensional beings.

True dreams or fantasies?

The same question might be put to the "mass dreams of the future" that have been reported and studied. One survey of contemporary dreams that seem to preview the distant future groups them in four categories, ranging from the horrifically apocalyptic (we fry, bring on nuclear winter, or die from toxins of our own manufacture) to the exoplanetary (we're all space cadets in other parts of the galaxy) to the Edenic, in which our homes and cities often seem to be constructed in a style that is part Buckminster Fuller, part Polynesian Village.

To the extent that such dreams may reflect a possible *collective* future, as well as a current or developing personal situation ("my world is gonna change") all that can be said about them with any confidence is that they suggest that the future of our species is no more fixed than the future of the individual. The global and collective futures we may be able to foresee are *possible* futures. Maybe different groups of dreamers, all over the world, are dreaming their way towards the realization of *different* collective futures. Who says that if any of them is going to realized, then it will only be one of them? Isn't it possible that, just as we dream ourselves different environments in the afterlife (as the movie *What Dreams May Come* delightfully illustrates), we may be dreaming different biofutures for the planet?

For our species, as for individuals, changing the future may involve a hololeap from one pattern of manifestation to another. David Loye contends that "when we act upon a premonition and appear to alter the future, what we are really doing is leaping from one hologram to another."[2] What he calls holograms could also be parallel worlds. The future of any given holographic universe may be determined, but we can jump holograms. We can do this not only in our personal lives, but for our communities—and maybe for our species and our planet.

Visionary psychologist Dick Nodell puts it beautifully: "We need to remember we have choice in the worlds we inhabit. Real change is the shift in perspective that allows for a change of worlds. Let's suppose our beings are probabilistic. We inhabit one world and then another. Each new world has its physics, chemistry and medicine. To be healed from cancer, or from war, we simply need to inhabit a world that is free of cancer or war for enough of the time."[3]

We are best able to accomplish this through dreaming. Dreams show us what may come in this world, but they also take us to other worlds. Dreaming, we not only jump time, but we leap from world to world of possibility. We can dream our dream and we can dream our world, if we remember, like Harriet Tubman, that we can fly.

notes

PREFACE: DREAMING TRUE

1. Paul J. Nahin, *Time Machines,* 2d edition (New York. AIP Press/ Springer, 1999).

INTRODUCTION: THE UNDERGROUND RAILROAD OF DREAMS

1. On Harriet Tubman's life and dreams, I have used the earliest biography, Sarah Hopkins Bradford, *Scenes in the Life of Harriet Tubman* (Auburn, NY: W. J. Moses, 1869), her later *Harriet Tubman: The Moses of Her People* [1886], (Bedford, Massachusetts: Applewood, 1993) and a clear and useful modern retelling, Ann Petry, *Harriet Tubman: Conductor on the Underground Railroad* (New York: Archway/Pocket Books, 1971). Virginia Hamilton, *The People Could Fly* (New York: Alfred A. Knopf, 1993), is a wonderful collection of black American folktales evoking the power of dream flight. Children will love a beautifully illustrated recent book on the same theme: Faith Ringgold, *Aunt Harriet's Underground Railroad in the Sky* (New York: Dragonfly/Crown, 1995).
2. Bradford, *Harriet Tubman,* 92–3.
3. A. H. Parmalee, Jr., et al., "Sleep States in Premature Infants," *Developmental Medicine and Child Neurology* 9, (1967): 70–77. See J. Allan Hobson, *The Dreaming Brain* (New York: Basic Books, 1988), and, for an excellent survey of recent research, Anthony Shafton, *Dream Reader: Contemporary Approaches to the Understanding of Dreams* (Albany: State University of New York Press, 1995), Chapter 1.
4. British neurologist Mark Solms has launched a formidable challenge to the linkage of dreaming and REM sleep that has been a staple of

sleep and dream laboratory research since 1953. He summarizes his case in "Dreaming and REM Sleep are controlled by Different Brain Mechanisms," *Behavioral and Brain Sciences* 23 (6), (2000).

5. See Marina Roseman's superb study, *Healing Sounds from the Malaysian Rainforest: Temiar Music and Medicine* (Berkeley: University of Califirnia Press, 1991). Her recordings of Temiar dream songs are available on CD, as *Dream Songs and Healing Sounds in the Rainforests of Malaysia,* Smithsonian/Folkways, 1995.

CHAPTER 4: WHEN DREAMS SEEM FALSE

1. Herodotus, *Histories,* trans. Aubrey de Selincourt (Harmondsworth: Penguin, 1983), 215, 230–31.
2. Dawn's experiences were mirrored and reflected in a curious series of synchronicities and overlapping dreams involving other dreamers. Just prior to Dawn's attendance at one of my own workshops, I had a dream in which I received my "telegram from the professor" containing a message about Gogol. Waking, I grabbed Gogol's books from the shelves in the "Russian" section of my personal library to see where the dream might be leading. The first volume—*Tales of Good and Evil*—fell open at the first page of a story entitled "The Nose," in which a "foreigner" wakes up to find his nose inexplicably missing and roams the city, trying to mask its absence with a bandage, in search of it.

CHAPTER 5: LISTENING TO NIGHTMARES

1. Arthur Osborn, *The Future Is Now: The Significance of Precognition* (New York: University Books, 1961).
2. Excerpt in J. B. Priestley, *Man and Time,* 225–27.
3. L. E. Rhine Collection of Spontaneous Psi Experiences, Institute for Parapsychology, excerpted in Richard S. Broughton, *Parapyschology: The Controversial Science* (New York: Ballantine, 1991), 20–21.
4. W. T. Stead, *Borderland: A Casebook of True Supernatural Stories* (New York: University Books, 1970), with introduction by Leslie Shepard. Stead's story of a shipwreck, "From the Old World to the New," was published in 1894 in his magazine *Borderland;* it is reprinted in Martin Gardner, *The Wreck of the Titanic Foretold?* (Amherst, NY: Prometheus Books, 1998), together with Morgan Robertson's precognitive novella, *Futility, or The Wreck of the Titan,* which first appeared in 1898.

5. Ian Stevenson, "A Review and Analysis of Paranormal Experiences Connected with the Sinking of the *Titanic*," *Journal of the American Society for Psychical Research* [*JASPR*] 54 (1960): 153–71, and "Seven More Paranormal Experiences Associated with the Sinking of the *Titanic*," *JASPR* 59 (1965): 211–25.

CHAPTER 7: BECOMING A BETTER DREAM JOURNALIST

1. Cynthia Pearson, "Earwigs and Arabesques: Dreaming in the Multiverse," available online at Cynthia's web site *www.nauticom.net.*

CHAPTER 8: WAYS OF DREAMING

1. Milton Kramer et al., "A City Dreams: A Survey Approach to Normative Dream Content" in *American Journal of Psychology* 127 (1971): 1350–56.
2. C. G. Jung, "Seminar on Children's Dreams 1938–9," quoted in Charles Rycroft, *The Innocence of Dreams* (Oxford: Oxford University Press, 1981), 32.
3. Anthony Shafton, ed., *Dream Reader: Contemporary Approaches to the Understanding of Dreams* (Albany: SUNY Press, 1995), 31.
4. Holger Kalweit, *Shamans, Healers and Medicine Men* (Boston: Shambhala, 1992), 81.
5. Serinity Young, "Dream Practices in Medieval Tibet" in *Dreaming* vol. 9, no. 1 (March 1999): 23–42. Young observes that a key distinction between this approach and Western lucid dreaming is that "Dream yoga is a practice designed to dissolve the notion of an enduring self or of an enduring world, not . . . to enhance the sense of self and make it more successful in a reified world." She has recently published an elegant new study, *Dreaming in the Lotus: Buddhist Dream Narrative, Imagery and Practice* (Boston: Wisdom Publications, 1999), that contains important documentary material not previously available in English and a no less important corrective to the mistaken impression that Buddhism dismisses dreaming as a realm of illusion. As Young demonstrates, without dreaming there would be neither Buddhism nor the Buddha.
6. Marc de Civrieux, "Medatia, a Makiritare Shaman's Tale," in David M. Guss, ed., *The Language of the Birds: Tales, Texts & Poems of Interspecies Communication* (San Francisco: North Point Press, 1985).

7. Tenzin Wangyal Rinpoche, *The Tibetan Yogas of Dream and Sleep* (Ithaca, N.Y.: Snow Lion, 1998).
8. Robert Moss, *Dreamgates: An Explorer's Guide to the Worlds of Soul, Imagination and Life Beyond Death* (New York: Three Rivers Press, 1998).
9. This account of the three selves and the dreams that reflect them is based on Suhrawardi's *'Awariful-Ma'arif*, which awaits a contemporary translator. The only translation I have found was made from a Persian recension by an Indian Army officer, Colonel H. Wilberforce Clarke, one of those remarkable independent scholars who sometimes flourished under the Raj. It was reprinted as *A Dervish Textbook* (London: Octagon Press, 1990).
10. Robin Ridington, "Beaver Indian Dreaming and Singing" in Guss, ed., *The Language of the Birds.*

CHAPTER 9: DREAM RECYCLING

1. Francis Crick and G. Mitchison, "The Function of Dream Sleep" in *Nature* 304 (1983): 111–14, and "REM Sleep and Neural Nets" in *Journal of Mind and Behavior* 7 (1986): 229–49.
2. John Antrobus, "Dreaming: Could We Do Without It?" in Alan Moffitt, Milton Kramer and Robert Hoffman, eds., *The Functions of Dreaming* (Albany, N.Y.: State University of New York Press, 1993), 549–58.
3. J. DeKoninck et al., "Intensive language learning and increases in rapid eye movement sleep," cited in Gayle Delaney, *Breakthrough Dreaming* (New York: Bantam, 1991), 5.
4. Montague Ullman and Stanley Krippner, *Dream Studies and Telepathy* (New York: Parapsychology Foundation, 1970), 105–119.

CHAPTER 10: DREAM MOVIEMAKING

1. James Hall, *Patterns of Dreaming* (Boston: Shambhala, 1991), 127.
2. "General Aspects of Dream Psychology" reprinted in C. G. Jung, *Dreams* (Princeton: Princeton University Press, 1974), 31, 36.
3. Brian Inglis, *The Power of Dreams* (London: Paladin Grafton, 1988), 51.

CHAPTER 11: DREAMING WITH THE BODY

1. Lewis Carroll, *Alice in Wonderland* and *Through the Looking-Glass* [double edition] (New York: Quality Paperback Book Club, 1994), 248.

2. Holger Klintman, "Is there a paranormal (precognitive) influence in certain types of perceptual sequences?" *European Journal of Parapsychology,* Part I:519–49 (1983), Part II:125–40 (1984).
3. Dean Radin, *The Conscious Universe: The Scientific Truth of Psychic Phenomena* (San Francisco: Harper Edge, 1997), 122.
4. Galen, *On Diagnosis from Dreams.* I am grateful to Lee T. Pearcy, chair of classics at the Episcopal University, for this translation.
5. *Ibid.*
6. Serinity Young, "Dream Practices in Medieval Tibet" in *Dreaming* vol. 9, no. 1 (1999).
7. William C. Dement, *Some Must Watch While Some Must Sleep* (New York: W. W. Norton, 1976).
8. *Dream Network,* vol. 16 no. 2, 1997.
9. Alan B. Siegel, *Dreams That Can Change Your Life* (New York: Berkley Books, 1992), 69–71.

CHAPTER 12: PSYCHIC DREAMING

1. Montague Ullman and Stanley Krippner, *Dream Studies and Telepathy* (New York: Parapsychology Foundation, 1970), 105–119.
2. Michael Talbot, *The Holographic Universe* (New York: Harper Perennial, 1992), 62.
3. David Ryback and Letitia Sweitzer, *Dreams That Come True* (New York: Doubleday, 1988), 7, 15.
4. Frederic W. H. Myers, *Human Personality and Its Survival of Bodily Death* (New York and London: Longmans, Green, 1903), 1: xxii.
5. *Ibid,* 5. Myers' great work, *Human Personality,* was published posthumously at the start of the twentieth century, just a couple of years after Freud's *The Interpretation of Dreams.* Myers should be as much of a household name as Freud, because he was an equally brilliant explorer of the unconscious and his insights are far more relevant to us today—indeed, they give us highly practical guidelines for investigating and working with precognition and developing a science of the soul.
6. Stanley Krippner, *Call of the Siren: A Parapsychological Odyssey* (New York: Harper & Row, 1975), 290.
7. *Dream Studies and Telepathy,* op.cit.
8. For these and other examples of the shaman's X-ray or "elastic" vision, see Mircea Eliade, *Shamanism* (Princeton: Princeton University Press/Bollingen, 1984).

9. On the U.S. remote viewers, see Joseph McMoneagle, *Mind Trek* (Charlottesville, VA: Hampton Roads, 1993), and Dale E. Graff, *Tracks in the Psychic Wilderness* (Boston: Element, 1998).
10. Martin Prechtel, *Secrets of the Talking Jaguar* (New York: Putnam, 1998), 120.
11. Rev. Canon Callaway, *The Religious System of the Amazulu* (London: Trubner & Co., 1970), 232.
12. S. Krippner, M. Ullman and C. Hornoton, "A Precognitive Dream Study with a Single Subject," *Journal of the ASPR,* vol. 65 (1971): 192–203, and "A Second Precognitive Dream Study with Malcolm Bessent," *Journal of the ASPR,* vol. 66 (1972): 269–279.
13. Russell Targ and Jane Katra, *Miracles of Mind* (Novato, CA: New World Library, 1998), 125–26.
14. Priestley, *Man and Time,* 300.
15. Targ, *Miracles of Mind.*

CHAPTER 13: TRANSPERSONAL DREAMING

1. For interesting accounts of group experiments in interactive or "mutual" dreaming, see Jean Campbell, *Dreams Beyond Dreaming* (Virginia Beach: Donning, 1980), and Linda Lane Magallon, *Mutual Dreaming* (New York: Pocket Books, 1997).
2. Dorothy Eggan, "Hopi Deams in Cultural Perspective" in G. E. von Grünebaum and Roger Caillois, eds., *The Dream and Human Societies* (Berkeley: University of California Press, 1966), 242.
3. Louis Ginzberg, *Legends of the Jews* (Baltimore: Johns Hopkins, 1998), 1:385.
4. Gustav Davidson, *A Dictionary of Angels* (New York: The Free Press, 1971), 359.

CHAPTER 14: SACRED DREAMING

1. Bob Brier, *Ancient Egyptian Magic* (New York: Quill, 1980), 224.
2. Augustine Fitzgerald, trans. and ed., *The Letters of Synesius of Cyrene* (London: Oxford University Press/Humphrey Milford, 1926).
3. From *De insomniis,* translated by Augustine Fitzgerald in *The Essays and Hymns of Synesius of Cyrene* (London: Oxford University Press, 1930).
4. *Ibid.*
5. *Ibid.*

6. Cf. Peter Brown, *The Cult of the Saints.* (Chicago: University of Chicago Press, 1981).
7. Henry Corbin, *The Man of Light in Iranian Sufism* (New Lebanon, N.Y.: Omega, 1994), 21.

CHAPTER 15: DREAMBRINGING

1. I have to quote this in the original because of the memory of the shivers Dante's celebrated opening brought me when I read it in the original at about the same age as the kid in Jane's story. I have often felt, as Helen Luke suggests in her beautiful book about the *Divine Comedy,* that the second line has a dual meaning: in order to find ourselves—literally, to find ourselves *again*—we must first lose ourselves. Cf. Helen M. Luke, *Dark Wood to White Rose* (New York: Parabola, 1993).
2. Jane White-Lewis, "Dreams and Social Responsibility: Teaching a Dream Course in the Inner-City" in Stanley Krippner and Mark Robert Waldman, eds., *Dreamscaping* (Los Angeles: Lowell House, 1999), 27.
3. Carolyn Myss, *Anatomy of the Spirit* (New York: Harmony Books, 1997), 84.
4. Kalweit, *Shamans, Healers and Medicine Men,* 80.

CHAPTER 16. DREAM HUNTERS AND DREAM HEALERS

1. Reuben Gold Thwaites, ed., *The Jesuit Relations and Allied Documents* (Cleveland: Burrows Brothers, 1896–1901), 73 volumes [hereafter *JR*] 53:251–3.
2. Robert Moss, "Missionaries and Magicians" in Peter Benes. ed., *Wonders of the Invisible World: 1600–1900* (Boston: Boston University Press, 1995).
3. *JR* 6:159–61.
4. James W. Schultz and J. L. Donaldson, *The Sun's Children* (New York: Houghton Mifflin, 1930), 177–78.
5. Mary Chinkwita, *The Usefulness of Dreams: An African Perspective* (London: Janus, 1993).
6. Plutarch, *Fall of the Roman Republic: Six Lives,* trans. Rex Warner (Harmondsworth: Penguin, 1962), 316.
7. Nerys Dee, *Your Dreams and What They Mean* (Wellingborough: Aquarian Press, 1984), 28–29.

8. Ward Hill Lamon, *Recollections of Abraham Lincoln, 1847–1865* (1911) (Lincoln: University of Nebraska Press, 1994). Lincoln's death dream is excerpted in Stephen Brook's excellent compilation, *The Oxford Book of Dreams* (Oxford: Oxford University Press, 1992), 143–44.
9. Inscription over the Propylaia at Epidaurus. The inscription over the gate of another Asklepeion, in North Africa, read: "Enter a good man, leave a better one." Emma J. Edelstein and Ludwig Edelstein, *Asclepius: Collection and Interpretation of the Testimonies* (Baltimore and London: Johns Hopkins University Press, 1998), 164.
10. These details of Tibetan dream incubation are based on the *Milam Tagpa* ("Examination of Dreams") ritual preserved in the ninth-century *Tangyur* collection, and discussed by Serinity Young in her important essay "Dream Practices in Medieval Tibet" in *Dreaming* vol. 9, no. 1 (1999): 23–42.
11. Cornelius Agrippa, *Three Books of Occult Philosophy,* trans. James Freake (St Paul, MN: Llewellyn, 1993).
12. The lines from Suhrawardi are my adaptation of a translation of his prayer to the personal guardian in Henry Corbin, *The Man of Light in Iranian Sufism.* (New Lebanon, N.Y.: Omega Publications, 1994), 21.
13. See A. Leo Oppenheim, *The Interpretation of Dreams in the Ancient Near East* (Philadelphia: American Philosophical Society, 1956).
14. Louis Ginzberg, *The Legends of the Jews* (Philadelphia: Jewish Publication Society of America, 1968), 1:245–46.
15. Thomas Berry, *The Dream of the Earth* (San Francisco: Sierra Club, 1990), 211.
16. Larry Dossey, *Reinventing Medicine* (Harper San Francisco, 1999).
17. "Spiritual telegraph" is a phrase that may have first appeared in the preface to Isaac Post's *Voices of the Spirit World* (Rochester, N.Y.: Charles H. McDonell, 1852). Post attributed the preface to no less an author than Ben Franklin, speaking to him from the other side. It is well worth reading as a commentary on communication by the departed and telepathy in general.
18. See Ann Braude, *Radical Spirits: Spiritualism and Women's Rights in Nineteenth-Century America* (Boston: Beacon Press, 1989).
19. Elizabeth Cady Stanton and Susan B. Anthony, eds., *History of Woman Suffrage* (Rochester, N.Y.: Fowler & Wells, 1881–1902), 4 vols., 3:530.

CHAPTER 18: BRINGING DREAMS INTO WAKING LIFE

1. Wendy Doniger O'Flaherty, *Dreams, Illusion and Other Realities* (Chicago: University of Chicago Press, 1984), 62.
2. *Ibid,* 63.
3. *Ibid,* 289.
4. See my book *Conscious Dreaming.*
5. Anjali Hazarika, *Daring to Dream: Cultivating Corporate Creativity Through Dreamwork* (New Delhi and Thousand Oaks, CA: Response Books, 1997).

CHAPTER 19: DREAMING AND FUTURE SCIENCE

1. David Bohm, *Wholeness and the Implicate Order* (London: Ark Books, 1985).
2. Patrick Morton "Mathematics and Dreaming," *IONS Noetic Sciences Review,* August–November 1999.
3. Our experiment was conducted independently from one proposed by Jean Galliano, a wonderfully venturesome and dedicated dream voyager in the Philadelphia area who quite frequently posts protocols and results for similar group journeys at the *alt.out-of-body* newsgroup. For details of other group travels I have led, see my book *Dreamgates.*

CHAPTER 20: CHANGING THE PAST

1. Jane Roberts, *The Nature of Personal Reality: A Seth Book* (New York: Bantam, 1980), 290.
2. Paul J. Nahin, *Time Machines: Time Travel in Physics, Metaphysics and Science Fiction,* 2nd edition (New York: AIP Press/Springer Verlag, 1993), xv.
3. Details of the University of Kent research and access to the computer experiments are available at the Retropsychokinesis Project website, *http://www.fourmilab.ch/rpkp.*
4. Julian Brown, "Martial arts students influence the past," *New Scientist,* July 1994.

CHAPTER 21: DREAMING HUMANITY'S PATH

1. Ann Petry, *Harriet Tubman,* 195–98.
2. David Loye, *The Sphinx and the Rainbow: Brain, Mind and Future Vision* (New York: Bantam, 1984).
3. Personal communication from Richard S. Nodell, October 8, 1999.

bibliography

Achterberg, Jeanne, *Imagery and Healing* (Boston: Shambhala, 1985).

Berry, Thomas, *The Dream of the Earth* (San Francisco: Sierra Club, 1990).

Bohm, David, *Wholeness and the Implicate Order* (London: Ark, 1985).

Bosnak, Robert, *Tracks in the Wilderness of Dreaming* (New York: Delacorte, 1996).

Bradford, Sarah, *Harriet Tubman, The Moses of Her People* [1886] (Bedford, MA: Applewood Books, 1993).

Braude, Ann, *Radical Spirits: Spiritualism and Women's Rights in Nineteenth-Century America* (Boston: Beacon Press, 1989).

Broughton, Richard S., *Parapsychology, The Controversial Science* (New York: Ballantine Books, 1991).

Bulkeley, Kelly, ed., *Among All Those Dreamers* (Albany, NY: State University of New York Press, 1996).

Caillois, Roger, ed., *The Dream Adventure* (New York: Orion Press, 1963).

Campbell, Jean, *Dreams Beyond Dreaming* (Virginia Beach: Donning, 1980).

Carrington, Dorothy, *The Dream-Hunters of Corsica* (London: Weidenfeld and Nicolson, 1995).

Chinkwita, Mary, *The Usefulness of Dreams: An African Perspective* (London: Janus, 1993).

Corbin, Henry, *The Man of Light in Iranian Sufism* (New Lebanon, N.Y.: Omega, 1994).

Davidson, Gustav, *A Dictionary of Angels* (New York: The Free Press, 1971).

Davies, Paul, *About Time: Einstein's Unfinished Revolution* (New York: Touchstone, 1996).

Dossey, Larry, *Recovering the Soul: A Scientific and Spiritual Search* (New York: Bantam, 1989).

———, *Reinventing Medicine.* (Harper San Francisco, 1999).

Dunne, J. W., *An Experiment with Time.* 3rd edition. (London: Faber and Faber, 1934).

Edelstein, Emma J. and Ludwig, *Asclepius: Collection and Interpretation of the Testimonies* (Baltimore and London: Johns Hopkins University Press, 1998).

Ellis, Normandi, *Dreams of Isis* (Wheaton, IL: Quest Books, 1995).

Flaherty, Gloria, *Shamanism and the Eighteenth Century* (Princeton: Princeton University Press, 1992).

Garfield, Patricia, *The Dream Messenger* (New York: Simon & Schuster, 1997).

———, *The Healing Power of Dreams* (New York: Fireside, 1992).

Garrett, Eileen J., *Telepathy* (New York: Creative Age Press, 1941).

Ginzberg, Louis, *The Legends of the Jews,* trans. Henrietta Szold (Baltimore and London: Johns Hopkins University Press, 1998) [reprint], 7 vols.

Graff, Dale E., *Tracks in the Psychic Wilderness* (Boston: Element, 1998).

Greene, Brian, *The Elegant Universe: Superstrings, Hidden Dimensions and the Quest for the Ultimate Theory* (New York: Norton, 1999).

Hazarika, Anjali, *Daring to Dream: Cultivating Corporate Creativity Through Dreamwork* (New Delhi and Thousand Oaks, CA: Response Books, 1997).

Humphrey, Caroline, with Urgunge Onon, *Shamans and Elders: Experience, Knowledge and Power Among the Daur Mongols* (Oxford: Clarendon Press, 1996).

Hunt, Harry T., *The Multiplicity of Dreams* (New Haven and London: Yale University Press, 1989).

Irwin, Lee, *The Dream Seekers: Native American Visionary Traditions of the Great Plains* (Norman and London: University of Oklahoma Press, 1994).

Jung, C. G., *Dreams,* trans. R. F. C. Hull (Princeton: Princeton University Press, 1974).

Kalweit, Holger, *Dreamtime & Inner Space: The World of the Shaman* (Boston: Shambhala, 1988).

———, *Shamans, Healers and Medicine Men* (Boston: Shambhala, 1992).

Kelsey, Morton T., *God, Dreams and Revelation,* revised edition (Minneapolis, MN: Augsburg, 1991).

Kirsch, James, *The Reluctant Prophet* (Los Angeles: Sherbourne Press, 1973).

Krippner, Stanley, *Song of the Siren: A Parapsychological Odyssey* (New York: Harper & Row, 1975).

Krippner, Stanley, and Mark Robert Waldman, eds., *Dreamscaping* (Los Angeles: Lowell House, 1999).

Krippner, Stanley, and Patrick Welch, *Spiritual Dimensions of Healing* (New York: Irvington, 1992).

Lightman, Alan, *Einstein's Dreams* (New York: Warner Books, 1994).

Loye, David, *The Sphinx and the Rainbow: Brain, Mind and Future Vision* (New York: Bantam, 1984).

Magallon, Linda Lane, *Mutual Dreaming* (New York: Pocket Books, 1997).

Mavromatis, Andreas, *Hypnagogia* (London and New York: Routledge, 1987).

McMoneagle, Joseph, *The Ultimate Time Machine* (Charlottesville, VA: Hampton Roads, 1998).

Mitchell, Edgar D., *Psychic Exploration.* (New York: G. P. Putnam's Sons, 1974).

Moss, Robert, "Blackrobes and Dreamers: Jesuit Reports on the Shamanic Dream Practices of the Northern Iroquoians" in *Shaman's Drum* 28 (1992).

———, *Conscious Dreaming* (New York: Crown, 1996).

———, *Dreamgates* (New York: Three Rivers Press, 1998).

———, "The Return of Asklepios: Recovering the Arts of Dream Healing" in *Dream Network,* vol. 18, no. 3 (1999).

———, "When We Become a Dreaming Culture" in *Dream Network,* vol. 16 no. 4 (1998).

Myers, Frederic W. H., *Human Personality and Its Survival of Bodily Death* (New York: Longmans, Green, 1903), 2 vols.

Nahin, Paul J., *Time Machines: Time Travel in Physics, Metaphysics and Science Fiction* (New York: AIP Press/Springer-Verlag, 1999).

O'Flaherty, Wendy Doniger, *Dreams, Illusion and Other Realities* (Chicago and London: University of Chicago Press, 1984).

Peek, Philip M., *African Divination Systems* (Bloomington & Indianapolis: Indiana University Press, 1991).

Petry, Ann, *Harriet Tubman, Conductor on the Underground Railroad* (New York: Archway, 1971).

Post, Isaac, *Voices from the Spirit World* (Rochester, N.Y.: Charles McDonell, 1852).

Priestley, J. B., *Man and Time* (London: Aldus Books, 1964).

Radin, Dean, *The Conscious Universe* (New York: Harper Edge, 1997).

Rhine, Louisa E., *ESP in Life and Lab* (New York: Macmillan, 1967).

Ridington, Robin, "Beaver Dreaming and Singing" in David M. Guss, ed., *The Language of the Birds* (San Francisco: North Point Press, 1985).

Roberts, Jane, *The Nature of Personal Reality* [a Seth book] (New York: Bantam, 1980).

Roseman, Marina, *Healing Sounds from the Malaysian Rainforest: Temiar Music and Medicine* (Berkeley: University of California Press, 1993).

Ryback, David, with Letitia Sweitzer, *Dreams that Come True* (New York: Doubleday, 1988).

Savary, Louis M., Patricia H. Berne and Strephon Kaplan Williams, *Dreams and Spiritual Growth* (Mahwah, N.J.: Paulist Press, 1984).

Schultz, Mona Lisa, *Awakening Intuition* (New York: Three Rivers Press, 1999).

Shafton, Anthony, *Dream Reader: Contemporary Approaches to the Understanding of Dreams* (Albany, NY: State University of New York Press, 1995).

———, "African-Americans and Predictive Dreams" in *Dream Time,* vol. 16, no. 3 (1999).

Shlain, Leonard, *Art & Physics: Parallel Visions in Space, Time and Light* (New York: William Morrow, 1991).

Stead, W.T., *The Blue Island* [recorded by Pardoe Woodman and Estelle Stead], facsimile edition (Pomeroy, WA: Health Research, 1970).

Talbot, Michael, *The Holographic Universe* (New York: Harper Perennial, 1992).

Targ, Russell, and Jane Katra, *Miracles of Mind* (Novato, CA: New World Library, 1998).

Tenzin Wangyal Rinpoche, *The Tibetan Yogas of Dream and Sleep* (Ithaca, NY: Snow Lion, 1998).

Ullman, Montague, Stanley Krippner and Alan Vaughan, *Dream Telepathy* (London: Turnstone Books, 1973).

Van de Castle, Robert L., *Our Dreaming Mind* (New York: Ballantine Books, 1994).

Von Franz, Marie-Louise, *On Divination and Synchronicity* (Toronto: Inner City Books, 1980).

Von Grünebaum, G. E., and Roger Caillois, eds., *The Dream and Human Societies* (Berkeley: University of California Press, 1966).

Wolf, Fred Alan, *The Dreaming Universe* (New York: Simon & Schuster, 1994).

Young, Serinity, "Dream Practices in Medieval Tibet" in *Dreaming,* vol. 9, no. 1 (1999).

———, *Dreaming in the Lotus: Buddhist Dream Narrative, Imagery and Practice* (Boston: Wisdom Publications, 1999).

resources

DREAMING ONLINE

Please visit my website, *www.mossdreams.com* for further advice on becoming an *active* dreamer, information on upcoming programs, new publications and research projects and links to many other online resources, including the Association for the Study of Dreams, Electric Dreams, Dream Tree, and Cynthia Pearson's Dream Journalist site.

WORKSHOPS

I give workshops and presentations in active dreaming, creativity, shamanism and personal growth in North America, Australia and Europe. The format ranges from lectures and two-hour introductory sessions to five-day advanced trainings in areas such as dream healing, creative expression, shamanic approaches to death and dying, and the exploration of nonordinary reality. For schedules and information, please visit my website or write to:

Way of the Dreamer
P.O. Box 215
Troy, N.Y. 12181
Fax (518) 274–0506

AUDIO TRAINING PROGRAMS

Dream Gates: A Journey into Active Dreaming is my six-cassette training program (not a book on tape, and with different content from *Dreamgates* the book). It includes guided inductions into conscious dreaming, shamanic drumming for dream journeyers, guidance on psychic protection and stories and dream practices that can transport you into other realities or bring the power of dreaming into everyday life. A two-tape condensed version is also available. You may order the tapes via *www.mossdreams.com* or direct from the publisher:

Sounds True
413 South Arthur Avenue
Louisville, CO 80027
Tel: (800) 333–9185 (U.S.callers)
Tel: (303) 665–3151 (international callers)
E-mail *SoundsTrue@aol.com*

RESEARCH PROJECTS

I am actively leading research projects, as well as experiential workshops, in the following areas:

The Home Precognition Experiment
Documenting and validating personal experiences of dream precognition and telepathy of dreamers all over the world.

Recovering the Arts of Dream Healing
Exploring the healing power of dream imagery and our ability to embark on conscious dream journeys to seek healing and soul recovery for ourselves and others. Through the new Dream Transfer technique, we can bring a dream—a healing image, a life vision, perhaps a path to the next world—to someone in need of a dream.

Creating from the Source
Using conscious dreaming techniques to tap into our creative Source and enter the flow state in which our best and most original work is generated most easily.

Bringing Dream Education to Schools
Dreamsharing and dream journalism foster creativity, storytelling and communication skills. Study projects like "The Underground Railroad of Dreams" and "Einstein's Dreams" provide history lessons kids can use to "dream their dream" today.

Dreams to Help the Dying
Using dreamwork and conscious dreaming techniques to help both the dying and their caregivers to use the last phase of this life experience as an opportunity for learning and growing—and move gracefully into the next one.

Dreaming and Future Science
Using conscious dreaming techniques, including group dream travel, to explore and map other "frequency domains" and contribute to our understanding of time, physics and reality creation in the multidimensional universe.

Building a Dream Community
Bringing the gifts of dreaming into everyday life to build better relationships, heal organizations, foster creative innovation and mutual understanding and help move communities beyond barriers of intolerance and prejudice.

For updates, please visit *www.mossdreams.com.*

Share Your Experiences
I welcome any experiences you would like to share, including those you may have after reading this book! You may write to Way of the Dreamer, Box 215, Troy NY 12181 or e-mail *robert@mossdreams.com.*

acknowledgments

I am deeply grateful to the thousands of dreamers in all walks of life who have shared their experiences with me, not only in workshops but by letter, e-mail, fax and in "chance" encounters on planes and trains, at beaches and bookstores, in a line at the post office or the supermarket checkout. Once you start working your dreams and sharing them with others, you'll find the same thing: this kind of enthusiasm is viral. Strangers and coworkers will be drawn to share dreams with you without quite knowing why, giving both of you the opportunity to confirm and validate each other's experience, and *grow your dreams.*

I have learned a huge amount—and continue to learn—from the active dreamers who take part in my advanced circles, especially my five-day trainings, the "Dreamgrowing," "Soul Recovery," and "Death" workshops and the private gatherings on the "magic mountain" from which the dream transfer technique emerged fully-fledged. These circles include physicians and scientists, artists and software designers, therapists and priestesses, all drawn together by a common desire to pursue deeper adventures *inside* the dreamstate, and to bring the gifts of dreaming into the community.

My understanding of the many schools of dreamwork and dream analysis has been greatly furthered by many delightful encounters with fellow-explorers in the Association for the Study of Dreams, including Rita Dwyer (who generously contributed some of her moving personal experiences for this book), Stanley Krippner, Patricia Garfield, Bob Van de Castle, Deirdre Barrett, Wendy Pannier, Edward Bruce Bynum, Jane White-Lewis, Aad van Ouwerkerk, Richard Russo, Kathleen Sullivan, Phil King, Linda Lane Magallon, David Gerbi, Tom Crockett, Naomi Epel, Robert Gongloff, Jodine Grundy, Fran Harris, Joanne Rochon, Bob and Lynne Hoss, Marcia and Jim Emery, Strephon Kaplan-Williams, Jeremy Taylor, Alan Worsley, Alan Siegel, Kelly Bulkeley and Henry Reed.

In the applications of dreaming and imagery to healing, I have benefited greatly from the splendid work of Larry Dossey and Jeanne Achterberg. In my understanding of the larger dimensions of dream healing, I continue to benefit from my early training in shamanic soul retrieval with Sandra Ingerman. My principal teachers, throughout my life, have been inside the dreamworld itself. This is something all active dreamers will understand.

My work is sustained and strengthened daily by the loving support of my dream family. I send love to my soul sisters, Wanda and Carol, and the members of our "home circle" of frequent flyers. I give thanks from the heart to the wonderful community dreambringers and healers who have helped me to grow this dream in many different environments: to Alex Sprinkle (keeper of my dream garden in Manhattan), Nancy Lunney, Albert Meyerer and Anna Sanchez; to Roberta Ossana and Noreen Wessling, dream artist and source of breathtaking dream theatre; to Barbara Bluck, who brought active dreaming to Prospero's island; to Juanita, who grew the dream of the "capital of dreams"; to Polly, Chonlada and "Miss Teresa"; to Derek, Ruth, Janet and our Toronto circle; to Joe Green, who brought Active Dreaming into John Wayne territory; to Ron Burch; to MiShalla, who helped bring the dance of the dream creator to the Heartland; to Gayle Seminara Mandel; to Dominick Sorrentino, gatekeeper of the Miami Dreaming; to

Elly, who kept dreaming me back to my native Australia; to Eileen and Judy, who kept me coming to Cincinnati; to Kathy, who called me to the high desert; to Jim, who brought us to dance with Death in the shadow of Gettysburg; to Lillian and Mary Ellen, who hold wonderful sacred space at Stillpoint; and to many, many others. I am grateful, as ever, for the love of my wife Marcia and my daughters and all our shared explorations. My youngest daughter, Sophie, who was ten when I completed this book and to whom it is dedicated, is a born dreamer and storyteller who constantly reminds me that "grown-ups" *must* listen to children's dreams and record them; in this area, our kids may be our teachers.

I was fortunate to find a dream publisher in Judith Curr and a dream editor in Mitchell Ivers, who has a sculptor's eye for the shape inside the stone. Stuart Krichevsky proved himself, once more, to be a dream agent: caring as well as professional, keenly interested in bringing out the best, a friend in all seasons.

In the last stages of working on this book, I found two soul brothers who quickened my excitement over two lines of research that were laid down by my dreams, and deepened my understanding of what they would require. The first is Dick Nodell, a marvelously gifted and caring psychotherapist and teacher, schooled in physics at M.I.T., who helped me interpret my "Einstein dreams" and expand the vision of how dreaming can contribute not only to emerging science but to peace and the evolution of our species. The second is Tony Cohen, a brilliant young black historian who has walked the routes of the Underground Railroad, sometimes in his bare feet, and helped me grasp the human experience and the spiritual legacy of the slaves who made their way to freedom. When we sat together for the first time in a coffee shop after I had given a talk, we both felt the benign influence of the ancestors—especially the Ashante, Harriet Tubman's people—pressing close in upon us, signalling, *Right on!* When Tony later came to one of my workshops, he asked me to write something he could paste inside his dream journal, as a prod to remember more of his dreams, and dream stronger. I wrote this:

> *I wish to dream true, the way Harriet Tubman, and my wise ancestors, dreamed—and remember.*

I wish this for *you.*

index

South [illegible]

Gogol
Dostoyevski